THE ASIA-PACIFIC ECONOMY

Also by Dilip K. Das

IMPORT CANALISATION

INDIA AND THE INTERNATIONAL FINANCE MARKETS

INTERNATIONAL CAPITAL MARKETS AND THE DEVELOPING
COUNTRIES

INTERNATIONAL FINANCE: Contemporary Issues (*editor*)

INTERNATIONAL TRADE POLICY

KOREAN ECONOMIC DYNAMISM

MIGRATION OF FINANCIAL RESOURCES TO DEVELOPING
COUNTRIES

THE YEN APPRECIATION AND THE INTERNATIONAL
ECONOMY

The Asia-Pacific Economy

Dilip K. Das
Visiting Professor
Graduate School of Business
University of Sydney, Australia

First published in Great Britain 1996 by
MACMILLAN PRESS LTD
Houndmills, Basingstoke, Hampshire RG21 6XS
and London
Companies and representatives
throughout the world

A catalogue record for this book is available
from the British Library.

ISBN 0–333–64549–9

 First published in the United States of America 1996 by
ST. MARTIN'S PRESS, INC.,
Scholarly and Reference Division,
175 Fifth Avenue,
New York, N.Y. 10010

ISBN 0–312–15825–4

Library of Congress Cataloging-in-Publication Data
Das, Dilip K., 1945–
The Asia-Pacific economy / Dilip K. Das.
p.   cm.
Includes bibliographical references and index.
ISBN 0–312–15825–4 (cloth)
1. Asia—Economic integration.   2. Pacific Area— Economic
integration.   3. Pacific Area cooperation.   4. Japan—Economic
conditions—1989–   5. International economic relations.   I. Title.
HC412-D33   1996
337.5—dc20   95–36942
                                                          CIP

10   9   8   7   6   5   4   3   2   1
05   04   03   02   01   00   99   98   97   96

Printed in Great Britain by
Ipswich Book Co Ltd, Ipswich, Suffolk

To Vasanti
with love and gratitude

Contents

Contents

List of Maps

List of Tables and Figures

Figures

Preface

Writing a preface is like presenting a justification for writing the book. I wrote this book on the Asia-Pacific economies because, first, over the last three decades the regional economies and industries have done miraculously well and thereby have attracted international attention. Secondly, in the foreseeable future this brisk growth and industrialisation pattern is going to pick up momentum and the region will be one of the largest suppliers as well as the largest markets in several products. When the US and European economies were mired in recession during the early 1990s, the Asia-Pacific region succeeded in bucking the trend and steam-rolled ahead with an annual growth rate approaching double figures. Between 1995 and 2000, an upswing in the world economic cycle is expected. The robust Asia-Pacific economies will be part of this upswing. While the world economies pick up speed, the Asia-Pacific economies are projected to zip ahead faster. At the end of 2000, the industrial and business scenario of the world will look discernibly different from now.

Much of the confidence about the immediate future emanates from the region's continued ability to attract foreign direct investment. The growth and prosperity of the region have made the emerging capital markets of the Asia-Pacific region a new investment frontier. The new investment is typically concentrated in export industries and brings technological and managerial know-how. The appreciating yen during 1994 once again forced Japanese industries to restructure and go off-shore, to the benefit of several neighbouring countries. Until a decade ago, people in the region only manufactured Nike shoes for the rest of the world. Now, for the first time, they are buying them as well. The region is in a strong buying position and showing clear signs of opening up its markets. Most of the countries in the region have one or more of the following attributes: a current account surplus, a healthy corporate sector investing profits in new equipment, and a swelling middle class eager to purchase the symbols of success. The regional consumer markets are the most rapidly growing in the world. These economies will demand many more products, particularly capital goods, which will enhance their international significance immensely.

Multinational enterprises operating in the region are helping in opening up the regional market. They are creating new production networks by siting plants and factories around the region and shipping parts and components around to a final assembly point. The doctrine of free trade is well understood and admired in the region. According to the governmental pronouncements made during the Asia Pacific Economic Co-operation (APEC) forum conference in November 1994, the regional leaders vowed to lower tariff barriers, harmonise investment regulations and integrate their economies. Their declared objective was to push the dynamic Asia-Pacific region forward as the world's economic powerhouse for the next century. This agreement rivals in significance the formation of the European Community almost four decades ago.

If innovation is defined as improving products and processes, several Asia-Pacific economies are now considered fairly innovative and competitive. Clearly, they could not possibly have developed so rapidly without the innovative streak. The newly-industrialising economies of Korea, Taiwan, Hong Kong and Singapore have long since mastered the art of imitation and moved on to the higher plateau of improving products and commercialising new products. Countries like Malaysia and Thailand are at the lower end of the spectrum but are fast moving up the innovation curve. The World Competition Report 1994, published by the International Institute of Management Development, Lausanne, Switzerland, ranked Hong Kong, Japan, Singapore, Malaysia and Taiwan among the top ten in getting new products to market quickly. These countries will have to continue to master innovation.

This book is pitched at the level of MBA students and can be used by any who are in related disciplines, like finance and economics, and have a desire to learn about the Asia-Pacific

economies. It will be useful for the executive development programmes in this area. As for the tectonic composition of the
book, it comprises six parts.

Chapter 1 traces the growth path of the Asia-Pacific
economies over the last thirty years. It does so for individual
economies, for sub-groups of them and *en masse* for the
region. The chapter serves as an introduction to the contemporary regional dynamism. Secondly, it tries to explain to the
reader how this subset of international economies grew so
rapidly and became so important internationally.

Chapter 2 deals with the initial endeavours made by the
regional economies to integrate. During the 1960s and 1970s,
the Asia-Pacific region made definite, albeit feeble, efforts to
integrate economically. Efforts to turn the region into a 'flying
geese paradigm' began during this period. Certainly, the
Japanese economy – the largest in the region – has played an
active integrating role, and Chapter 3 first focuses on Japan's
emergence as an economic superpower and then on its integrating role in the region.

Chapter 4 starts with the diversities in the regional
economies and then looks at the current economic integration
process through trade, investment and economic assistance
on the one hand and through micro-level corporate integration endeavours in the region on the other. Next, it posits that
the integrating forces are entirely market-driven and are
effectively bringing the regional economies together. It
concludes that there are distinct possibilities of the region
becoming more cohesive in the intermediate term.

Another kind of regional integration which is under way in
the region is discussed in Chapter 5. This entails the emergence
of small sub-regional economic zones, prominent among which
are the Baht zone, the Hong Kong–Shenzhen nexus and the
Fugian–Taiwan nexus. These economic zones have come to
acquire a dynamism of their own and are no longer so small.

Finally, Chapter 6 deals with the classical dilemma of regionalism versus multilateralism in the context of the swiftly
growing Asia-Pacific economies. After following the principal strands of this debate, this chapter supports the doctrine
of 'open regionalism' adopted by the region.

I owe a debt of gratitude to several libraries that helped me with my research for this book. Principal among them are those of the Australian National University, Canberra; the European Institute of Business Administration (INSEAD), Fontainebleau, France; and the University of Sydney. I held visiting professorships in these institutions while researching or writing this book. The usual caveat applies.

Graduate School of Business   DILIP K. DAS
University of Sydney

The beginning of all things lies in the beyond, in the form of ideas that are yet to become real. The Creative sees with great clarity the causes and effects, and lends form to these ideas through perseverance. The course of the Creative alters and shapes things until each attains its true, specific nature. Then he strives to keep them in conformity with the way of the universe, with the *tao*. Knowing the calm strength of patience, the Creative waits for the time of fulfilment.

Wisdom of the *I Ching*

1 The Changing Morphology of the Asia-Pacific Region

THE ECONOMIC TAKE-OFF

To medieval Europeans, the Asia-Pacific region was something of a cornucopia and for a long time thereafter it was admired for the exotic aspects of its life and cultures. To the post-war world, it is the land of effervescent economic growth. Its rise can be traced back to the early 1960s when the Japanese economy came into its own. Since then several fundamental and far-reaching economic changes have taken place in the region and a new era of economic expansion has begun: it has outpaced all other regions in terms of economic growth over the last three decades. Throughout the 1960s, Japan's GNP grew over 10 per cent annually and it successfully exported its way out of all the exogenous economic disturbances of the 1970s. Japan was followed by the 'four dragons' whose economic achievements surpassed that of Japan. Other Southeast Asian countries[1] and China followed close on the heels of the dragons. One country's economic growth helped others in the region and it almost became a self-perpetuating economic expansion. These countries concentrated their energy on economic growth, pursued pragmatic macroeconomic policies and climbed the spiral of industrialisation to become the most dynamic region of the international economy in a short period of time. They demonstrated to the rest of the world that vigorous economic growth does not take a miracle. Herman Kahn, with some prescience, noted that the Asia-Pacific economies were turning into the centre of world economic power. The centre of international economic dynamism that used to be in the Mediterranean in the remote past, moved to north-western Europe and then to the north Atlantic. During the post-war period it moved again to the Asia-Pacific region (Kahn, 1979). This notion has acquired not only credibility but also considerable international support, and scholars have began to use expression such as 'the Pacific century' unabashed (Vogel, 1984; Linder, 1986; Gibney, 1992). In what follows, we shall trace the growth path of the Asia-Pacific economies from poor, struggling economies to international economic stardom; analyse the economic characteristics of each subregion; and delve into the causal factors underlying their hyper-growth and economic transformation.

THE REGION DEFINED

The Asia-Pacific economies have been a subject of active interest and animated discussion among economists, industrialists, bureaucrats and politicians. Since the mid-1960s, when Professor Kiyoshi Kojima put forth his concept of an Asia-Pacific region, it has been variously defined, with each definition including its proponent's favourite country group, policy coverage and institutional arrangements. Kojima envisioned a two-tier Asia-Pacific region which included the five industrialised countries – namely, the USA, Canada, Australia, New Zealand and Japan – as the core group. The developing countries of the region were of secondary importance and were to be the secondary partners in the regional economic grouping. In 1966 he posited a Pacific free trade area (PAFTA) involving mutual elimination of tariffs among the member economies while retaining them for the non-members. Country groupings, and therefore acronyms, that developed over time included: (i) the Pacific Trade and Development Conference (PAFTAD), which had a strong economic flavour; (ii) the Organization for Pacific Trade and Development (OPTAD), which was intended to be an OECD-like organisation and had Sir John Crawford and Subiro Okita as its protagonists; (iii) the Pacific Economic Co-operation Conference (PECC), which brought academics, businessmen and government officials informally together for the exchange of views regarding regional and international economies, and which publishes several economic and statistical publications regarding the Asia-Pacific region; (iv) the Pacific Basin Economic Council (PBEC), which had complete business community orientation; (v) the East Asia Economic Caucus (EAEC), which was proposed by the ASEAN (Association of South-East Asian Nations) to unite it economically with Japan, China, Taiwan, Hong Kong, South Korea, Vietnam, Myanmar and the Pacific island nations, but Japan declined to commit itself to the idea; and (vi) the Asia-Pacific Economic Co-operation (APEC) forum, which was floated by the erstwhile Australian Prime Minister, R. L. J. Hawke, in 1989 and initially received unenthusiastic support from Japan, but by 1992 had grown into a formal body of fifteen regional members: the USA, Canada, Mexico, Japan, Australia, New Zealand, China, Hong Kong, Taiwan, South Korea, Thailand, Indonesia, Malaysia, Singapore and the Philippines. By the time of its fourth meeting in 1992, the membership question was still not settled. Questions were being asked, such as why Mexico should be a member when several nations of Indochina and the Pacific islands are not.

With this background of a surfeit of definitions and concepts of Asia-Pacific regional groupings, I am venturing to propose my own to include:

- Japan, the largest and pivotal Asia-Pacific economy;
- Australia and New Zealand, two prosperous economies;
- South Korea, Taiwan, Hong Kong, Singapore, four newly-industrialising economies;
- Indonesia, Malaysia, Thailand, the Philippines, the ASEAN-4, the first three of which are among the better performing developing economies; and
- China, a large developing economy which has recorded rather high growth rates over the 1980s and the 1990s.

The grouping of these twelve economies is based on economic norms. It brings together those economies of east and south-east Asia and the western Pacific that – with minor exceptions – have experienced dynamic growth in the immediate past because of their liberal, pragmatic and market-orientated macroeconomic policies, outward-orientated industrialisation strategy, and efficient resource allocation by way of rational prices; and whose governments are consciously committed to economic growth. The second feature of this group of economies is complementarity in terms of natural resources, technology and market size. The third characteristic which vindicates their grouping together is an increasing dynamic co-operation and deepening interdependence among them since the early 1980s. The economies of the eastern Pacific are excluded because their inclusion will make this compact, mutually co-operative and interactive – and therefore symbiotic – group sprawling and cumbersome, both functionally and conceptually. This is not to contend that the eastern Pacific economies will not interact closely (as do the USA and Japan) with those of the Asia-Pacific. They will, and some of them do so intensely, but they will relate to the Asia-Pacific group without belonging to it and will remain active external participants.

As seen in Figure 1.1, the Japanese economy, by virtue of its financial prowess, technological lead and the strength of the yen, and because it is the largest economy of the region, will be the epicentre of this economic grouping. It is an important determinant of the prosperity of the Asia-Pacific region. A lot of what Japan does will determine the future direction of the regional economy. With the four newly-industrialising economies of east Asia and the two industrialised economies of Australasia interacting more closely with Japan than with the ASEAN-4 and China the Asia-Pacific region makes a compact, three-tier growth pole of the international economy. In the foreseeable future, it promises to be as dynamic as the other two growth poles of the international economy – the European Union (EU) and the two north Atlantic economies, the USA and Canada.

VIVE LA DIFFÉRENCE!

The rich diversity of the Asia-Pacific region is visible in land area, population, size of GDP and other indicators. For instance, the region includes China, which has a huge land area

Figure 1.1   Composition of the Asia-Pacific Region

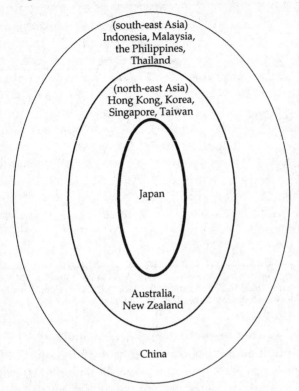

of over 9.5 million km² and a population of 1.1 billion. The region also includes small countries, called microstates, with areas under 1000 km² and populations under 10 million. Japan, the largest economy of the region, is an economic superpower having per capita income of $ 25 430 (Table 1.1). At the other extreme are the small economies such as the Philippines, New Zealand, Malaysia and Singapore, with GDP less than $ 50 million. The Philippines, Indonesia and China are the low-income economies, with per capita incomes of $ 730, $ 570 and $ 370 respectively. Japan, with 67 per cent of regional GDP, overwhelmingly dominates the regional economic stage. China and Australia are the second and third largest economies, accounting for 8.2 per cent and 6.6 per cent of the regional GDP respectively.

Table 1.1   GDP and GNP of Asia-Pacific Countries

	GDP in 1990 ($ m.)	GDP as proportion of total regional GDP(%)	GNP per capita (1990)
Japan	2 942 890	66.8	25 430
Korea	236 400	5.4	5 400
Taiwan	144 820	3.3	7 997
Hong Kong	59 670	1.3	11 490
Singapore	34 600	0.8	11 160
Indonesia	107 250	2.4	570
Malaysia	42 400	0.9	2 320
Thailand	80 170	1.8	1 420
Philippines	43 860	1.0	730
Australia	296 300	6.6	17 000
New Zealand	42 760	0.9	12 680
China	364 900	8.2	370
Total	4 396 060	100.0	

Source: World Bank, *World Development Report 1992*, Washington, DC, 1992. Data for Taiwan come from *Taiwan Statistical Data Book 1992*, Council for Economic Planning and Development, Taipei, Republic of China.

Some countries are very densely populated, others are very sparsely populated. Most countries are a contiguous whole, but Indonesia and the Philippines are archipelagos, together having over 20 767 islands, ranging from small reefs to areas about the size of France. Japan, Korea and Taiwan are ethnically homogeneous societies, whereas Malaysia, Indonesia, Singapore and Hong Kong are multi-racial and multi-cultural.

When growth began in the region, during the early 1960s, Japan was reconstructing its war-ravaged economy, China was in the throes of revolutionary turmoil, Korea and Taiwan were abjectly poor. At this point Australia and New Zealand were prosperous countries, although they were far from being mature industrial economies. Thus, while the majority of countries started growth from a low level, some started from a high base. There is also a striking disparity in natural resource endowments, where the countries range from very poor to very rich. This diversity has been harnessed to deepen economic interdependence and maintain high growth in the region. As alluded to above, Japan posted high growth rates in the 1960s. In the 1970s and 1980s it slowed, but the four Asian newly-industrialising economies (ANIEs) and the ASEAN-4 began to register high growth rates. The expansion of trade and investment in the region during the 1980s further stimulated growth in the ANIEs and the ASEAN-4. In addition, rapid growth in China during the 1980s was achieved through active economic interaction with the market economies of the region, which in turn contributed to the growth of the region. As set forth earlier, an interesting economic symbiosis has developed among the regional economies, with Japan providing capital, technology and markets; Australia, New Zealand and the ASEAN-4 providing natural resources and markets; and the ANIEs drawing in natural resources and providing capital and exports of manufactured goods. The stark complementarity between the Chinese and Japanese economies has been sharply evident and has facilitated collaboration between the two.

PIONEERING GROWTH

The Asia-Pacific region, particularly Japan and the ANIEs, has established itself as a trail-blazer in the arena of economic growth. A person active in *haute couture* will naturally be drawn to Paris, a connoisseur of art will head for Florence, but an economist interested in the rapid growth and industrialisation will find it impossible to take his or her mind away from Japan and the ANIEs because it is the most interesting and dynamic region of the world economy. The achievements of the Asia-Pacific economies were neglected during the 1960s, but Myrdal's *magnum opus*, published in 1968, saw south Asian economies as the prototype of growth and the economies of the future. The world was enthralled by the superficial intricacies of their five-year plans and the vigour and direction that their governments were going to impart to these economies. The ANIEs did not come into focus until the publication of the Asian Development Bank's report in 1971. It was an influential work and set the new line of thinking about the Asia-Pacific economies. The superlative performance of Japan and the

ANIEs changed what economists knew about economic growth and initiated a new orthodoxy. Adam Smith and classical economists could only partly explain this performance. Standard theories about the rise of capitalism and industrialisation, *à la* Garnaut, have begun to appear as inadequate as pre-Galilean astronomy.

The Asia-Pacific economies expanded faster than those of any other region in the world. During the post-war period four waves of economic dynamism swept through them. The first swept through Japan in the 1950s, and the ANIEs followed close on its heels in the 1960s. The third wave struck the ASEAN group in the 1970s, and the fourth struck and transformed the Chinese economy during the 1980s. Kuznets' (1966) authoritative work has no record of an economy doubling its GDP in a decade, although Australia and the USA came close to doing so when the former averaged 5.7 per cent growth rate between the early 1860s and the mid-1880s and the latter averaged 5.5 per cent a year for a period between the late 1860s and the early 1890s. However, over the post-war period, five economies of the Asia-Pacific region achieved the rare feat of doubling GDP in a decade: Japan, South Korea, Taiwan, Hong Kong and Singapore. During the 1980s China, through actively reforming its domestic economy and interacting with the market economies, became the sixth economy to achieve this distinction (Garnaut, 1988). Thailand has maintained high growth rates for a long time and is heading the same way. When other countries in the Asia-Pacific region were experiencing rapid economic expansion, Australia and New Zealand had achieved the status of industrialised – albeit small – economies, growing at a sedate pace.

Certainly, there are considerable differences in the economic policies of the Asia-Pacific countries. For instance, on the one hand there is the *laissez-faire* Hong Kong and on the other hand there is Korea, where there has been significant industrial policy interventionism. Yet there are several basic commonalties in macroeconomic policy as well as common determinants of rapid growth in these economies. For example: they have recorded the highest rates of saving in the world – government policies and fiscal incentives have contributed indirectly to high domestic savings, and real interest rates have been positive and, from an international perspective, high. The government sector has also made direct contribution to saving, particularly in Korea, Taiwan and China. High saving rates was one reason behind strong investment performance; external capital was another. Several Asia-Pacific economies supplemented domestic savings with external capital inflows whenever the resource gap seemed large. These countries, except the Philippines, were careful about not jeopardising their external stability. High savings leading to high investment soon became a virtuous cycle, with one feeding on the other in a circular causation. Since a large proportion of national income was continually invested, capital stock expanded rapidly. Several Asia-Pacific economies kept a firm grip over their financial markets and forced them to serve the needs of the industrial sector during the initial phases of growth.

High investment certainly leads to technology upgrading and expansion of capital stock and explains better growth performance – but only partly. The classical view that factor input determines economic growth is now considered limited. Studies like Denison (1962) and Otani and Villanueva (1988) have shaken the classical view. Capital formation seemed to explain only a small part of cross-country differences in growth rates. Cross-country comparisons, while confirming some correlation between high investment ratios and high growth rates, report weak correlation coefficients. In addition, there is the unanswered riddle of the direction of causality. A major part of growth performance is attributed to total factor productivity, generated by all-encompassing, albeit ill-defined, 'residual factors'. These include the human factor and Lee Kwan Yew's 'vital intangible',[2] macroeconomic policy and improvement in resource allocation, institutional and structural characteristics, absorption of technology, efficiency of investment or incremental capital output ratio (ICOR), provision of public goods, management and entrepreneurship, and the like.

Let us, therefore, turn to the residual factors in the case of the Asia-Pacific region. The high points of policy stance and economic characteristics enumerated below applied, in varying degrees, to all of them. First, an outstanding characteristic of the Asia-Pacific economies was their outward-orientated growth process, that is, growing ratio of foreign trade to GDP and domestic expenditure. International economic orientation contributed to both growth and stability. Economies that are internationally insolvent or have binding international liquidity constraints cannot grow. They are also highly vulnerable to debt traps. Rising exports of manufactures from these countries helped diversify export structures away from primary exports and thereby steadied their terms-of-trade. Outward economic expansion also establishes a second virtuous cycle, that of linking trade expansion to technological upgradation of the domestic industrial sector. Exporting firms come to acquire the wherewithal of importing advanced capital goods embodying state-of-the-art technology. Trade exposes them to the newest techniques and helps them focus on the art of the possible. These firms realise the importance of the technological edge necessary to stay competitive in the international markets. Brisk expansion of trade provided them with opportunities to specialise according to comparative advantage which, in turn, encouraged the exploitation of scale economies as well as maintenance of high capacity-utilisation (Balassa and Williamson, 1990). Asia-Pacific economies ranging from Japan to the ASEAN-4 have been able to capture these dynamic gains from trade in addition to the static gains that were provided by improved resource allocation. Although only Hong Kong is a free-trading economy, other governments on various occasions have expanded the manufacturing sector, including manufacturing exports. Import tariffs were slapped on consumer imports at times for balance of payments reasons, but the bias introduced by these tariffs was largely offset by export subsidies. Policy neutrality was more or less maintained.

Secondly, to stimulate export-orientated industrialisation, countries of the Asia-Pacific region used both credit subsidies and financial repression (as in Korea) and fiscal subsidy (as in Taiwan). The former had side-effects: for instance, with capital costs subsidised, the favoured sectors tended to become capital-intensive and large-scale. In addition to providing loans at below the market rates and possibly to buy government debt at low interest rates, banks were forced to suppress deposit rates which discouraged savings in the financial sector. Conversely, a fiscal subsidy on output or exports of favoured industry does not have these side-effects. Besides, the cost of fiscal subsidies is hidden in low deposit rates, whereas the cost of fiscal subsidies is explicit in the tax structure (Bradford and Branson, 1987).

Thirdly, economic growth in the Asia-Pacific region was accompanied by rapid change in the structure of production. The agricultural sector declined relatively while the importance of manufacturing and service sectors rose (see pp. 39–44 below) and export specialisation underwent identical transformation. Structural changes continued steadily, and by the 1970s the developing economies of the Asia-Pacific region had made a considerable degree of progress in industrialisation. Their economies had acquired a significant level of capital intensification.

Fourthly, prudent and cautious macroeconomic management was another hallmark of these economies. In general, they were low-inflation economies. Over the period 1980–90, in seven of them, the average long-term inflation rate was 5 per cent or less. The best performers were Japan (1.5 per cent), Malaysia (1.6 per cent) and Taiwan (2.2 per cent). The Philippines and New Zealand were the poorest performers, having average inflation rates of 14.9 and 10.5 per cent respectively. The World Bank associated higher growth with lower price distortions. *The World Development Report 1983* contained a price distortion index for thirty-one countries. It was prepared using measures of distortion of foreign exchange pricing, factor pricing and product pricing. It demonstrated that in the 1970s countries with higher government-induced distortions grew slowly. The *World Development Report 1985* showed that large price distortions also lead to slower growth of exports and greater likelihood of debt-servicing difficulties. Although distortions were there (as in Korea), in general the Asia-Pacific economies were identified with low levels of price distortions. In spite of this, these economies implemented numerous reforms in their industrial and trade policies as well as financial systems. During the 1980s several of them adopted macroeconomic reforms that were conducive to growth. Some of them (Japan, Taiwan and Korea) had to adjust to external surpluses, while others (Australia, New Zealand, Indonesia, Malaysia and Thailand) had to adjust to external deficits. Adoption of reform measures drove these economies to liberalisation and efficiency-enhancing macroeconomic policies. Although Australia and Thailand were exceptions in this regard – because while making structural adjustments they were forced to impose controls on capital movement – in general governments in the region saw an opportunity to liberalise the economy while making macroeconomic adjustments. Freeing of market forces helped achieve optimal allocation of resources on the given production possibility curve in these economies and dynamic gains from international orientation of their economies helped in moving this curve outward.

Fifthly, governments in these economies had a high level of commitment to economic growth, which is a precondition of economic growth. It was given higher priority than social and welfare objectives. These governments intervened directly in economic affairs to promote growth. Yet they were less intrusive in resource allocation than other developing economies and did not stifle market forces. Government policy in all these economies, including Indonesia after 1965, rejected public ownership over the means of production and centralised planning. These economies discovered early that the private sector is the high-achiever. Market orientation of these economies facilitated the operation of price mechanisms, therefore resources were able to move with relative ease from less to more productive uses. Reliance on markets for resource allocation also facilitated adjustments to domestic and external economic shocks. An exemplary case of market and government collaborating is the phasing out of industries that were losing comparative advantage in Japan and ANIEs. These governments did not suffer from the soft-state syndrome and were authoritarian in varying degrees, therefore rent-seeking groups were not able to dominate them.

These groups have had a powerful influence on policy-making in other market economies. Therefore these societies were able to pursue their economic goals in a more determined manner without frittering away their creative energy.

Sixthly, much is made of the cultural values of the Asia-Pacific societies as a promoter of economic growth. These societies assigned high value to formal education, personal discipline and an attitude of thrift. These proclivities are central to what is popularly described as Confucianism. This cultural tradition is the common property of north-east and south-east Asia, more so in the former than in the latter. Several of these traits, such as thrift, higher education, and meritocracy, can be easily and closely associated with a capacity to sustain high levels of growth. Individual and social disciplines impart social cohesion and a readiness to accept change. Individuals and families react passively to the short-term costs of change because of its long-term promise and potential. They tend to rationalise the short-term pain and in the process create an environment of political stability, so necessary for stable economic growth. In addition, for centuries the Sinic societies – Chinese, Japanese, Koreans – have shown intense respect for bureaucracy and officialdom. This has made it possible for the modern governments to get away with their soft authoritarianism. Yet another trait was an almost religious regard for education, scholarship and learning. In the Confucian world the loci of wisdom and virtue were seen to intersect. This has helped in creating skilled and well-educated workforces in the region. All these characteristics have decisive economic ramifications.

The rise of the Asia-Pacific countries to economic prominence has given new relevance to the age-old question reposed by Simon Kuznets (1966). In the preface of his seminal book he wondered whether the economic principles devised and followed in the West were suitable for universal application or were culture-bound and had meaning and relevance only for societies where they were created. In its quest for productive efficiency, the West came upon its rational model through its belief in individualism and successfully harnessed the forces of scientific creativity and technological innovation. As opposed to this, the Asia-Pacific societies traditionally emphasised human relations, group cohesion and harmony. When they launched into economic growth, they borrowed technology from the West through various modes of technology transfer. By marrying machines with their human-centred cultures, the Asia-Pacific countries achieved unparalleled economic growth. Western technology and Eastern ethos produced laudable economic results (Tai, 1989). Though on the one hand this mix is not a sufficient condition for economic growth, on the other its success insinuates that if Western individualism was appropriate for the pioneering period of industrialisation, it is likely that post-Confucianism 'collectivism' is better suited to the age of mass industrialisation and mass production (MacFarquhar, 1990). The east Asian model has emerged as the first alternative to the rational Western model which was born at the dawn of industrial revolution.

A little-known tendency of the post-Confucian countries (namely, Japan, Taiwan, Hong Kong, Singapore and Korea) is that they are extremely meritocratic; this has decisive economic ramifications. In their belief that people vary in calibre and have inherent genetic differences, these societies are Platonic. Plato categorised people into gold, silver and brass (Dore, 1987). Meritocracy begins with children in schools, continues to universities and then in bureaucracies, both public and private. At all levels high performers are separated repeatedly from mediocres. The system assumes that people legitimately deserve material rewards, prestige and power by virtue of their capabilities. Meritocracy identifies the high achievers, separates wheat from chaff, and rewards the deserving. Academic achievements, although important, are not the only determinants of success in a career. Other qualities like drive, determination and dynamism also play a role. The individuals who belong to the top of the ability spectrum are also judged for these qualities. They differentiate the high-flyers on the seniority-promotion fast track from plodders on the slow track. Meritocracy thus allows the best possible use of human resources and contributes to institutional efficiency, which becomes easily visible in general X-efficiency and economic performance. As opposed to this, in other developing countries – for instance, those in south Asia – an individual of any calibre can be anywhere because these societies are not meritocratic. A capable individual can plod all through his career while a mediocre, low-drive, lacklustre individual can be a high-flyer on the fast track. The outcome of this tendency is also evident from the tardy economic performance of these resource-rich economies.

Japan, the pioneer economy of the region, is also close to the other Asia-Pacific economies; such proximity – and propinquity – has to influence the other economies. They benefit from it both in a tangible and an intangible manner: tangibly, because they can easily and cheaply benefit from the exchange of goods and services, including financial services; intangibly, because they will be more prone to exchanging ideas and ambitions with the pioneer of their own geographical region than with those that are equally alluring but remotely located.

SUB-REGIONAL TRANSFORMATIONS

Let us now focus on the economic metamorphoses of each sub-group in the region, beginning with Japan.

Japan

In the early 1950s, the Japanese economy had a dualistic structure and it depended heavily on US military procurement orders. The Engel coefficient for urban households in the mid-1950s was 45 per cent, that is, almost half of the disposable income was being spent on food (Kosai, 1986). This is considered a characteristic of a developing economy. The first good year that the economy had was 1955 when it recorded a 10 per cent growth rate in real terms. This is referred to as Japan's beginning of *suryo* or quantitative prosperity. Industry consciously began to bridge the technology gap that existed between Japan and other industrialised economies and also began to develop export sectors. The earliest success was achieved by the shipbuilding industry. Export success gradually began to spread to other sectors and domestic consumption and investment began to boom. The sudden rise in plant and equipment investment during the latter half of the 1950s produced a sea change in the economy, and by 1959 Japan had entered a period of prosperity called the Iwato boom. This upswing of the business cycle was durable and lasted for 42 months. It had an all-pervading effect over the economy and the Japanese economy found itself on the crest of a technological revolution. Growth and modernisation processes moved at a fast rate and facilitated the development of consumer durable sectors like automobiles and electric machines and appliances. The international economy was entering an era of mass production in several key consumer durable industries and worldwide demand for such products was strong. The establishment of the General Agreement on Tariffs and Trade (GATT) promoted free trade, which was to benefit Japan immensely.

The institutional competitiveness of Japanese exports continually increased because of its well-conceived domestic and international strategy in this regard. It was based on properly laid down objectives, clear ideas on how to achieve them and the provision of necessary institutional support by the government. Varying degrees of success in international competitiveness are explained by the differences in growth-productivity-resource orientation on the one hand and distribution-security-opportunity orientation on the other (Scott, 1985), with Japan falling into the former category. Although business and government collaborated closely and purposefully, the vital success ingredient was the growth and productivity orientation of both. The growth orientation of *kaisha*, or the corporations, was strengthened and nurtured by fierce domestic competition, and then they were supported by a well-laid out government strategy, turning them into formidable international competitors (Abegglen and Stalk, 1985). The growth-productivity orientation was based on the dynamic comparative advantage (Higashi and Lanter, 1990). Japan's export production was dominated by large firms because they had greater financial, personnel and material resources than small or medium-sized firms and could absorb the effects of export price changes while deciding whether to slash prices or to shift into new products or businesses, and so forth.

After the mid-1960s, Japan maintained its growth momentum and steadily caught up with the other industrialised economies. Measures of total factor productivity growth show (Balassa and Noland, 1988) that it outperformed all the major industrial economies during the 1966–73 period. It fell behind France and Germany during the 1973–85 period, but remained well ahead of the USA. However, Japan constantly maintained its lead in capital formation – its growth rate of capital formation was about double that of the other major industrial economies. By 1980, Japan had become a power to reckon with in the areas of industrial development, technological advancement, trade, managerial and organisational capability and by the mid-1980s it had emerged as the second-largest economy, third-largest trader and the largest creditor nation in the world. Towards the end of the decade it also became the largest donor and largest foreign investor (Das, 1992).

Australia and New Zealand

Australia and New Zealand are two small, land-rich, better-off, industrial economies and, like Japan, they are members of the OECD (Organization for Economic Co-operation and Development). They have high per capita incomes and moderate growth rates. Their pattern of trade conforms more to their highly favourable endowment of land. Measured in terms of the volume of GDP, Australia is larger than Sweden and Switzerland but smaller than Spain. Its per capita GNP is comparable to Italy and the Netherlands. The GDP of New Zealand is comparable to that of Ireland, whereas its per capita GNP is close to that of Belgium. Both the countries are sparsely populated. A rich natural resource base, together with domestic and external capital, and a long history of economic growth has helped provide the foundation for high living standards.

Yet the two countries have found it hard to sustain their relative position among the affluent countries. Since they have traditionally relied on agriculture and extractive industries for a great proportion of their export earnings, they have found it progressively more difficult to create wealth which is comparable to that being generated by the technological societies into which other industrial countries have transformed themselves. Natural resources and primary products are still a large part of their foreign trade. Australia is a large exporter of coal, wool, wheat, beef and mineral ores, while New Zealand exports are dominated by meat, dairy products, wool and forestry products. Thus, these two economies depend heavily on exports of primary products for earning foreign exchange. Much as developing countries do, they export primary goods to finance their imports of capital goods. Both economies have been recipients of foreign direct investment which brought technology and managerial skills with it. Since they relied on the other OECD economies for keeping up with technology, they had to rely on foreign direct investment. During the last three decades, in terms of growth rate and economic performance in general, Australia has been far more dynamic than New Zealand.

The two economies have had three distinct eras: the first was the emigrant colonialism of the pre-war period when they were providers of food and raw materials for industrial societies, particularly Britain. After 1945, slow transition towards economic independence began. Traditional dependence on Britain in both trade and finance ended. This phase was marked by extensive government interference in all aspects of the economy, financial controls and exchange restrictions. The third phase can be dated from the late 1970s, when the two economies began to adjust to the international economy and discovered their place in the Asia-Pacific region.

The two economies have had periods of concern because their commodity and foodstuff exports to traditional markets in Europe and north America faced restrictions because of intensification of protectionistic policies since the mid-1970s. Their exports failed to keep pace with the growing import bills and, therefore, they tended to give in readily to protect their domestic manufacturing sectors, at times at high costs. Japan's rise as a major industrial power changed the scene profoundly for them. With its voracious needs for industrial raw materials, it became a major trading partner of Australia and New Zealand. Japan also saw a large market for its manufactured and durable consumer goods exports in these two regional neighbours. Economic interdependence and common strategic interests have brought the three economies close and the mutual affinity is likely to grow. During the 1980s, Korea also became a significant trading partner of Australia and New Zealand, and the economic ties were substantially strengthened with China, Taiwan and ASEAN-4. In the process the two economies have successfully carved a regional niche for themselves. Their future growth prospects largely depend on their success in increasing efficiency within their economies as well as growth in the regional and international economies.

The two countries entered into a free trade agreement called the New Zealand-Australia Free Trade Agreement (NAFTA) in 1965 and another one called the Australia-New Zealand Closer Economic Relations Trade Agreement (ANCER) in 1983. The key difference in the new agreement is that it aimed at freeing trade in all goods across the Tasman from restrictions, although a small number of products were specifically set aside for later consideration, whereas the objectives of NAFTA were less ambitious, aiming at progressively liberalising trade in specified goods. The ANCER had far larger scope: it was intended eventually to establish a trans-Tasman free-trade zone by phasing out all tariff, quantity and other restrictions on trade between the two partners. Subsequently the agreement was extended to free trade in services and to consider ways of harmonising business laws (Australian Government Publishing Service, 1986). Both the partners benefited from the ANCER, with New Zealand deriving greater benefits than Australia. This difference in gains is partly accounted for by the fact that Australia is a much more important trading partner for New Zealand than New Zealand is for Australia (Australian Government Publishing Service, 1989).

Asian Newly Industrialising Economies (ANIEs)

The success of the four ANIEs has attracted a great deal of professional and popular interest. They have been extensively studied and immense literature exists on their economic growth and its rationale. For instance, see Berger and Hsiao (eds), 1988: Corbo *et al.*, 1985; Lau 1990; Muton, 1986; Smith *et al.*, 1985; and Woronoff 1986. This list is far from exhaustive. As indicated earlier, although the 'four-dragons' began to breathe fire in the 1960s, their achievements were not recognised until the early 1970s. Publication of *Industry and Trade in Some Developing Countries*[3] (Little *et al.*, 1990) was an important step in this direction. These four economies took a leaf out of the book of Japan's economic success and pursued an export-orientated strategy of deliberate promotion of manufacturing goods exports in keeping with their comparative advantage. They saw wisdom in shunning import-substitution after the initial stages of growth and exploited dynamic gains from trade and reaped the benefits of their comparative advantage. The result was an exemplary economic performance. They recorded very high rates of GDP growth, which in turn was associated with their high rate of export volume growth. These countries were poorly endowed with natural resources. Initially their exports were concentrated on traditional and labour-intensive manufactured products, then they progressed to capital-intensive and technology-intensive manufactured goods. By the early 1990s, they had begun to make forays in the knowledge-intensive product markets.

A certain set of preconditions existed in these economies when they began their hypergrowth, including: a well-educated and disciplined labour force; a competent bureaucracy; social and governmental commitment to economic growth; a market-orientated domestic economic strategy; and a dominant role of the private sector. The small public sector that existed was largely regarded as a good performer (Amsden, 1989; Chang and Singh, 1992). In addition, the international economic environment of the 1950s and 1960s was aptly suited for the outward-orientated growth strategy of the ANIEs. These unusual preconditions assisted their brisk take-off into high and sustained growth.

The high level of human capital raised the technological level in the ANIEs in a short time span. They also maintained significant growth rates in savings and capital accumulation. However, there were other developing economies that failed to take off despite comparable rates of saving and investment. The ANIEs must have done something extra to achieve what they did. While most other developing economies remained wedded to ideologically-orientated development doctrines promoted by institutions like the UNCTAD and stressed basic needs, income distribution (before growth and production) and other social objectives, the ANIEs were influenced by the resurgence of neoclassical economics in the 1960s and adopted clear, pragmatic neoclassical policy lines. Sound macroeconomic policies and, in general, high quality economic management, were among the basic reasons for their economic success. Their economic strategy and management was characterised by pragmatism and flexibility. Conversely, the outcome of ideologically-orientated economic policies and poor quality economic management can be seen in the shoddy performance of south Asian developing economies, which has continued decade after decade.

The mainstream neoclassical economists and the Western model of free enterprise both preclude governments from the running of the economy and spurn government intervention. Three of the ANIEs had all-pervasive government presence in their economic affairs, Hong Kong was the only exception. So much so that governments went into such detailed decision-making as 'picking the winners'. However, the intervention was of a rather different kind. It did not replace markets, only guided them. It was not the market subduing or distorting intervention but of a market-conforming variety, little understood in the context of Western-style capitalism. The soft authoritarianism of these governments gave the ANIEs their basic directions without smothering the market forces and destroying domestic competition. This strategy supported the 'survival of the fittest' kind of industrialisation and thereby improved the efficiency of resource allocation. Instead of being counterproductive, this kind of government intervention enhanced economic efficiency because governments adopted policies to compensate for the weaknesses of the free enterprise system. The negative externalities were identified and taken care of by the governments. For instance, an important externality for developing countries is the cost of selling in the world market. The developing country exports have to counter the quality bias, and individual enterprises cannot bear the cost of countering the bias and creating a market niche without government support. Another area which benefits from government intervention is that of the market cost of labour, which often tends to be higher than the social cost of labour. Thus, in the ANIEs, intervention lubricated the economies instead of thwarting them.

Lastly, emphasis on private enterprise, concomitantly existing with domestic and international competition, contributed to making ANIEs resilient. Private sector enterprises, without competition, would have resulted in private monopolies which in turn would have been as pernicious as the public sector ones. The experience of the ANIEs buttresses the dictum that competition is value-creating.

The ASEAN-4

In the oft-used metaphor of 'flying geese', where Japan leads a formation of Asia-Pacific economies, followed by the ANIEs, the ASEAN-4 come last. This sub-group has learned a great deal from the economic and technological experiences of the economies that preceded it in the 'flying geese' formation. Japan and the ANIEs were *sui generis* only to a limited extent, because the ASEAN-4 were able to replicate their performance to a considerable degree. The ASEAN-4 also gained immensely from economic co-operation with them. Noteworthy, in this context, is the Malaysian campaign of 'look East' and 'learn from Japan'. ASEAN was established in a low-key manner in 1967, initially without any economic ambitions. However, it soon began to make economic co-operation-related overtures and the Federation of ASEAN

Chamber of Commerce and Industry was established in 1971 for co-operation among private enterprises.

Although the ASEAN-4 were neighbours, their economic ties were initially tenuous. They were well-endowed with natural resources, and, therefore, were suppliers of industrial raw materials and foodstuffs. Their exports were strongly specialised in primary products. With rapid industrialisation, significant structural change occurred over the 1970s. Growth in manufactured exports began, which received impetus from the huge expansion in world trade that took place in the early 1970s. The share of manufactured goods in total exports increased considerably in all of them except Indonesia, where it was negligibly small to begin with. Trade expansion enabled these countries to establish extensive links with a wide range of countries, especially the industrialised economies. While promoting industry, these economies did not neglect their agricultural sectors because they were essentially land-based economies. Consequently, per capita food production rose steadily. Indonesia recorded the minimum rate of growth of food production.

The economic philosophy of the ASEAN-4 was generally one of pragmatic flexibility, bending with international economic developments and responding to external changes with economic prudence. At an early stage in their industrialisation process they began to show a healthy respect for outward-looking strategy. This strategy is known to create pressure for adopting better monetary, exchange rate and labour policies. Their macroeconomic management is considered to be of high quality (Arndt, 1989). These countries increasingly allowed market forces to drive their economies, which, coupled with outward orientation, enhanced functional efficiency and the efficiency of resource allocation. Also, it is generally agreed that external factors influenced the growth process in the ASEAN-4 significantly (Chintayarangsan *et al.*, 1992).

Owing to recession, the early 1980s were lean years for these economies but their decadal average growth rate was the highest for any region in the world. They attracted a good deal of foreign direct investment due to rapid growth and prudent economic management. A major part of foreign direct investment went into high-tech industries. By the early 1990s, Malaysia became the largest exporter of integrated circuits in the world. Their eagerness to emulate the ANIEs and Japan is obvious.

China

During the economic restoration period of 1950–7, the Chinese economy grew at an average rate of around 8 per cent per annum but the brisk growth abruptly collapsed with the 'Great Leap Forward' (1958–60) strategy. However, despite reversals and the chaos of a decade-long (1966–76) cultural revolution, China's economic performance was not abjectly dismal. Long-term average output grew by over 5 per cent per annum, although the per capita rise was much lower. Initially growth in output was entirely made through the contributions made by increasing the labour force. The high saving rate helped build capital but the ICOR was also high and the efficiency of investment remained low. Being a neighbour, China could not help being impressed by the achievements of Japan and the ANIEs. Through the socialistic economic haze it saw the economic benefits potentially attainable from dismantling its myriad price and quantity controls, having a market economy and adopting open trade policies. The realisation that the complexities of the socialistic economic system were taking a heavy toll in terms of efficiency and output had set in well by the end of the cultural revolution, and 1976 was marked for the beginning of implementation of what became the political economy of reform and economic opening. The reform measures were introduced gingerly at first, but decisively after the Third Plenary Meeting of the Eleventh Communist Party Central Committee in December 1978. This became an epochal point in modern Chinese economic history, the beginning of a sweeping set of economic reforms, popularly known as the 'open door' policy.

Several liberalisation and open market reform measures were initiated in the early 1980s and they were strengthened in a stronger wave of reforms in 1984. The former, import-substituting industrialisation, strategy was almost abandoned. Commitment to reform was steady and several missing elements of the Japan-ANIEs formula were eagerly institutionalised. Society supported the new economic ideology and accepted the use of markets for the allocation of resources in lieu of the central planning authority. The operation of market forces first began in the rural economy and after 1984 entered the urban economy. Opening up of the economy enabled the absorption of much-needed technology from abroad as well as the inflow of foreign direct investment (World Bank, 1985, 1989). The consequences of liberalisation and reforms were clearly visible in China's growth rate: real GNP grew by an average of almost 9 per cent per annum over the 1978–91 period, a rate that doubles the size of the economy every eight years. Thus liberalisation and reforms paid off handsomely. The economy acquired a great deal of momentum and by the early 1990s was bursting with life. When the republics of the former USSR next door were close to bankruptcy, China had over $ 40 billion in foreign exchange reserves and was attracting plenty of foreign direct investment. More than $ 1 billion-worth of chinese funds were floated in the West in the early 1990s and investors' response was highly favourable (*The Economist*, 1992a). China has tried to integrate with the surrounding Asia-Pacific economies, especially with Japan.

Hindsight reveals that in spite of commitment to economic reforms, China's course has been zig-zag. It needs to stay on course because the part of the economy that was being run by the central planning authorities was operating poorly even in the early 1990s. A third of the state-owned enterprises were money-losers and twice as many were really in the red. Fortuitously, half the industrial output at this point was accounted for by firms that were not state-owned but by market-sensitive lower-tier governments, private individuals and foreign investors. In addition, problems related to poor infrastructure continue to dog the economy. The 14th National Congress of the Chinese Communist Party (October 1992) attempted to institutionalise politically the open market reforms and turn China into a 'socialist market economy', which appears to be an oxymoron. During the Congress it was acknowledged that the operating principles should be as follows: the macroeconomic tools are better instruments of economic control; the plan should be nothing more than strategic targets; infrastructure investment should be government's prerogative; government should no longer manage industrial enterprises; the bureaucracy must be shrunk, as must employment in state enterprises; and more attention should be paid to the services sector for absorbing surplus labour (Byrnes, 1992). This is the famous thesis of patriarch Deng Xiaoping and represents the current proclivity of the managers of the Chinese economy. Japan will serve as a key model for the relationship between government and industry as China switches to a market economy (Mitsumori and Meshino, 1992). Indications are that the reform revolution will roll on, and in the short term consumerism will supplant communism.

ECONOMIC ASCENSION

The long-term growth rate is a good indicator of economic dynamism because (i) it eliminates short-term variations; and (ii) it reveals whether the growth was a sustained feature or a mere period-specific event caused by some favourable internal or external developments. Average GNP growth of the Asia-Pacific economies and that of other country groups over the 1965–90 period is given in Table 1.2. The group average for Asia-Pacific was 4.6 per cent. The performance of none of the other country groups is comparable to that of the Asia-Pacific region. The second best performing region, the OECD economies, had an average GNP growth rate of only 2.4 per cent, which is half the Asia-Pacific growth rate.

The brisk growth rate of the Asia-Pacific economies led to more than four-fold economic expansion of their GDP in real terms over the 1965–89 period (Table 1.3). The north American and west European economies, which comprised the other two growth poles of the global economy, doubled

Table 1.2   Comparative Average Annual GNP Growth Rates, 1965–90

Country/region	(%)
Japan	4.1
ANIEs	7.1
ASEAN-4	3.6
Australia and New Zealand	1.5
China	5.8
Asia-Pacific region	4.6
Sub-Saharan Africa	0.2
South Asia	1.9
Middle-East and north Africa	1.8
Latin America and the Caribbean	1.8
OECD countries	2.4
USA	1.7

Source: World Bank, *World Development Report 1992*. Data for Taiwan come from: *Taiwan Statistical Data Book 1992*, Council for Economic Planning and Development, Taipei, Republic of China.

Table 1.3   Comparative GDP at Constant Prices, 1965–90

	1965	1970	1980	1989
Asia-Pacific countries	919 (13.6)[a]	1515 (17.6)	2473 (20.6)	3759 (25.3)
USA	2597 (38.6)	3030 (35.2)	4016 (33.4)	5271 (35.4)
European Community (of 12)	2252 (33.5)	2821 (32.7)	3771 (31.3)	4548 (30.6)
World	6719 (100)	8618 (100)	12030 (100)	14867 (100)

[a] Figures in parentheses stand for percentage of total world GDP.
Source: International Economic Data Bank, Australia National University, Canberra.

their respective GDPs over the same period and the world GDP increase by 2.2 times. This growth pattern enhanced the weight of the Asia-Pacific region in the international economy. Its GDP was 13.6 per cent of the total world GDP in 1965. By 1989, its share rose to 25.3 per cent, while both the pre-established growth poles lost ground.

Rapid economic expansion has established the Asia Pacific region as the third pole of the international economy.

However, as seen in Table 1.4, it is still the smallest of the three in terms of the volume of GDP. The future need not be a repetition of the past, and economic growth during the 1990s may not be at a fast clip. The expansionary phase of the business cycle that began in Japan in November 1986 ended in 1991. Several indexes began to show 'plateau condition' and corporate earning rate hit ceiling. Notwithstanding the slow down of the domineering Japanese economy, no one expects the region to lose its momentum. Its catching-up process with the other two growth poles will, therefore, continue.

As seen in Table 1.4, there were marked intra-regional differences in economic expansion. The mantle of greatest dynamism fell on the ANIEs because their long-term (1965–90) average GNP growth rate was 7.1 per cent. Taiwan and Korea recorded an outstanding 8.5 and 7.1 per cent respectively. China, as noted earlier, did not do poorly, as this indicator shows, recording a respectable 5.8 per cent long-term

Table 1.4　　GDP and GNP Growth, 1965–90

	GDP as a proportion of world GDP (%)				Average annual growth rate of GNP per capita over 1965–90 (%)
	1965	*1970*	*1980*	*1989*	
Japan	10.0	13.5	14.9	17.7	4.1
Korea	0.3	0.4	0.6	1.1	7.1
Taiwan	0.2	0.3	0.5	0.8	8.5
Hong Kong	0.1	0.1	0.2	0.4	6.2
Singapore	0.1	0.1	0.1	0.2	6.5
Indonesia	0.3	0.3	0.4	0.6	4.5
Malaysia	0.3	0.4	0.6	1.0	4.0
The Philippines	0.2	0.2	0.3	0.3	4.4
Thailand	0.2	0.2	0.3	0.4	1.3
Australia	1.2	1.3	1.2	1.4	1.1
New Zealand	0.2	0.1	0.1	0.1	1.9
China	0.8	1.1	1.4	2.3	5.8
Regional average	13.6	17.6	20.6	25.3	4.6

Source: International Economic Data Bank, Australia National University, Canberra.

average. Japan followed with 4.1 per cent. By the early 1980s it had become a mature industrial economy and its growth rate had stabilised at a lower level than that in the earlier decades. In addition, it suffered from the *endaka* recession in the mid-1980s (Das, 1992). Among the ASEAN-4, the Philippines remained a languorous economy and pulled down the long-term average of the group to 3.6 per cent. The other three members averaged 4 per cent or higher. Since this group was a late bloomer, their decadal average for the 1980s was close to 10 per cent, though again the Philippines was an exception. Australia and New Zealand recorded a sedate 1.5 per cent average annual growth over this period. Table 1.4 also shows that between 1965 and 1989, the share of GDP of the ANIEs in the world GDP quadrupled. It soared from 0.7 per cent of the world GDP in 1965 to 2.5 per cent in 1989. Korea, Taiwan and Hong Kong all quadrupled their respective shares. China raised its share by a multiple of 2.9 and the ASEAN-4 by a multiple of 2.3. Japan came close to doubling its share of the world GDP. Australia and New Zealand did not expand their share but stood their ground and maintained their share of the world GDP.

Starting from a low economic level, several countries of the Asia-Pacific region achieved per capita income levels comparable to the poorer countries of the European Community. Korea surpassed Portugal in terms of 1990 per capita income and Taiwan went ahead of Greece as well as petro-rich Saudi-Arabia. Singapore and Hong Kong were better off than Spain and almost as rich as New Zealand, and their living standards were not very far from those of Italy and Britain. Malaysian per capita income was 71 per cent higher than that of Turkey.

The openness of the Asia-Pacific economies progressively increased. If exports as a proportion of GDP is taken as a measure of openness (Table 1.5), the performance of the ANIEs turns out to be outstanding. In the short space of a quarter of a century exports soared from 18 per cent of the GDP to 72.1 per cent. ASEAN-4 did well but their endeavours on this count were concentrated during the latter half of the 1970s and the 1980s. In 1989, exports were 35.8 per

Table 1.5   Exports as Percentage of GDP

	Japan	ANIEs	ASEAN-4	ANZ	China	Regional average
1965	5.2	18.0	26.6	11.9	6.8	8.5
1970	6.6	26.4	26.7	13.4	8.2	9.2
1980	10.8	50.1	31.0	15.4	10.8	15.2
1989	14.2	72.1	35.8	17.7	15.2	21.2

Source: International Economic Data Bank, Australian National University, Canberra.

cent of their GDP. The ANIEs and the ASEAN-4 became the most open economies in the world. Australia and New Zealand, like other industrial economies, were fairly open even in the mid-1960s and have since slowly opened their economies further. As the statistics indicate, China's opening-up began in earnest after the adoption of the 'open door' policy – that is, during the 1980s. Also, Japan has shown a steady rise in opening-up. For the region as a whole, the progress seems steady, appearing to have accelerated after the 1970s.

The openness of the economy must be closely associated with the export growth rate and economic integration with the regional and non-regional economies. In conformation with this observation, the ANIES recorded the highest long-term real growth rate of exports. During the period 1965–89, their exports grew annually at the average rate of 15.5 per cent (Table 1.6). The ASEAN economies came next, with a group average of 7 per cent. Indonesia and the Philippines lagged because they were slow to open and, therefore, were the least open economies in the group. Note that all these economies began their exports from a very low level, therefore statistics do hide the low-base effect. Japan recorded 9.9 per cent – again, the long-term average has been adversely influenced by languid performance over the 1980s. For China, the long-term average was 8 per cent and, unlike Japan, this figure has been favourably influenced by its performance over the 1980s. The average growth rate of exports for the Asia-Pacific region was 10.1 per cent, which is almost twice as high as that for USA, and the European

Table 1.6   Real Growth Rate of Exports, 1965–89[a]

	(%)	(%)
Japan	9.9	
Korea	18.7	
Thailand	9.5	15.5
Hong Kong	11.1	
Singapore	11.3	
Indonesia	5.4	
Malaysia	8.2	7.0
The Philippines	5.5	
Thailand	9.6	
Australia	5.1	
New Zealand	4.2	4.9
China	8.0	
Average for Asia-Pacific countries		10.1
USA and Canada		5.9
European Community of 12		5.6
Developing countries		5.6
World		6.0

Source: International Economic Data Bank, Australian National University, Canberra.
[a] Exports measured in constant 1987 dollars.

Community of 12, as well as the developing countries. Thus, the region's export performance was outstanding: its outward-orientation paid off richly.

Was the trade-related dynamic growth of the Asia-Pacific countries externally driven or internally generated? Was it the demand-side variables that principally determined the dynamic export growth, or was it the supply-side factors? In his statistical investigation James Riedel went to considerable lengths to answer these queries and concluded that for the Asia-Pacific region, international trade expansion only worked as 'the handmaiden' of growth, not the 'engine of growth'. He found evidence that suggested that it was the supply-side rather than demand factors that were primarily responsible for the dynamic export performance, and he categorically rejected the premise that the exports performance of the region was externally driven (Riedel, 1984).

Such an aggressive export performance resulted in steep rises in the volume of exports from the region. They doubled to $ 37 million between 1965 and 1970 and increased to $ 291 million in 1980, which was an eight-fold increase in a decade (Table 1.7).

In 1990, they reached $ 715 million, which is again two and a half times of the level of a decade before. In 1965, the Asia-Pacific countries accounted for a puny 11.4 per cent of total world exports. This proportion did not rise much in 1970, but in 1980 they had begun to account for 15 per cent of total world exports. In 1990, this proportion was as high as 22 per cent. Japan has traditionally dominated exports from the region. In 1965, it accounted for 42.6 per cent of total exports from the region. In 1970, the corresponding proportion rose to 52.1 per cent and further to 66.1 per cent in 1980. That is, Japan's domination of the regional exports went on increasing. However, the situation was reversed in 1990 when Japan's dominance came down to 40.1 per cent of the total exports of the Asia-Pacific region. Other large exporters in the region are China, Taiwan, Korea and Singapore.

Between 1965 and 1990, Japan doubled its share in world exports and accounted for 8.81 per cent of the total (Figure 1.2). The ANIEs expanded their share of world trade from 1.4 per cent of the total to 6.6 per cent, while the ASEAN-4 expanded its share from 1.9 per cent to 2.7 per cent over the same period. These dramatic jumps should be interpreted carefully: the small base effect is obvious for these two sub-groups. China succeeded in raising its share of world trade by a multiple of 2.6. Conversely, the share of Australia and New Zealand slipped drastically from 2.3 per cent to 1.4 per cent, because the two countries lacked drive in exports.

Table 1.8 indicates that the Asia-Pacific economies have gained in international trade at the expense of the USA and Canada, but the EU has strengthened its position. Until the mid-1970s, the Asia-Pacific region did not hold a position of significance on the international trade scene, albeit certain countries were doing well. However, largely because of the extraordinarily good performance of the ANIEs, Thailand

Table 1.7   Export Expansion from Asia-Pacific Economies, 1965–90

Country	1965		1970		1980		1990	
	Exports ($ million)	As proportion of total world exports (%)	Exports ($ million)	As proportion of total world exports (%)	Exports ($ million)	As proportion of total world exports (%)	Exports ($ million)	As proportion of total world exports (%)
Japan	8 452	4.87	19 319	6.61	129 542	6.67	286 768	8.81
Korea	175	0.10	830	0.28	17 446	0.90	64 837	1.99
Taiwan	450	0.26	1 428	0.49	19 837	1.02	67 040	2.06
Hong Kong	880	0.51	2 037	0.70	13 672	0.70	29 002	0.89
Singapore	981	0.57	1 554	0.53	19 375	1.00	62 627	1.62
Indonesia	722	0.42	1 055	0.36	21 909	1.13	25 553	0.78
Malaysia	1 206	0.69	1 687	0.58	12 939	0.67	31 505	0.97
Philippines	766	0.44	1 060	0.36	5 751	0.30	9 134	0.28
Thailand	607	0.35	685	0.23	6 369	0.33	23 002	0.71
Australia	2 971	1.71	4 482	1.53	21 279	1.10	35 973	1.10
New Zealand	979	0.56	1 203	0.41	5 262	0.27	9 045	0.28
China	1 643	0.95	1 768	0.60	17 481	0.90	80 529	2.47
Regional average	19 831	11.42	37 108	12.69	290 863	14.98	715 016	21.96

Source: International Economic Data Bank, Australian National University, Canberra.

Figure 1.2 Exports of the Asia-Pacific Economies as Share of Total World Exports, 1965–90

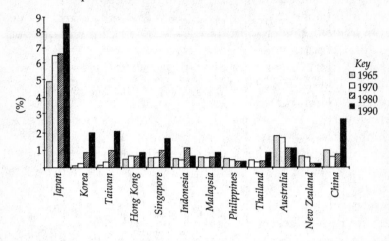

Table 1.8 Comparative Export Performance, 1965–90 ($ m.)

	1965	1970	1980	1990
Asia-Pacific countries	19 831	37 108	290 863	715 016
	(11.42)	(12.69)	(14.98)	(21.96)
USA and Canada	35 110	58 775	275 992	496 522
	(20.22)	(20.10)	(14.22)	(15.25)
European Union (of 12)	65 885	116 125	687 847	1 349 580
	(37.94)	(39.70)	(35.43)	(41.45)
World	173 650	292 475	1 941 181	3 255 825
	(100)	(100)	(100)	(100)

ª Figures in parentheses stand for percentage of total world trade.
Source: International Economic Data Bank, Australian National University, Canberra.

and China, during the decade of the 1980s, the region has gained a high profile on the international trade scene.

Initially a dominant part of their exports comprised labour-intensive and resource-based products. This is how industrialisation begins. However, soon these economies began to export light manufactured products. Manufactured goods are high value-added goods and their exports are an important indicator representing the competitive strength of the industrial sector and economic maturity in general. In 1965, the Asia-Pacific region accounted for a mere 10.85 per cent of the total exports of manufactures in the world (Table 1.9). In 1990, this proportion was 24.78 per cent or a quarter of total world exports of manufactures. In the early years these exports were heavily dominated by Japan – for instance, in 1965 Japan accounted for 73 per cent of manufactured exports from the region and in 1970 for 74.4 per cent. However, by 1980 other countries in the region were participating more actively and Japan accounted for only 61.1 per cent of the total. In 1990, this proportion had further plummeted to 46.9 per cent due to active manufactured export drives by China, Taiwan, Korea and to a lesser extent by Singapore and Hong Kong. Over the 1965–90 period, the ANIEs raised their share of world markets in manufactured goods from 1.5 per cent to 7.9 per cent, while the ASEAN-4 share rose from 1.6 per cent to 2.9 per cent. As in the case of exports, the low-base effect is obvious for these two subgroups. Australia and New Zealand did not capture markets in manufactures in 1990 to any greater extent than they had in 1965. Conversely, China, after a poor performance until 1980, succeeded in raising its market share by three-and-a-half times during the 1980s (Figure 1.3).

Growing participation of the Asia-Pacific economies in international trade in manufactures is apparent from Table 1.10. Their significance grew considerably over the 1980s. At the beginning of the decade, the Asia-Pacific economies and the north American growth pole were neck and neck in terms of volume of manufactured exports. However, by 1990, the Asia-Pacific region had left north America far behind and had almost 70 per cent higher exports. The EC has maintained its position of strength, essentially due to intra-trade in manufactures.

Japan, Taiwan and Korea have emerged as net foreign investors in the international economy. Of course, Japan is the largest. Going by the *International Financial Statistics*, net foreign direct investment made by Japan in 1980 was a skimpy $ 2.1 billion. It soared to $ 46.3 billion in 1990 and at this point Japan was the largest foreign investor in the world. In 1991, the investment level fell to $ 29.4 billion because of financial

Table 1.9 Export of Manufactures from Asia-Pacific Economies, 1965–90

Country	1965		1970		1980		1990	
	Export of manufactures ($ m.)	As % of total world exports of manufactures	Export of manufactures ($ m.)	As % of total world exports of manufactures	Export of manufactures ($ m.)	As % of total world exports of manufactures	Export of manufactures ($ m.)	As % of total world exports of manufactures
Japan	7 704	7.92	18 024	9.92	124 028	11.32	279 436	11.63
Korea	104	0.11	635	0.35	15 686	1.43	60 675	2.53
Taiwan	187	0.19	1 087	0.60	17 441	1.59	62 112	2.59
Hong Kong	823	0.85	1 954	1.08	13 194	1.20	27 784	1.16
Singapore	336	0.35	474	0.26	10 452	0.95	38 315	1.60
Indonesia	27	0.03	15	0.01	533	0.05	9 061	0.38
Malaysia	73	0.07	125	0.07	2 464	0.22	17 263	0.72
Philippines	43	0.04	80	0.04	2 118	0.19	5 905	0.25
Thailand	19	0.02	55	0.03	1 788	0.16	14 783	0.62
Australia	432	0.44	846	0.47	5 588	0.51	13 004	0.54
New Zealand	53	0.05	132	0.07	1 062	0.10	2 255	0.09
China	752	0.77	797	0.44	8 517	0.78	64 693	2.69
Regional average	10 552	10.85	24 224	13.33	202 872	18.51	595 289	24.78

Source: International Economic Data Bank, Australian National University, Canberra.

Figure 1.3   Asia-Pacific Economies' Exports of Manufactures, 1965–90

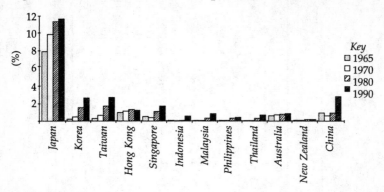

Table 1.10   Comparative Performance in Export of Manufactures ($ m.)

	1965	1970	1980	1990
Asia-Pacific countries	19 831 (11.42)[a]	37 108 (12.69)	290 863 (14.98)	715 016 (21.96)
USA and Canada	35 110 (20.22)	58 775 (20.10)	275 992 (14.22)	496 522 (15.25)
European Union (of 12)	65 885 (37.94)	116 125 (39.70)	687 847 (35.43)	1 349 580 (41.45)
World	173 605 (100)	292 475 (100)	1 941 181 (100)	3 255 825 (100)

[a] Figures in parentheses stand for percentage of total world trade in manufactures.
Source: International Economic Data Bank, Australian National University, Canberra.

turmoil in Japan. Korea recorded a tiny net foreign investment of $ 7 million in 1980. This amount rose to $ 105 million in 1990 and to $ 241 million in 1991. Taiwan also turned into a substantial net investor during the latter half of the 1980s: its investments rose and touched $ 5.3 billion in 1990.

Table 1.11 shows that Japan turned into a net exporter of capital through portfolio investment in 1983. Taiwan, Korea, Malaysia and Singapore also began to make portfolio invest-ment abroad in a relatively small way during the latter half of the 1980s. China began to do so in 1989, although invest-ments were not substantial until 1991.

Table 1.11 Portfolio Investment in and by the Asia-Pacific Economies (in $ m.)

Country	1965	1970	1975	1980	1981	1982	1983	1984	1985	1986	1987	1988	1989	1990	1991
Japan	80	250	2 590	9 430	7 670	840	−2 900	−23 960	−41 750	−102 040	−91 330	−51 750	−32 530	−14 490	35 450
Korea				40	60	15	188	333	982	301	−113	−482	−29	811	
Taiwan				45	85	145	41	−50	−46	69	−371	−1 711	−902	−1 006	45
Hong Kong															
Singapore			−2	13	−48	−29	−49	−151	175	−549	252	−293	324	287	232
Indonesia				46	47	315	368	−10	−35	268	−88	−98	173	0	0
Malaysia	88	−28	268	−11	1 131	601	668	1 108	1 942	30	140	−448	−107	−255	170
Thailand		13	1	96	44	68	108	155	895	−29	346	530	1 486	−38	110
The Philippines		3	27	4	3	1	7	−3	5	13	19	50	280	−50	
Australia	128	456	417	1 896	673	2 399	1 183	736	2 144	1 188	4 325	5 834	377	1 970	4 842
New Zealand													88	30	
China						41	20	83	742	1 567	1 051	876	−180	−241	−7 558

Source: International Economic Data Bank, Australian National University, Canberra.

The foregoing exposition has convincingly established that the Asia-Pacific region has emerged as the third growth pole of the international economy. Unprecedented growth in GDP, fast clip expansion in exports, especially exports of manufactured products, expansion in foreign direct investment and portfolio investment and other economic achievement point in the same direction – a new actor is entering the stage of the international economy. The economic dynamism of the Asia-Pacific economies is rejuvenating the global economy. Some countries see new threats rather than new opportunities in the phenomenon of the Asia-Pacific growth, because they suffer from severe constraints on factor mobility and have limited capability to take initiatives to make the necessary structural adjustments.

STRUCTURAL AND INDUSTRIAL TRANSFORMATION

As alluded to earlier, economies in the Asia-Pacific region consistently maintained high rates of investment. The only exception to this rule is the Philippines, which could not maintain its investment during the 1980s due to non-economic reasons (Table 1.12). The ANIEs were the highest investors, recording average investment rates of 12.8 per cent for the period 1965–80 and 5.8 for the period 1980–90. ASEAN-4 recorded 10.5 per cent for the first period and 6.2 per cent for the second, if the Philippines are excluded from the group average. China recorded an average of 10.7 for the first period, which is as high as that for the ASEAN group, but for the 1980s it recorded an average of 13.7 per cent which is the highest rate of investment not only in the Asia-Pacific region but also in the world. Australia and New Zealand, particularly the latter, increased their rate of investment during the 1980s. The average rate of investment for the Asia-Pacific region over the period 1965–80 was 9.5 per cent and 9.0 per cent during 1980–90. Both of these averages are higher than those for any other region in the world. The 1980s was a difficult period and several regions recorded negative growth in their investment. Latin America recorded negative growth of 2 per cent and sub-Saharan Africa –4.3 per cent. The developing economies of Europe recorded a growth rate of –0.1 per cent over this period. Another feature of investment was that whereas there was a resource gap for many countries in the region before 1980 and they had to borrow from external sources, during the 1980s several countries not only financed investment out of their own savings but also generated surplus over investment. The principal surplus-generating countries were Japan, Taiwan, Hong Kong, Singapore and China.

Growing investment leads to accumulation of physical capital and thereby to the transition from being a less-developed to a more-developed economy. The implicit assumption is that the ICOR is not inimical. The central feature of this transition is the transformation of the production structure and, therefore, the GDP composition. The structural changes occur in the following sequence: (i) the share of industry in total output rises while the agricultural sector shrinks both in relative and absolute terms; and (ii) with continued rise in investment and income, the share of the services sector begins to expand largely at the expense of the

Table 1.12   Gross Domestic Investment, Average Annual Growth Rate (%)

	1965–80	1980–90
Japan	6.9	5.7
Korea	15.9	12.5
Taiwan	12.9	3.4
Hong Kong	8.6	3.6
Singapore	13.3	3.6
Indonesia	16.1	7.1
Malaysia	10.4	2.9
Thailand	8.0	8.7
The Philippines	7.6	-2.5
Australia	2.7	3.0
New Zealand	0.8	4.4
China	10.7	13.7

Source: World Bank, *World Development Report 1992*, Washington, D.C. Data for Taiwan come from *Taiwan Statistical Data Book 1992*, Council for Economic Planning and Development, Taipei, Republic of China.

manufacturing sector. The causal factors behind this transition are, first, changes in comparative advantage resulting from ongoing accumulation of physical and human capital; secondly, Engel's law posits decline in relative expenditure on food and necessities with rising income, and a concomitant increase in the share of manufactured products and services; and thirdly, choice of macroeconomic policies and trade orientation of the economy also influences the structural transformation (Chenery and Syrquin, 1975). As shown in Table 1.13, the relative contribution of the agricultural sector has contracted considerably in the region over the 1965–90 period. In Japan the agricultural sector contributed only 3 per cent of the GDP in 1990. In Korea and Taiwan the relative contribution of this sector was also reduced considerably, while in Hong Kong and Taiwan it disappeared. In the ASEAN countries the relative decline of the agricultural sector was significant; however, the Philippines was an exception, where the relative decline was only marginal. In Australia the agricultural sector shrank further, while in New Zealand it still contributed 9 per cent to GDP in 1990. In China there was a marked reduction, but the agricultural sector still contributed over a quarter of GDP. Being a highly populous country, it has to continue having a substantial agricultural sector, although its relative contribution will continue to decline. For the region, the contribution of the agricultural sector fell by more than a half, which implies that the regional economic structure was swaying towards industrial and services activities.

In Japan, the relative contribution of the industrial and manufacturing sectors declined, because at its stage of development the service sector becomes more important and grows faster: its contribution to Japan's GDP grew by 10 per cent over the 1965–90 period. In Korea and Taiwan both industrial as well as manufacturing activities expanded and so did the service sector. All three sectors expanded at the expense of the agricultural sector. Hong Kong recorded a decline in the industrial sector and virtually became a service economy. However, in Singapore the contribution of the industrial sector expanded at the cost of the service sector,

Table 1.13   Structure of Production: Distribution of GDP (%)

	Agriculture		Industry		Manufacturing		Services	
	1965	1990	1965	1990	1965	1990	1965	1990
Japan	10	3	44	42	34	29	46	56
Korea	38	9	25	45	18	31	37	46
Taiwan	26	4	30	46	21	37	44	49
Hong Kong	2	0	40	26	29	18	58	73
Singapore	3	0	24	37	15	29	74	63
Indonesia	51	22	13	40	8	20	36	38
Malaysia	28		25		9		47	
Thailand	32	12	23	39	14	26	45	48
Philippines	26	22	27	35	20	25	47	43
Australia	9	4	39	31	26	15	51	64
New Zealand		9		27			19	64
China	38	27	35	42	28	38	27	31
Regional average	24	11	30	37	20	26	47	52

Source: World Bank, World Development Report 1992, Washington, DC. Data for Taiwan come from Taiwan Statistical Data Book 1992, Council for Economic Planning and Development, Taipei, Republic of China.

where contribution to GDP declined by 11 per cent. Rapid industrialisation in the ASEAN-4 countries is evident from the considerable expansion of the industrial and manufacturing sectors. Their relative contribution to GDP virtually doubled. The Philippines was an exception, where industrial sector growth was slow. These countries only recorded minor expansion in the contribution of the service sector to GDP. Again, the Philippines was an exception because the relative contribution of the service sector declined. Like Japan, Australia has grown to become an economy where the service sector dominates the rest: its relative contribution expanded at the cost of other sectors. Just as the ASEAN-4 did, China industrialised fast and its efforts are visible in the change in distribution of its GDP over the 1965–90 period – the relative contribution of the manufacturing sector rose by 10 per cent. For the region, the manufacturing and services sectors have expanded, while the agricultural sector has declined in importance.

Although statistics for the latter half of the 1980s are incomplete, Table 1.14 illustrates reasonably well the progress of various sub-sectors in industrialisation during the 1980s. Countries having high levels of per capita value-added in manufacturing, like Japan, Australia, New Zealand, Singapore and Taiwan, show a higher proportion of value-added in machinery and capital-intensive industries. In Japan, the combined share of machinery and capital-intensive industries reached 65 per cent. Conversely, countries having relatively low per capita value-added in manufacturing – such as Indonesia, Malaysia, Thailand, the Philippines and China – have a higher proportion of value-added in labour-intensive and food-processing industries. The resource-abundant countries show a higher concentration in resource-processing

Table 1.14   Share of Value-Added in Manufacturing Industries (%)

	Year	Resource-processing	Food-processing	Labour-intensive	Capital-intensive	Machinery
Japan	1980	17.2	9.7	12.5	24.4	36.2
	1988	15.2	10.0	9.8	23.6	41.4
Korea	1980	19.9	17.3	23.3	20.5	19.0
	1988	17.1	11.8	21.0	19.3	30.0
Taiwan	1980	24.5	12.5	26.9	21.4	20.6
	1988	24.1	10.3	16.0	22.9	26.6
Hong Kong	1980	11.7	5.3	47.0	11.3	24.7
	1988	11.7	6.4	47.6	8.9	25.9
Singapore	1980	24.7	5.1	10.3	11.6	48.3
	1988	11.6	5.8	5.9	20.2	56.4
Indonesia	1980	14.4	30.3	23.5	18.3	13.5
	1988	14.6	26.5	26.8	21.9	10.1
Malaysia	1981	23.6	23.7	18.0	11.5	23.2
	1987	19.4	19.6	16.5	21.4	23.0
Thailand	1982	16.3	54.1	12.0	8.3	9.3
	1986	15.6	35.6	24.0	8.6	7.2
Philippines	1980	17.8	31.0	17.1	22.9	11.1
	1987	19.8	43.5	13.6	15.4	8.6
Australia	1980	19.1	18.6	14.4	23.9	24.0
	1987	19.5	20.4	15.8	23.0	21.0
New Zealand	1981	17.4	27.7	20.3	16.2	18.4
	1986	22.3	26.9	18.6	14.9	17.3
China	1980	12.3	12.4	22.2	25.1	27.9
	1986	20.7	11.9	18.4	22.2	26.9

Source: Gleaned from Table 1.4, MITI, 1992a.

and food-processing industries. Among the ANIEs, Singapore has a high concentration in the machinery and capital-intensive industries. This is a country-specific example of concentration. Hong Kong is characterised by emphasis on labour-intensive manufacturing.

Both Korea and Taiwan briskly expanded their machinery sectors during the 1980s. The share of value-added in labour-intensive and food-processing industries declined in both countries, whereas those in machinery and capital-intensive industries exceeded 50 per cent. Among the ASEAN-4, Malaysia has a 45 per cent concentration in machinery and capital-intensive groups. Doubling of the share of value-added in capital-intensive industries has a lot to do with this. As opposed to this, Malaysia's natural resource production and food production shares fell rapidly. In Thailand, Indonesia and the Philippines the share of food-processing industries has traditionally remained large due to abundant food resources in these countries. However, in Indonesia and Thailand the share of this group declined over the 1980s and that of labour-intensive industries has risen. It should be remembered that a great deal has happened in Thailand since 1986, the last year for which the statistics are included. The share of value-added in capital-intensive and machinery sectors in China is close to 50 per cent. These two sub-sectors were large and state-controlled (MITI, 1992a). In most Asia-Pacific countries the industrial sector has climbed several rungs of the ladder of comparative advantage. With steadily rising investment and increasing stock of physical and human capital, the ability of these economies to export new products and compete successfully in the international markets has increased markedly.

Along with the physical capital, human capital also accumulated fast in the region. Japan and the ANIEs have attained high general literacy levels and the result is remarkable human capital endowment in the labour force. These countries have also trained a good number of scientists and engineers and have ensured an indigenous capacity for technological adaptation. This is essential for successful industrialisation. In the ASEAN-4 countries the situation is far from uniform. The

Philippines has a strong educational tradition, but trains inadequate science and technology-related personnel. Thailand has made impressive strides in the past in this regard. Malaysia has as much as 30 per cent of its adult population illiterate, although the number of college graduates in various disciplines has soared impressively. Among the ASEAN countries, Indonesia's educational achievements are the least impressive. If there is a common feature in this country group, it is that it has the lowest proportion of technically-trained people in the Asia-Pacific region which is liable to slow the efficient adaptation of technology from abroad in the future (Noland, 1990a). In urban China the labour force is not as well-trained as in the ANIEs. China is also expected to face bottlenecks of science and technology-related personnel.

CONCLUSION

Over the last three decades, the Asia-Pacific region developed into the third growth pole of the international economy and scholars began to wonder if this was the beginning of a Pacific century. During this period, several informal groupings and fora involving varying combinations of the Asia-Pacific countries have emerged, although they are far from institutionalising these arrangements in the manner of an Asian OECD. No matter how the region is defined, the Japanese economy has to be its hub. A great deal of diversity exists in the economic and social indicators of these countries. The Asia-Pacific region has established itself as a trailblazer in the area of economic growth. Six regional economies doubled their output in a decade. Their dynamic trade-orientated growth posed an intellectual challenge. They appear to be an alternative model of development, a model which is more relevant and therefore more successful than the standard neoclassical model in which the world had put its faith. There were considerable differences in the macroeconomic policies pursued by these countries, yet there were several basic commonalities. For instance, they all recorded high savings and investment rates and adopted outward-orientated economic strategies after an initial spell of import-substitution. It led to a change in the structure of production as well as that of trade. High export growth, along with un-usually rapid structural change in manufactured trade, sug-gests that economic policy played a decisive role, shifting specialisation of production towards higher value-added goods. The supply push and export promotion strategies were among the key elements underpinning dynamic transi-tional growth. The other causal factors included lower levels of price distortions, adoption of pragmatic liberalisation mea-sures, market orientation, high commitment to economic growth of both the governments and the societies, and Confucionist cultural orientation. Proximity to Japan, the pioneer regional economy, stimulated the other regional economies both directly and indirectly. Despite striking simi-larities in the growth process, each economy or group had its own characteristic growth path. The ultimate result, for the majority of them, was the same.

The brisk growth rate led to more than four-fold economic expansion of GDP for the Asia-Pacific region in real terms over the 1965–89 period. North America and the EC, which comprised the other two growth poles of the global economy, doubled their respective GDPs over the same period. This growth pattern enhanced the weight of the Asia-Pacific region in the international economy. Of course, there were marked intra-regional differences in economic expansion. The mantle of greatest dynamism fell on the ANIEs: these countries opened their economies considerably. In fact, the ANIEs and the ASEAN-4 have become the most open coun-tries in the world. In a region which in general was highly successful in export expansion, these two country groups also recorded the highest long-term average growth rates of exports. This trade-related dynamic growth was principally supply-driven, although the demand-side factors did assist. Such an outstanding export performance resulted in a steep rise in the volume of exports from the region, and by 1990 it accounted for almost a quarter of total world exports. In terms of volume, Japan dominated the regional exports; however, during the 1980s this domination markedly declined. China, Taiwan, Korea and Singapore developed as substantial exporters in their own right. Export of manufactured products has special significance, because it represents the competitive strength of the industrial sector. In the mid-1960s, the region accounted for 11 per cent of total exports of manufactures, and almost the whole of this was from Japan. By 1990, the region accounted for as much as a quarter of total exports of manufactures and Japan no longer dominated them, although it retained its position of being the largest exporter of manufactured products in the region. Exports from China, Taiwan and Korea, and to a lesser extent from Singapore and Hong Kong, had expanded significantly. In terms of value of manufactured exports, by 1990 the Asia-Pacific region had left North America far behind. Japan, Taiwan and Korea have emerged as net foreign investors. These countries, along with Malaysia and Singapore (and, to a lesser extent, China) have also begun to make portfolio investments abroad.

The economic structure has undergone considerable transformation. The relative contribution of agriculture to GDP has contracted considerably in the region. The regional economic structure has swayed towards the industrial and service sectors. In as many as five economies, the service sector has become the dominant sector. Countries having high levels of per capita value-added in manufacturing – such as Japan, Australia, New Zealand, Singapore and Taiwan – showed a higher proportion of value-added in machinery and capital-intensive industries while others recorded a marked expansion in food processing and labour-intensive sectors. In addition, over the last three decades considerable accumulation of human capital endowment has taken place in the labour force in this region.

2 From Economic Integration to Economic Co-operation: Institutional Initiatives

INTRODUCTION

In the mid-1960s, there were vigorous efforts to unite the Asia-Pacific region in some form of economic integration. It was largely a knee-jerk reaction to the formation of the Economic Community (EC) in another part of the globe. The region's economic diversity and the fast expansion of international trade increased economic interdependence in the region. Furthermore, brisk growth and the outward-orientated economic policies followed by the economies of the Asia-Pacific region had brought them closer together. These countries also felt that they were being discriminated against by the established economic powers. A variety of institutional initiatives were taken for regional economic unification. These endeavours can be divided into three phases. The earliest initiative, in the 1960s, aimed at the formation of a formal free-trade area. This zeal cooled off in the 1970s, and various regional economic co-operation schemes were carefully studied. They were found to be more suitable for the region. After a great deal of purposeful activity and experimentation, the Pacific Economic Co-operation Council (PECC) and the Asia-Pacific Economic Co-operation (APEC) forum emerged and were accepted as institutions of lasting value. As the names indicate, they were to promote economic co-operation; APEC is a unique institution, created to promote open regionalism. It is a regional institution with a global vision. It is outward-orientated, nondiscriminatory and committed to preserving the GATT-based multilateral economic and trade system. In numerous ways the APEC economies can co-operate to mutual advantage as well as for global benefit. Although it took a quarter of a century to reach the concept of APEC and to institutionalise it, APEC represents a level-headed and sagacious achievement by the Asia-Pacific economies.

ECONOMIC INTEGRATION VERSUS ECONOMIC CO-OPERATION

The term 'integration' has a precise meaning in the discipline of economics. It implies extending the market limits for products and factors of production beyond national boundaries. For its normal operation, economic integration calls for supra-national legal and institutional arrangements. Extension or elimination of market boundaries may well begin with a reduction in traditional market impediments – namely, tariffs and quota restrictions (QRs). Economic integration generally begins with the economic co-operation which, in turn, emerges naturally from the operation of market forces (Machlup 1976). Economic integration takes several stages or has a variety of forms. For instance, it can be limited to a preferential trading area, which only has partial reduction of trade restrictions on intra-trade flows, as in the case of ASEAN. As a text book would define it, a free trade area is created when member states completely dismantle all tariffs and non-tariff barriers to mutual trade, albeit they are free to retain restrictions on their trade with the rest of the world. The European Economic Community (EC)[1] achieved this stage of integration in 1968. It subsequently developed into a customs union which is characterised by the complete elimination of restrictions on mutual trade and the imposition of a common external tariff against trade with the rest of the world. A customs union is transformed into a common market when all restrictions against factor mobility among the participating economies are eliminated. The final stage of economic integration is an economic union, which is achieved when, in addition to common market arrangements, member countries harmonise their economic policies.

Unlike integration, 'economic co-operation' can have several meanings, ranging from issue-specific consultations on the one hand, to collusion in non-competitive market behaviour on the other. Co-operation primarily begins with trade in goods and services and may advance to exchange of factors of production, somewhat on the lines of economic integration. Any meaningful economic co-operation endeavour involves agreements to reduce or eliminate the traditional market impediments named in the preceding paragraph. If, among the economies that are trying to co-operate, (a) information is imperfect, (b) externalities are present and (c) market imperfections retard co-operation, government action can facilitate movement towards establishing co-operation arrangements. Academic and business leaders can also lubricate the process. In what follows, we shall see how the Asia-Pacific economies institutionalised for themselves an ingenious and highly functional form of economic co-operation arrangement.

THE PRINCIPAL STIMULI

No efforts towards integration or grouping were made during the two decades following the Second World War, because the Japanese economy was engaged in reconstruction and other Asia-Pacific economies were too tiny to be considered significant for any grandiose economic integration endeavour. In addition, the USA not only dominated the economies of the region but also the entire 'free' world. Its leadership was not merely economic, but had definite strategic and geopolitical overtones and was comprehensive, if not hegemonic. From the perspective of the Asia-Pacific region, the most important public good that the US leadership provided was its moral guardianship of a liberal international economic order. The GATT-based multilateral trading system burgeoned and provided a framework within which the Asia-Pacific economies flourished (Kindleberger, 1986). Given their economic diversity and highly-skewed resource endowment, the economies of the region benefited a great deal from the development of a liberal trading system, successive tariff reductions and the expansion of world trade. The end of the Vietnam War saw the beginning of a denouement, as US hegemony steadily declined and its economic leadership was eroded. The Japanese economy grew at a fast clip which raised its absolute and relative importance for the region. Australia and New Zealand effected a huge shift in their economic focus from the UK to east and south-east Asia and Japan (Garnaut 1989). The four Asian newly-industrialising economies (ANIEs) came into their own and the south-east Asian countries took to the fast track and tried to emulate the 'four dragons'. Owing to these developments, the GDPs of the regional economies grew constantly and the Asia-Pacific region became far stronger economically.

Several factors contributed to increased economic interdependence in the region. Foremost was the rapid growth of the Japanese economy which enhanced trade intensity among the regional economies. The impact of growth was felt through huge Japanese imports of industrial raw materials and foodstuffs, as well as through the large exports of capital goods and technology that the countries in the region needed badly. The second causal factor was industrial growth and trade expansion in the north-east and south-east Asian economies, in that order. It was underpinned by two exogenous influences: the resource-rich countries of south-east Asia and Australia benefited from the opening-up of new trading opportunities with Japan; and the success and therefore popularity of an outward-looking, trade-orientated industrial strategy in the region (Anderson and Smith, 1981). The third causal factor was the high degree of complementarity in the regional economies. Rapid growth and industrialisation brought about changes in the economic structures which in turn reinforced trade complementarity between the resource rich countries of the Pacific and the rapidly growing economies of East Asia further. Bilateral relationships between Australia and Japan during the 1960 and 1970s were firmly based on the strong complementarity of the two economies. This bilateral trade soon supplanted and outstripped trade with other leading trade partners. The two countries benefited from specialisation and exchange arising from enormous differences in resource endowments which played an important role in their economic growth (Crawford and Okita, 1976). During the 1980s and 1990s, there existed between China and Japan the same genre of stark complementary, which they attempted to exploit. Proximity, and therefore low transport costs, further promoted trade in the region. This included trade in raw-materials. So penetration of regional markets for resource-related goods from other regional members increased. These forces made interdependence, co-operation and integration economically logical as well as feasible.

In as much as the regional economies were fast-growing, outward-orientated and complementary, the notion of mutual co-operation occurred to them naturally. The creation of the EC and prospects for its further expansion supported this notion and made it emotionally congenial. There was an apprehension among the Asia-Pacific economies that the established economic powers, especially the EC, would discriminate against and thwart their legitimate efforts to grow through trade expansion. The EC's completion of internal tariff elimination by 1968 fanned their fears of the creation of a progressively inward-looking, self-sufficient European bloc, damaging the interests of the Asia-Pacific economies in terms of global market access. It had destabilised trade in Australia, New Zealand and Japan. The first two had suffered due to the Common Agricultural Policy (CAP) and had lost their traditional agricultural markets. Therefore, both of them turned towards the Asia-Pacific region to develop new markets. Similarly, Japan found that its exports were being discriminated against in the EC; this, in turn, encouraged Japan to develop closer ties with its regional neighbours. Subsequently, the concept of EC unification – which was initially given shape in 1985 at the EC summit conference in Milan – further exacerbated the apprehensions of the Asia-Pacific countries, as did the Single European Act of 1987. Clairvoyant academics, pragmatic business leaders and statesmen with foresight began to discuss the need and desirability for close, effective consultations among the regional economies. Greater mutual co-operation was considered necessary for sustained growth in the region as well as to counter any possible discriminatory treatment in the future. Professor Kiyoshi Kojima (of Hitotsubashi University, Tokyo), Dr Saburo Okita and Sir John Crawford emphasised the closer co-ordination of policy-making at a regional level in order to identify new economic opportunities, resolve potential friction in trade and to make the presence of the Asia-Pacific economies felt as a growth pole in the future.

INSTITUTIONAL INITIATIVES

The intellectual lineage of regional integration and co-operation efforts is not long and can be traced back to Kojima's plan in the mid-1960s (Kojima, 1968). Subsequently, various initiatives were devised, which fall into three distinct phases (see Table 2.1). The first phase ran between 1960 and 1966. It was led principally by Japan and was very much a response to the creation of the EC. Japan was beginning to assume a bigger role in the region in order to preserve its own economic interests, such as the steady supply of industrial

Table 2.1   Institutional Initiatives

Phase	Year of inception	Institution
I	1966	The Pacific Free Trade Area (PAFTA)
II	1967	The Pacific Trade and Development Conference (PAFTAD)
	1967	The Association of South East Asian Nations (ASEAN)
	1967	The Pacific Basin Economic Community (PBEC)
	1979	The Organisation for Pacific Trade and Development (OPTAD)
III	1980	The Pacific Economic Co-operation Conference (PECC)
	1989	The Asia Pacific Economic Co-operation (APEC) forum

raw materials and a shipping lane through the Malacca Straits, and for the development of markets for its exports. Japan's new interest in the region was manifested by its strong and enthusiastic support for the establishment of the Asian Development Bank in 1966 and its proposal for an 'Asian-Pacific sphere in co-operation'[2] in 1967. It was intended to be the first tentative step towards regional economic co-operation to promote both trade among the developed countries of the region, and also increased economic assistance to the developing economies of the region. Kojima's proposal for a Pacific Free Trade Area (PAFTA) attracted a good deal of regional attention and stimulated a debate on the issue of regional economic integration versus economic co-operation. The free trade area was to consist of the five developed economies – namely, Australia, Canada, Japan, New Zealand and the USA.

The second phase stretched over the period 1967–79, and saw several initiatives. The Pacific Trade and Development Conference (PAFTAD) of 1967 covered issues related to both trade and economic policy. The Association of South East Asian Nations (ASEAN) was also established in 1967. It started life as a non-economic organisation and was to focus on politico-security issues, shunning any idea of regional economic co-operation for a long while. The Pacific Basin Economic Community (PBEC) was born in the same year as a private business-orientated organisation. The last meaningful proposal for regional integration during this phase was that of Drysdale and Patrick, who recommended to the US congress an OECD-like organisational framework to be called the Organisation for Pacific Trade and Development (OPTAD). True to its name, it was to concentrate on trade and development-related issues (Drysdale and Patrick, 1979). The concept of economic integration had lost its sheen by the 1970s. None of the institutions proposed during the second phase had economic integration as their priority, or even consideration. They were all intended for consultation and co-operation.

The third phase, during the 1980s, saw the birth of the Pacific Economic Co-operation Conference (PECC). It drew from the experiences of the establishment of the past institutions, including the Drysdale-Patrick proposal. Australian-Japanese efforts helped establish the PECC. At the end of the decade, the Asia-Pacific Economic Co-operation (APEC) forum was established (Higgott *et al.*, 1991). Of the seven noteworthy initiatives of regional integration and co-operation taken over the period of 1966–89, the APEC promises to be the most substantive. The following exposition deals with the principal institutions, and focuses especially on the APEC.

The Pacific Free-Trade Area (PAFTA)

As alluded to earlier, the PAFTA was proposed to develop measures for expanding trade among the five developed countries of the Pacific rim, and trade and economic assistance with the regional developing economies. The latter group was to have the status of associate members in the PAFTA (Kojima 1971, 1976). The objectives of the free trade area were to be served by eliminating tariffs among the five developed members – Australia, Canada, Japan, New Zealand and the USA. Each member was to maintain its own tariff schedule for trade with outsiders. The PAFTA proposal was comparable to the European Free Trade Area (EFTA) which provided for freeing of mutual trade among members without aiming at common external tariffs. The associate membership for the developing countries of the region was modelled on the Yaondé convention of the EC – subsequently overtaken by the Lomé convention – which covered economic relations with countries in Africa, the Caribbean and the Pacific. The developing countries of the region were accorded non-reciprocal tariff concessions. Completion of the Kennedy Round of negotiations in June 1967 assigned an added relevance to the PAFTA proposal. Since the next round of multilateral trade negotiations was not due for at least a decade, the PAFTA formation could effectively give a fillip to expanding trade among the large Pacific economies and, thereby, contribute to the momentum of international trade liberalisation.

Enormous attention was paid to the proposal, but no concrete steps were taken to institutionalise the PAFTA. For several reasons, it was both a political and an economic impossibility. First, the five economies lacked the necessary degree of complementarity. Secondly, the policy environment in the USA was against any potentially discriminatory arrangement. Becoming part of the PAFTA was against the global commercial interests of the USA: this course was not only incompatible with its stature in the world economy at that time, but also contrary to the main thrusts of its approach to international trade policy (Drysdale, 1988). This was the most important factor working against the PAFTA. Thirdly, Kojima's analysis indicated that establishing a free trade area would result in trade expansion. Using 1965 statistics, he concluded that trade in the region will increase by $ 5 billion and that Japan would benefit more than any other member country (Kojima, 1968). The large gains for Japan derived from the fact that as much as 37 per cent of Japan's exports depended upon the PAFTA markets at that time. Also, as much as 95 per cent of Japan's exports to other Pacific economies were manufactures which would have enjoyed greater expansion from trade liberalisation. At the same time, 71 per cent of Japan's imports were primary products which would not have increased appreciably as a consequence of tariff reduction.

The developing countries of the region saw PAFTA as a rich man's club and remained unenthusiastic about the proposal. Trade liberalisation among the five industrialised countries would not have helped them enough to foster their trade and growth. Japan past nationalist-expansionist economic position did not inspire confidence among them either.

The Pacific Trade and Development Conference (PAFTAD)

This was another Japanese proposal to promote regional cooperation based on an 'awareness of common principles'. Japan lent official support to a series of Pacific Trade and Development Conferences (PAFTAD). This conference series has involved policy-orientated academic economists, many of whom have served as advisers to their governments, business leaders and some government officials, attending in their private capacity, who were interested in analytical and policy-related dialogue on trade, investment and development issues in the Asia-Pacific region. Japanese and Australian academics have taken notable initiatives in PAFTAD conferences. The conferences rotate among the cities of the region and are devoted every time to a research programme on pre-specified theme. These are frequently related to regional economic issues as well as co-operation and integration. Research results are deliberated upon, along with their implication for policy, and the conference papers and proceedings are published and widely publicised. Also under the sponsorship of PAFTAD, major joint research projects have been undertaken by a group of Australian economists at the Australian National University and another group of Japanese economists working at the Japanese Economic Research Center.

Association of South East Asian Nations (ASEAN)

Under the obviously misdirected recommendations and faulty framework of policies emanating from the Kansu Report,[3] the ASEAN group took off poorly. Their initial industrialisation strategy was inward-orientated and resource allocation was made inappropriately by heavy-handed bureaucracies: the outcome was lethargic economic performance. The first meaningful economic proposal that came out of ASEAN was that of the ASEAN Free Trade Area in 1977, a decade after its formation. This aimed at encouraging greater intra-trade among the six members of ASEAN, the principal instrument for trade liberalisation being the grant of tariff preferences to each other. At first, tariff cuts were of the order of 10 per cent, but later they were made as large as 25 per cent. Although the list of preferential trading items exceeded 15 000 items, the tariff concessions affected only 1 per cent of total intra-trade, because products of greater importance in trade were not accorded preferential tariffs, while numerous irrelevant items like snow ploughs were on the list of preferential trading items (Chang, 1990).

The dynamic economies of the ANIEs had profound demonstration effect on the ASEAN economies. They borrowed the outward-orientated development strategy from them and began to reform their financial sectors, trade and exchange rate policies and the general macroeconomic policy structure, as well as to address the problem of inefficient parastatals. The liberalisation measures were identical to those carried out in Korea and Taiwan over the period 1960–65, when they shifted their policy gear from import-substitution to export promotion. The four ANIEs started making large investments in the ASEAN countries and soon, as a group, became the largest investors. The result of reforms and investment was an economic boom in the ASEAN economies in the latter half of the 1980s. Japan, ANIEs and ASEAN, in effect, became the three tiers of economies at varying levels of skills, technology, wage rates and stages of development (Yan *et al.*, 1992). The ASEAN group began to involve itself progressively with the Asia-Pacific region and an increasing web of economic linkages between ASEAN and other regional economies developed. During the 1980s, they became an active participant in the PECC conferences and extended their vision from Southeast Asia to the Asia-Pacific region.

The Pacific Basin Economic Council (PBEC)

The business community, including bankers and industrialists, from the five industrialised countries of the Pacific rim collaborated to establish PBEC for co-operating on commercial matters. Its objectives include liberalisation and consultation on issues related to trade and investment as well as the convergence of the roles of private sector and public sector in the region. Over 600 companies are members of the PBCC. Although it remains a low-key organisation, it has succeeded in creating an information network which was missing in the region. The PBEC is seen as the endeavour of business community to promote the concept of close economic ties among the regional economies.

Organisation for Pacific Trade and Development (OPTAD)

In the PAFTAD conferences, a proposal for an Organisation for Pacific Trade and Development (OPTAD), modelled on the OECD, was intensely debated for a long time. Two principal proponents of OPTAD were Kiyoshi Kojima and Peter Drysdale. Between 1968 and 1979 the proposal underwent several changes in terms of membership, organisational structure and functions – these various forms are available in several places in the literature. They have four broad objectives.

(i) OPTAD was conceived as a safety valve for settling trade and economic grievances that were likely to arise from the existing level of interdependence in the regional economies. Tensions were to be resolved rationally and without damaging the profitable national economic interests of any member.

(ii) It was to provide a framework for economic assistance to developing economies in the region and improve their relations with the industrial ones.

(iii) It was to plan the contours of the long-term economic transformation of the region.

(iv) It was to develop a secure framework of economic alliances among the countries of the region in such a manner that countries could develop closer economic ties in smaller groupings (Drysdale, 1978).

Thus conceived, OPTAD was an ambitious body, intended to weld the economic, political and diplomatic strands in the Asia-Pacific region.

In an earlier outline, Kojima saw OPTAD as an intermediate step towards the final goal of a PAFTA (Kojima, 1968). But the reluctance of the member countries to eliminate mutual tariffs and begin to integrate their economies became an obvious impediment to this. Therefore, institutional integration was given for functional integration. Drysdale emphasised the potential benefits of OPTAD, even in the absence of a comprehensive movement towards regional trade liberalisation. Yet since a reference point of the Pacific economic power was needed, an OPTAD-like body was necessary. The clearest enunciation, and generally accepted vision, of the OPTAD was made by Drysdale and Patrick, in a paper prepared for the Committee on Foreign Relations in the US Senate (Drysdale and Patrick, 1979). Their recommendations for the structure of OPTAD were that:

- OPTAD be a government body where member countries are represented by their government;
- the membership should include Australia, Japan, Canada, the USA, Korea, the market economies of south-east Asia and the other Pacific basin countries;
- the administrative apparatus and budget be small;
- issues be handled by functional task forces with specific policy-orientated assignments with high-level political involvement;
- the operational style be informal, consultative and communicative.

The substantive issues with which OPTAD had to grapple immediately included: (a) trade liberalisation and restoration of regional trade conflicts; (b) trade and industrial resolutioning; (c) financing regional development; (d) foreign direct investment strategy; (e) resource and energy security; and (f) economic relations with the non-market economies of the region. The Drysdale-Patrick report was a considerable refinement of the concept of regional economic co-operation. The notion of regional integration was fast receding into oblivion, its place being taken by an issue-specific, problem-solving, economic co-operation framework. Implicit in their proposal was regional collaboration aimed at rapid development, capitalising on economic complementarities, spontaneous growth of economic interaction between the regional economies and gradually increasing the institutional ties binding them. Their report valued the role of the business and academic communities highly and emphasised the need for its continuance.

The Pacific Economic Co-operation Conference (PECC)

The Drysdale-Patrick report capitalised on the creation of the PECC in 1980, following a seminar at the Australian National University in which the former prime ministers of Australia and Japan participated. True to the vision of its authors, the PECC was tripartite, comprising representatives of academia, the business world and governments. The representatives of governments attended in their non-official capacities, so that though governments were drawn into the deliberations, they were neither required to lead nor to make a commitment to the decisions taken. The tripartite character was an important institutional innovation serving the special needs to the Asia-Pacific region, if not the times (O. Harris, 1989). During the 1980s, several informal consultative meetings were held and issue-specific task forces were set up. They helped develop a Pacific perception on trade and development-related issues and facilitated communications on other regional and international economic developments. Another noteworthy achievement of the PECC was that it drew into its fold the ASEAN members and turned them towards the wider Asia-Pacific economic stage. Yet another breakthrough was acceptance by China and Taiwan of each other's full membership in the PECC.

The PECC commenced operations somewhat on the lines of the OECD. For instance, it published OECD-like publications that monitor the regional economies – *The Pacific Economic Outlook* is published on a similar pattern to the *OECD Outlook.* Becoming an exact replica of the OECD would have been unwise for PECC, because the former serves industrial economies of by and large the same level of economic development and similar economic structures. The same cannot be said about the Asia-Pacific region. PECC has a different role to play for a different set of economies. While the OECD has preoccupied itself with macroeconomic co-ordination, the mandate of the PECC is very different, as has been stated above. In addition, the opinion-forming and decision-making processes for the two organisations will have to be strikingly dissimilar.

The PECC operates though sectoral taskforces and *ad hoc* fora. Its operations have given impetus to the creation of transregional networks and linkages among the Asia-Pacific economies. The PECC has eschewed OECD-like bureaucratisation. Given the antipathy towards a large bureaucracy and its trappings, it was difficult to make the network denser than it was. Institutionalisation on a grand scale, it was feared, would not only lead to the ossification of decision-making but would also result in the loss of transparency and organisational flexibility.

Deliberations in the PECC during the 1980s succeeded in (a) gathering strong support in the Asia-Pacific region for the GATT-based open multilateral trading system and (b) reaching a consensus on the benefits of outward-looking, rather than a defensive form of co-operation. The working of the PECC also revealed that, despite the economic diversity of the region, members could co-operate effectively, accommodating regional interests. It perfected ways of policy-orientated economic consultations in the region. In January 1992, in a meeting held in Honolulu, the PECC International Standing Committee changed the name of the organisation from Conference to Council, so that the importance of the work of the sectoral task forces and fora can be reached in its name.

THE EVOLUTION OF APEC

The birth of the Asia-Pacific Economic Co-operation (APEC) forum was the consequence of two principal developments. First, the maturing of the initiatives outlined in the preceding section which in turn rendered continuity of endeavour; and, secondly, the international economic milieu during the decade of the 1980s. Since the former has been dealt with, let me turn to the latter.

Although various rounds of multilateral trade negotiations under the aegis of the General Agreement on Tariffs and Trade (GATT) had achieved a sharp fall in tariffs, non-tariff barriers and less transparent forms of protection became rife during the 1980s. To an extent, rising protectionism was in response to the success of the Asia-Pacific economies, led by Japan. Industrialisation and export expansion in the region required the slicing away of market shares of the established traders, first in labour-intensive manufactured products and then in capital and technology-intensive products. Japan and the ANIEs not only affected the export market shares of the USA, the UK and Europe in several sectors, but also successfully penetrated their domestic markets in a significant manner. The structure of international comparative advantage was undergoing transformation, and the Asia-Pacific economies were threatening the sunset industries in the industrial countries.

Instead of acting in a pro-active manner and undertaking structural adjustment measures, these economies chose to take negative defensive measures to restrict imports, imposing 'voluntary' and other restraints on several dynamic export lines of the Asia-Pacific countries. This certainly defied economic logic and had a deleterious effect not only over the regional economies, but also over the importing industrial economies. One justification offered frequently by the latter for the surge in protectionistic tendencies was that the Asia-Pacific economies were themselves protectionistic, therefore, giving them a dose of their own medicine was in order. But Japan has a conspicuously good record of supporting the GATT principles and of unilateral trade liberalisation. It also subscribed to all the Tokyo Round codes on non-tariff barriers and has the lowest level of tariff of all major OECD countries. Over the 1980s, measures were taken by the other Asia-Pacific economies to counter this accusation. The ANIEs took several important steps towards opening their economies, as did Australia, New Zealand, Indonesia, Malaysia and Thailand, although the last three still have high average tariffs.

During the latter half of the 1980s, the multilateral trading environment deteriorated. There was a drift away from Article I of the GATT, that is, towards discriminatory trade policies and bilateral solutions to trade problems. The EC's single market policy threatened the creation of a protectionist

'Fortress Europe'. The USA and Canada had concluded their Free Trade Area (FTA) agreement and a North America Free Trade Area (NAFTA) had become a distinct possibility. The mid-term review of the Uruguay Round in 1988 reported tepid progress and virtual stagnation in the negotiations on agriculture, services and intellectual property rights. The Asia-Pacific economies were aware that they had gained enormously from the post-war liberalisation of international trade regime and trade expansion, and that they stood to lose most from the disintegration of the GATT system. They were also aware that none of them, not even Japan, had played a significant role in shaping it in the past and could not ensure its success in the future. In such an international environment, the need to express regional anxiety for preserving an open trading system effectively promoted regional co-operation further.

It was against this background that R. J. L. Hawke, the erstwhile Australian Prime Minister, called on the regional leaders in 1989 to start ministerial-level consultations for defending the region's common economic interests, discussing the trade obstacles in the region and defending an open multilateral trading system.[4] In response, the first high-level meeting of the APEC took place in November 1989, where the ASEAN Secretariat, the PECC and South Pacific Forum participated as observers. There were minor disputes over the membership issue. The Australian suggestion of excluding Canada and the USA met with resistance, because it appeared that the proposed forum was intended to have a west Pacific slant. Perhaps the Australian motive for excluding North America was to avoid a situation of American dominance of the forum. However, Japanese pressure forced the inclusion of Canada and the USA, and the APEC was launched with twelve participants – the six members of ASEAN, plus Australia, New Zealand, Japan, South Korea, Canada and the USA.

The guiding principles of the APEC were set out in the Seoul Declaration, on which basis the nine principles of APEC were adopted by consensus at the initial November 1989 meeting.

1. The objective of enhanced Asia-Pacific Economic Co-operation is to sustain the growth and development of the region, and in this way, to contribute to the growth and development of the world economy.
2. Co-operation should recognise the diversity of the region and variations in the current levels of developments.
3. Co-operation should involve a commitment to open dialogue and be based on consensus, with equal respect for the views of all participants.
4. Co-operation should be based on non-formal consultative exchange of views among the Asia-Pacific economies.
5. Co-operation should focus on those economic areas where there is scope to advance common interests and achieve mutual benefits.
6. Consistent with the interests of the Asia-Pacific economies, co-operation should be directed at strengthening the open multilateral trading system, it should not involve the formation of a trading bloc.
7. Co-operation should aim to strengthen from interdependence, both for the region and the world economy, and should include encouraging the flow of goods, services, capital and technology.
8. Co-operation should complete and draw upon, rather than detract from existing organisations in the region, including formal inter-governmental bodies such as ASEAN and less formal consultative bodies like the PECC.
9. Participation by Asia-Pacific economies should be assessed in the light of the strength of economic linkages with the region, and they may be extended in future on the basis of consensus on the part of all participants.[5]

An institution based on the above set of guiding principles needs to be outward-orientated and to eschew any notion of trade-bloc formation. Some cynically shrug the latter part off as a mere noble intent. Who has ever admitted to a trading-bloc objective? However, those aware of the backdrop of APEC creation find these objectives orderly and logical. An inward-orientated trade-bloc notion has clearly been rejected. The outward-orientated, regional co-operation was indeed a unique objective and reflected APEC's concern regarding global economic interests instead of defending regional and domestic markets. Although APEC is not averse to promoting regional trade liberalisation, it will only do so if it is consistent with the tenets of the GATT and not detrimental to other economies (see principles 6 and 7).

The diversity of the region was also given due consideration. Although some of the regional economies are much larger than others, their relative weights are in a process of flux. Yet any functional co-operation process would need to recognise the regional diversity and endeavour to avoid domination of the process by anyone of the participants or a few of them. Therefore, due weight is to be given to the views of all participants, that is, to building a consensus of opinions. The original twelve participants also decided to keep it an open-ended organisation. Based on the strength of economic linkages, new participants can join the APEC in future (see principle 9).

Espousal of the concept of an outward-looking regional grouping was evidently an expression of the region's strong interest in preserving the non-discriminatory, multilateral trading system. It owes its intellectual birth to the work of PECC and to thinkers like Crawford, Okita and Drysdale. As a result of dynamic growth in the region, intra-regional trade is expanding fast. It has entered a circular causation, that is, it is contributing to regional growth and growing due to it. However, trade with the rest of the world is larger in volume and is also growing fast. The global market place provides the regional economies with niche and mass markets. Endangering that trade through the formation of an inward-orientated regional bloc will be as irresponsible as it would be imprudent (Hughes, 1991). In addition, the economies of the region are capable of competing in the international markets without the support of a narrow, regional bloc. It must be noted that the concept of an outward-orientated regional grouping is radically different from the discriminatory principles of the EU. As a proof of its outward-orientation and support of multilateralism, the APEC strongly supported the faltering Uruguay Round.

The major achievement of the third ministerial meeting of APEC held in Seoul in November 1991, was the acceptance of the three-China principle. China, Hong Kong and Taiwan participated as full members, bringing the membership to fifteen. The APEC is the first international institution in which they are all represented by ministers in their official capacities. The 1992 ministerial meeting was held in Bangkok (on 10 and 11 September 1992) when members agreed to establish a small permanent secretariat at Singapore, without creating a large bureaucracy, and with an annual budget of up to $ 2 million. Although the member countries were anxious in case the North America Free Trade Area (NAFTA) turned into a protectionist trade bloc, they reiterated their belief in 'open regionalism' and endorsed the view that 'regional and sub-regional trade arrangements [should] be outward-looking, GATT-consistent and support the process of broader trade liberalisation'(Joint Statement, 1992). A small study group was set up to delve into the 'vision for trade in the Asia-Pacific to the year 2000'. Since the APEC and the PECC both tread common ground, they have forged a close working relationship.

AN ALLIANCE FOR OPEN MULTILATERALISM

By the early 1990s, Kojima's vision of an Asia-Pacific free trade area was all but abandoned. The notion of economic integration has been reduced to the fading history of Asia-Pacific economic co-operation endeavours. As elucidated in the preceding section, APEC's contemporary stance in this regard is well-considered, educated, refined and overarchingly multilateral. Commitment to open regionalism in the Asia-Pacific economies has become deeply entrenched. If the fastest growing group of economies in the world spurns the idea of a trading bloc, it is sure to deter, if not prevent, the fragmentation of the world economy into similar defensive blocs. If they continue to adhere to multilaterialism, they provide a disincentive to economies in the other parts of the world to organise themselves into trading blocs, an anathema to the spirit of free trade. The APEC can further the cause of free, multilateral trade by reducing the traditional obstacles to regional trade, namely the tariffs and non-tariff barriers. Any reduction in trade barriers – even when it is non-discriminatory – will bring benefit to regional economies. The proximity and dynamism of the regional economies will ensure that a large part of the benefits of liberalisation accrue to the regional economies themselves.

The Uruguay Round is trying to bring the average level of tariffs down by 30 per cent (GATT, 1992). If the Asia-Pacific economies undertake unilateral trade liberalisation, they will strengthen the efforts being made under the Round as well as multilateral trade liberalisation in general. To corroborate this point, Elek cited the example of the USA-Australian-Japan beef negotiations of 1988. Beef producers around the world can compete for Japanese markets and those having maximum comparative advantage will have competitive edge over the others. The end result is better access to Japanese beef markets for exporting countries and cheaper beef for Japanese consumers (Elek, 1990). This example shows how everybody can benefit from market opening, even if it is negotiated bilaterally, provided the market liberalisation is non-discriminatory.

In an identical manner, measures taken after the Strategic Impediment Initiatives (SII) negotiations between Japan and the USA resulted in benefits for all economies that trade with Japan. It is a good illustration of reform measures in the APEC economies working favourably for all. More importantly, in the case of SII what the two negotiating economies agreed was not only GATT-consistent, but some of the issues went beyond the coverage of the GATT.

Where this regional alliance for multilateralism will go from here will, *inter alia*, depend upon developments in the EC and the NAFTA because they have worked in the past as two pressure points for the APEC. If they remain relatively open and work towards the expansion of trade liberalisation, the APEC – given its underlying philosophy – will continue its current posture. However, should they turn into an inward-orientated and protectionist bloc, then, given its past, the APEC will show a certain degree of restraint and then reconsider its strategy.

AN AGENDA FOR OPEN MULTILATERALISM

A substantive agenda for broad-based regional co-operation exists for the Asia-Pacific region. The measures to be implemented could be phased from relatively simple and non-controversial to the taxing and onerous issues. Some of the innocuous issues need to be tackled first. For instance, exchange of information regarding regional trade and foreign investment policies and increased transparency in these policies will reduce uncertainty in international transactions. Some progress in this regard has been made and an APEC Electronic Information Network was in operation in 1992. Secondly, Asia-Pacific trade fairs can be periodically organised. The first one of its kind has in fact already taken place in Japan during 1994. Thirdly, adopting co-ordinated measures to deregulate and liberalise economies will be difficult because, as alluded to earlier, most regional economies have taken such measures.

This is not to say that no measures need to be taken. The rice trade in Japan and Korea is an example of unattended absurdity in trade policy. Similarly, some APEC countries protect their textiles and clothing sectors. The rapid liberalisation of these sectors will benefit Indonesia, the Philippines and China directly and raw material producers, such as Australia, indirectly (Elek, 1992). Although the Uruguay Round is to phase out the trade-distorting Multi-Fibre Arrangement (MFA), the APEC countries can truncate the phasing out. This can be done by agreeing to raise quota limits more rapidly than prescribed by the Uruguay Round. Fourthly, inventories for services trade data are being developed which can be followed by trade liberalisation in services. It is a difficult issue, because services and trade in them are generally not easily understood. Under the Uruguay

Round, a new set of rules have been negotiated to govern international trade in services and to secure an initial package of liberalism measures (GATT, 1992). The APEC can choose the services of special significance for the region and promote the new regime.The four services sector that are ripe for the first phase of liberalisation are: banking, transport, telecommunications and tourism.

Rationalising and harmonising legislation and regulations regarding international transactions require a good deal of skill, because of their radical differences in different countries of the region. A good kick-off point could be regulations influencing foreign direct investment where rules specify basic rights and responsibilities of foreign investors. Harmonising these will cut protracted negotiations. Tax concessions for foreign investors could be next to be tackled. Uniformity in them will dispel distorting competition for investment.

The sensitive issue of market access will need to be tackled with imagination and drive. The present level of barriers is, perversely, the highest in sectors where there is greatest complementarity in terms of resource endowment and cost structures (Drysdale and Garnaut, 1989a). For instance, tariff and quota restrictions are the highest in sectors such as agriculture, textiles, clothing, processed minerals and so on. They reduce potential gains from trade and specialisation as well as befuddling decisions regarding location of production facilities in the region. Non-discriminatory trade liberalisation in the aforementioned sectors will benefit the Asia-Pacific by augmenting trade volume in the region (Elek, 1992). Addressing these and related issues in a carefully graduated manner is sure to have a salutary effect over the regional economies.

The APEC is ideally suited to become a regional lobby for free trade in the international fora. The USA is no longer championing the cause of free trade globally – it has not only abandoned its historical role, but has also made a veritable volte-face in this regard. The mantle of leadership of free trade will have to be taken on by the APEC: there are no other credible contenders for the job. The APEC has repeatedly made it known that a significant outcome of the Uruguay Round is indispensable for underpinning the growth of world trade, for forestalling protectionist pressures, for instilling confidence in markets and for facilitating the continuation of economic reforms in the Asia-Pacific region and in the international economy.[6] With its new mantle, the APEC as a country grouping and an institution will come to have a noteworthy role in the international economy.

CONCLUSION

In the immediate post-war period, no attempts were made to integrate the Asia-Pacific region because the Japanese economy was under reconstruction, other economies were too small to be considered significant for any such endeavour, and the USA overwhelmingly dominated not only the regional economy, but also the international economy. The fast growth of the Japanese economy, which was accompanied by trade expansion, and subsequently similar developments in the ANIEs, created some motivation for regional economic integration. Other stimuli included economic complementarity among the regional economies; bilateral trade and investment relations between Japan and the ANIEs and Japan and Australia; outward-orientation of the regional economies and dynamic growth in them; and the perception of being discriminated against by the established economic powers. The existence of the EC, and subsequent creation of the NAFTA, worked as a glue to promote regional integration.

The proposals for regional integration and co-operation can be divided into three phases; 1960–66, 1967–79 and the 1980s. In the mid-1960s, Kojima's plan of region integration, which had all the five industrial countries of the Pacific rim as participants, received a great deal of attention. However, for various reasons his Asia-Pacific free-trade area never came into being. It was, in fact, a political and economic impossibility. Several other institutions were proposed and created subsequently – namely, the Pacific Trade and Development Conference (PAFTAD), the Association of South East Asian Nations (ASEAN), the Pacific Basin Economic Community (PBEC), the Organisation for Pacific Trade and Development (OPTAD), the Pacific Economic Co-operation Conference (PECC) and the Asia-Pacific Economic Co-operation (APEC) forum. Of the seven noteworthy initiatives for regional integration and co-operation taken during the 1966–89 period, the APEC promises to be the most substantive. The academic community, business leaders and government bureaucracy all contributed in the creation of these institutions. During the 1970s, the members' interest in forming an organisation of regional economic integration declined sharply: they were more interested in creating institutions for pragmatic and purposeful regional co-operation.

The creation of APEC is considered to be a consequence of two principal developments: first, the maturing of earlier institutional initiatives; and, secondly, the international economic environment of the 1980s. It emanated from the so-called 'Hawke initiative'. The guiding principles of APEC were such that it has to be an outward-orientated institution which rejects any suggestion of an inward-orientated trade-bloc formation. These are indeed unique objectives and reflect APEC's concern for global economic interests. The dictum of open regionalism has become a firmly entrenched part of the Asia-Pacific economic psyche. Although the APEC is not averse to promoting regional trade liberalisation, it will only do so if it is consistent with the tenets of the GATT and not detrimental to other economies. The APEC has manifested a strong commitment to preserving the non-discriminatory, multilateral trading system and support for the Uruguay Round. By the early 1990s, Kojima's vision of an Asia-Pacific free-trade area was all but laid to rest.

The economies of the Asia-Pacific region are capable of competing in the international markets without the support of a narrow, regional bloc. These economies benefited a great deal from the opening of a multilateral economic system and trade expansion during the post-war decades, and an open multilateral trading system in the contemporary period suits them as much as it did in the past. Therefore, they created APEC as an alliance for open multilateralism. If the APEC – which comprises the fastest growing economies of the world – rejects the idea of a trading bloc, it is sure to prevent fragmentation of the world economy into defensive blocs.

Several unilateral measures of the APEC will promote multilateralism in the international economy. A substantive short-term agenda awaits the APEC: it includes the exchange of information regarding regional trade and foreign investment of policies; organising Asia-Pacific trade fairs; adopting co-ordinated measures to deregulate and liberalise the regional economies; bringing down the traditional market barriers and promoting trade in services; rationalising and harmonising legislations and regulations regarding international transactions; and imaginatively tackling the sensitive issue of market access. This apart, the APEC is ideally suited to become a regional lobby for free trade in the international fora.

3 The Ascension of the Japanese Economy to Pre-eminence

INTRODUCTION

In this chapter I shall present a broad-brush sketch of the Japanese economy, basic facts relating to it, its structure and changes therein. Also, I shall attempt to give a succinct overview of its operation. The approach, essentially, is that of mainstream economists. Although the treatment is in no way comprehensive, it does cover all the salient aspects of Japanese economic growth during the post-war period. From the ravages of the Second World War, the Japanese economy rose and rebuilt itself into the second largest economy in the world by the early 1970s. It is an achievement lauded by the world at large. A decade or so later, it became the largest creditor country in the world, and then, in quick succession, the largest donor and the largest foreign investor. By the mid-1980s, it was generally recognised as an economic, financial and technological superpower. This process of growth from an abjectly low economic level to international pre-eminence is analysed here. Japan's new status has significant international implications: in the world after the cold war, economic strength has a great deal of swaying capability. This has assigned Japan a meaningful role not only in the Asia-Pacific region, but also in the wider international economic arena.

AFTERMATH OF WAR

The Second World War devastated Japan's economic base and created all kinds of shortages, including a severe food shortage. Japan was occupied by the US Army under the Supreme Commander for Allied Powers who held absolute powers. Apparently, therefore, the USA dominated efforts to reconstruct and rehabilitate the Japanese economy. The reform measures adopted, *inter alia*, entailed reduction of concentration of business power and the establishment of more competitive markets. This involved steps such as the dissolution of family-owned *zaibatsu* conglomerates, the elimination of cartels and monopolies, and the break-up of some extremely large firms.

Since inflation was running menacingly high and the economy badly needed to be stabilised, the Dodge Plan was announced in 1948 by the General Headquarters of the occupation forces. It emphasised such measures as balancing the budget, restraining credit, stabilising wages and increasing the domestic production of raw materials and manufactured goods. The austerity programme was faithfully implemented. As a consequence, the volume of currency circulation contracted, black-market prices fell and, therefore (after some time) price control measures began to be abolished. Trends in the rationalisation of firms and in their efficiency increases were impressive. The Dodge austerity policy also dealt a blow to the labour union movement which was beginning to gather steam.

Since the economic base had been devastated, output was increased by eliminating war-caused bottlenecks and excess capacity in the existing industrial structure. The experience of the war-torn west European countries was identical. Although Japan became a giant supply base serving the American forces during the Korean war (which began in 1950) and experienced a mini-boom due to the war, the economy remained impoverished. The Allied occupation of Japan ended in April 1952 and Japan became an independent state. At this point, according to the OECD statistics, Japan's GNP was $ 16.3 billion and per capita GNP a paltry $ 188, which was lower than that of Brazil, Chile, Malaysia and several other developing countries. Structurally the economy was a quaint mix of characteristics of developing and developed countries.

In the early 1950s, the Japanese economy was widely considered to be in a decrepit state, one that would have to depend on the Western industrialised economies for a long time before stabilising at any level. This supercilious evaluation turned out to be incorrect and the economy achieved an outstanding record of recovery and growth, particularly since the adoption of the Yonzenso programme. This thrust Japan into a decade-long era of double-figure annual growth rate during the 1960s. This was the beginning of the *asahi* or 'rising sun' era. Sagacious macro-economic management, organisational acumen and plain hard work lifted Japan from the ravages of the war to middle-income level in little over a decade. By the 1970s, Japan had achieved keen industrial competitiveness in a good number of industries and Herman Kahn prognosticated that it would 'not be surprising if the twenty-first century were the Japanese century' (Kahn, 1970). The economy continued to expand, and the per capita income continued to rise, while income distribution in the society grew egalitarian. In 1960, its share of world GNP was 3 per cent, in 1980 it grew to 9 per cent, and in 1990 it was 13 per cent. In relative terms, at the beginning of the 1960s Japan's GNP was less than 10 per cent of that of the USA; by the early 1980s, it was 40 per cent of the US GNP; in 1990 it was 54 per cent. In the mid-1980s, Japan became the largest creditor of the world, while the USA became the largest debtor. Before the end of the decade, as stated earlier, Japan acquired other status symbols, such as being the largest foreign investor and the largest donor economy. It has remained the third-largest trading economy throughout the 1980s. The contrast between the Japan of the early 1950s and the mid-1980s is as startling as it is interesting. In what follows, we shall see how this contrast was created and what were the principal contributing factors behind it.

The Backdrop of Brisk Growth

In as much as the economic and cultural foundation of the future economic growth of Japan was laid after the collapse of the Tokugawa shogunate and restoration of the reign of Emperor Meiji in 1867, this should be the logical starting point of any study of the contemporary Japanese economy.

During the Tokugawa shogunate, Japan was an isolationist, semi-feudal and economically backward country. The shogunate was brought down by a remarkable group of reformers and cultural revolutionaries that included rising young merchants and disaffected *samurai* bureaucrats. This group abhorred the erstwhile 'box' society and went about the business of modernising Japan with a missionary zeal. They had an obsession for opening Japan to other influences, particularly for learning from the West.

The most influential of Meiji reformers was Yukichi Fukuzawa, an indignant samurai turned scholar-reformer, who was one of the prime movers in pulling Japan into the modern era. He led an intensely productive, albeit apolitical, life and almost single-handedly introduced and popularised the intellectual culture of the West along with the whole body of ideas of the Western Enlightenment (Gibney, 1992). Fukuzawa founded Keio University and led Japan towards empirical learning. He decried Confucianism as irrelevant and promoted 'the laws of number and reason' as understood in the West. (The wheel has since come full circle and Japan is now being fervently lauded in the West for its Confucian legacy.) Reformers such as Mori Arinori, who followed Fukuzawa, remained equally committed to modernising and industrialising Japan so that it caught up with the West. Thus, a national ethos for industrialisation was firmly established. It is little wonder that the Meiji period has come to be known as the beginning of an era, one of the modern economic expansion of Japan.

Textile factories were the first to develop. Japan had a comparative advantage in producing silk, therefore, as family silk farms expanded, silk exports expanded and became a major source of foreign exchange. This continued until the early 1930s. The Meiji government helped industrialisation endeavours by developing a centralised banking system under the Bank of Japan. It went a long way in capital formation, indispensable for economic growth. The burdensome land tax was supplanted by broad-based consumption and excise taxes. The government also helped develop steel and shipbuilding industries. A large steel mill, called the Yawata Steel, was established in 1901, so that scale economies could be exploited. The first of the *Sogo Shosha*, or great trading companies, called Mitsui Bussan, was established during this period with an objective to compete with the Western companies in acquiring commodities and raw materials in the international markets. The usual provision of public good, like infrastructure creation, was also undertaken by the government. By 1900, over 40 000 miles of railway tracks had been laid, linking all major cities. Mining, particularly coal, was paid a good deal of official attention. Working conditions in the mines and factories were unhealthy and took a heavy toll in terms of human life, and workers laboured for long hours in stifling sweatshops for minuscule wages.

Foreign capital was purposively shunned because Japan watched the economic colonisation of China next door and disapproved of it. The government and businessmen worked together to make up for the absence of foreign capital. Development finance institutions like the Industrial Bank of Japan provided the much-needed capital. The bond between the business and bureaucracy began to grow stronger, until it began to appear that all roads led to Tokyo. By the end of the nineteenth century, the foundation of a modern industrial society was in place. It was strengthened by the family-owned *zaibatsu* conglomerates that were subsequently to play a large part in the Japanese economy. At this point, the economy had reached what in modern parlance is known as, the 'take-off stage'. Japan thus became the first Asian country to acquire this distinction by a margin of at least seventy-five years.

Over the last quarter of the nineteenth century, Japan exploited its traditional agricultural sector, which was the largest in the economy. The revenue provided to the government was used in building infrastructure and importing technology. By 1900, the size of the agricultural sector had contracted somewhat and it employed 66 per cent of the total labour force. Investment ratio at this time was 13.0 per cent of GNP. During the first quarter of the twentieth century, the economy expanded at an annual average rate of 3.5 per cent in real terms. It even experienced a boom period during the

First World War years. Cotton had become a major industry and, as with silk, Japan had a good deal of comparative advantage in it. Its textile exports were competitive all over the world.

By 1930, the agricultural labour force had further reduced to 50 per cent of the total and the investment ratio had climbed to 17.7 per cent. Unlike other industrial countries, Japan posted a high growth rate for the 1930s: GNP grew at an average annual rate of 5 per cent during this decade. This was the time when militant nationalism gripped Japan and in its wake large industrial units in chemicals, metals and machinery were created. These soon dominated the industrial structure. By the end of the 1930s, it was considered a relatively advanced economy. The labour force in agriculture had further contracted to 40 per cent of the total and the investment ratio had topped 20 per cent. Japan had become an important exporter of manufactured products and importer of industrial raw materials. Although it was a rapidly expanding economy, it retained its so-called dual character, which is a characteristic of the developing economy (Ohkawa and Rosovsky, 1973). The story of Japan being involved in two military misadventures is too well-known to require further discussion here.

THE *ASAHI* PHASE

Over the 1950s and 1960s, the objective of economic strategy was clearly defined and it was consistently implemented. Economic growth topped the priority, while secondary emphasis was laid on stability, meaning thereby to reduce the crests and troughs of business cycles and keep inflation within moderate limits. The size of GDP was too small to attract any external attention. Growth was assisted during the Korean war years (1950–53) by US procurement orders. A tiny upswing of business cycle began in 1955 and ended in 1957. It was called the *Jimmu* boom[1] and was followed by a shortfall in growth and investment rates. But in 1958 another upswing of the business cycle started. It was a stronger and longer-lasting upswing, at a higher level of average growth rate than the previous one, and was called the *Iwato*[2] boom. It lasted forty-two months, between July 1958 and December 1961 and, like the first boom, was followed by a shortfall in real growth and investment rates. In 1961 the Doubling National Income Plan was announced, which envisaged a future growth rate of 7.2 per cent. Despite two booms in quick succession, sceptics abounded. But Japan not only attained this goal, its long-term (1950–73) average growth rate turned out to be 10.5 per cent. This was more than twice the growth rate of the world GDP for this period, which was 4.7 per cent. Among eleven industrial economies, this average was the highest. West Germany came second with 5.5 per cent, while the USA averaged 3.2 per cent (Denison and Chung, 1976).

Since saving and investment are so necessary – although not sufficient – for growth, let me first focus on the saving–investment balance. Private sector saving rates, which includes the savings of corporate and household sectors, were very high: during the rapid growth period they were 28.9 per cent of GNP in 1950, 26.0 per cent in 1955, 28.2 per cent in 1960 and 27.4 per cent in 1965. One rationale of high savings rate could possibly be that the rapid rate of growth produced an unequal distribution of income and raised savings rate. However, this scenario did not apply to the Japanese economy. Savings rose, instead, in the process of income equalisation. A wage differential had developed during the latter half of the reconstruction period and a two-tier dual economic structure had become quite prominent. As the economy moved into the rapid growth period, the two-tier structure dissolved and the surplus labour force was absorbed in the expanding economy, which in turn resulted in income equality and higher savings. Over the 1960s, private sector investment regularly exceeded savings. This imbalance was offset by (a) government surplus and (b) the current account deficit which occurred frequently during the decade.

As Table 3.1 shows, savings in the private sector were high and equally high investment demand in the corporate sector kept gobbling them up as fast as they accumulated. During these years, both savings and investment levels, as percentages of GNP, were double the levels in the USA. The average private sector saving–investment balance for the entire decade showed an excess of investment over savings of 1.9 per cent of GNP. Also, the household sector was a consistent net saver, averaging 4.4 per cent of GNP, while the corporate sector was a consistent net investor, averaging 6.3 per cent of GNP. These figures imply a voracious corporate demand and, therefore, a constant flow of savings from households to the corporate sector (Lincoln, 1988). Whenever the household sector was unable to fulfil the total demand of the corporate sector, the

Table 3.1   Savings–Investment Balances, 1960–91 as % of GNP

Year	Private sector			Corporate sector		
	Savings	Investment	Savings minus investment	Savings	Investment	Savings minus investment
1960	28.2	31.1	−2.9	16.5	24.6	−8.1
1965	27.4	27.5	−0.1	15.8	19.1	−3.3
1967	31.4	32.7	−1.3	18.4	23.8	−5.4
1968	32.9	33.0	−0.1	19.7	24.1	−4.4
1969	32.6	34.5	−1.9	19.8	25.3	−5.5
1970	33.3	34.0	−0.7	18.7	27.5	−8.8
1971	31.0	30.0	1.0	16.1	24.8	−8.7
1972	32.0	29.2	2.8	16.9	23.9	−7.0
1973	32.3	31.7	0.6	15.4	26.2	−10.8
1974	30.0	31.4	−1.4	10.3	23.1	−12.9
1975	29.0	26.8	2.2	8.4	17.9	−9.5
1976	30.4	26.0	4.4	9.1	16.2	−7.0
1977	29.5	24.6	5.0	9.5	15.2	−5.6
1978	30.7	23.9	6.8	11.4	13.9	−2.5
1979	29.0	25.2	3.8	11.7	16.1	−4.3
1980	28.4	25.1	3.2	11.3	17.0	−5.7
1981	27.9	24.2	3.7	10.6	16.9	−6.3
1982	27.2	23.3	3.9	11.2	16.2	−4.9
1983	26.9	21.9	5.0	11.0	15.3	−4.2
1984	26.7	22.3	4.5	11.4	19.5	−4.5
1985	26.8	22.8	4.0	11.8	17.2	−5.4
1986	27.2	22.1	5.1	12.6	16.2	−3.6
1987	26.0	22.6	3.4	12.9	16.7	−3.7
1988	26.0	24.4	1.6	13.3	18.9	−5.6
1989	25.6	25.6	0.0	12.9	20.4	−7.7
1990	25.2	26.4	−1.2	12.4	21.8	−9.4
1991	25.4	25.9	−0.5	12.1	28.9	−8.8

Table 3.1 Continued

Year	Household sector			Government sector		
	Savings	Investment	Savings minus investment	Savings	Investment	Savings minus investment
1960	11.8	6.6	5.2	7.7	4.7	3.0
1965	11.6	8.4	3.2	6.0	5.4	0.6
1967	13.0	8.9	4.1	6.3	5.1	1.2
1968	13.2	8.9	4.3	6.9	5.1	1.8
1969	12.7	9.2	3.6	7.5	5.0	2.5
1970	14.6	6.5	8.1	6.8	5.1	1.7
1971	15.1	5.3	9.8	6.2	6.3	−0.1
1972	14.9	5.2	9.7	7.0	5.8	1.2
1973	16.9	5.4	11.5	6.9	6.4	0.5
1974	19.7	8.3	11.5	6.3	6.0	0.4
1975	20.6	8.6	11.7	3.3	6.0	−2.8
1976	21.3	9.8	11.4	2.1	5.8	−3.7
1977	20.0	9.4	10.6	2.5	6.3	−3.8
1978	19.4	10.0	9.3	1.5	7.0	−5.5
1979	17.3	9.2	8.1	2.5	7.2	−4.7
1980	17.1	8.1	9.0	2.7	7.1	−4.4
1981	17.3	7.3	10.0	3.3	7.1	−3.8
1982	16.0	7.1	8.8	3.2	6.8	−3.6
1983	15.9	6.6	9.3	2.8	6.4	−3.7
1984	15.3	6.4	9.0	3.9	6.0	−2.1
1985	15.0	5.6	9.4	4.8	5.6	−0.8
1986	15.1	5.4	9.7	4.7	5.6	−0.9
1987	13.9	5.4	8.5	6.4	5.9	0.5
1988	13.3	4.9	8.6	7.6	6.1	1.5
1989	13.6	4.4	9.2	8.8	5.9	2.5
1990	13.3	3.7	9.4	8.9	6.1	2.9
1991	13.9	4.1	9.7	9.2	6.2	2.9

Source: Economic Planning Agency, *Annual Report on National Statistics*, Tokyo, various issues.

deficit was met by the government sector rather than from capital flow from abroad. This brings us to another important feature: government revenues exceeded expenditures. Thus, one can infer that, as a net saver, government made a direct contribution to investment endeavours.

In the 1970s, the scenario changed and in a way was the opposite of the 1960s. With moderation in growth and decline in investment, the private sector became a net saver (Table 3.1) and the government sector began to record deficits. The private sector began to record a surplus of savings over investment after the early 1970s. It rose rapidly and reached a peak of 6.8 per cent of GNP in 1978 (Ito, 1992). The outlet for the surplus was long-term capital outflow. Japanese banks expanded overseas and began to contribute to the international syndication of loans. Several leading city banks began to participate in international business. Over the 1980s and early 1990s, private sector savings continued to be at a very high level. By this period, Japan had become a mature industrialised economy. Compared to other mature economies, these rates were four to five times higher; therefore, Japan was accused of 'oversaving'. This helped in long-term capital outflows from Japan after 1981 (Table 3.2). The private sector investment rates between 1988 and 1991 ranged between 24.4 per cent and 26.4 per cent of GNP. At the time when the economy entered a recessionary phase in the latter half of 1992, it became obvious that Japan had over-invested during these years.

The direct impact of high levels of investment in plant and equipment was that the average age of the capital stock came down, leading to rapid productivity. The K/L ratio, or capital equipment per person, increased by leaps and bounds and so did the average productivity per person (Y/L) – see Table 3.3.

Initially, labour productivity was low because the capital stock per worker was small. This state continued even after recovery because capital formation in absolute terms was slow. As the statistics in Table 3.3 show, after the mid-1950s, capital began to grow more rapidly than the labour force. During the period spanning 1952–73, plant and equipment expenditure increased by an average of 14.4 per cent per annum. Over the 1950s, investment in real terms remained about 20 per cent of GNP, an impressive performance by any measure (Patrick and Rosovsky, 1976). The optimism in the business and managerial community was responsible for further improvement in capital formation in the 1960s. No other industrial economy matched this performance. Ploughing back such large proportions with reasonably low incremental capital–output ratio (ICOR) apparently had an income effect. The high investment phenomenon was

Table 3.2   Balance of Payments Indicators, 1965–91 (in $ m)

Year	Current account balance	Trade balance	Long-term capital flows (net)	Overall balance of monetary movement (net)
1965	932	1 901	415	405
1967	−190	1 160	−812	−571
1968	1 048	2 529	−239	1 102
1969	2 119	3 699	−155	2 283
1970	1 970	3 963	−1 591	1 374
1971	5 797	7 787	−1 082	7 677
1972	6 624	8 971	−4 487	4 741
1973	−136	3 688	−9 750	10 074
1974	−4 693	1 436	−3 881	−6 839
1975	−682	5 028	−272	−2 676
1976	3 680	9 887	−984	2 924
1977	10 918	17 311	3 184	7 743
1978	16 534	24 596	12 389	5 950
1979	−8 754	1 845	−12 976	16 662
1980	−10 746	2 125	2 324	−8 396
1981	4 770	19 967	−9 672	−2 144
1982	6 850	18 079	−14 969	−4 971
1983	20 799	31 454	−17 700	5 177
1984	35 003	44 257	−49 651	−15 200
1985	49 169	55 986	64 542	−12 318
1986	85 845	92 827	−13 461	−44 767
1987	87 015	96 386	−136 532	−29 545
1988	79 631	95 012	−130 930	−28 982
1989	57 157	76 917	−89 246	−33 286
1990	35 762	63 528	−43 586	−7 234
1991	72 598	103 289	36 628	76 369

Source: Bank of Japan, *Economic Statistics Annual, 1991*, Tokyo: Research and Statistics Department, March 1992.

Table 3.3   The Capital Labour Ratio and Capital Equipment per Worker

	1955	1965	1975
K/L (in ¥, 000)	492	982	274
Y/L (in ¥, 000)	443	883	1867

Source: Kosai and Ogino (1984).

economy-wide, therefore it did not create any situation of industry-specific excess capacity.

Japan was determined about not importing capital and made up for any gaps by domestic sources. The reason for this lays in its external account. The exchange rate for the yen was fixed at 360 to the dollar under the Bretton Woods system, which made the yen overvalued. At this rate Japan could not export enough to pay for its imports. Under the Bretton Woods system all the adjustments were to be made by the deficit country, if it did not wish to resort to devaluation. Japan did not, because it was trying to be seen as a responsible and productive member of the international economic community – it equated devaluation with national humiliation. To ward off any current account deficits, Japan instituted high tariffs, widespread import quotas and prevented corporations from borrowing abroad. Capital control measures were instituted and therefore, up to the mid-1960s, the effective interest rates were higher at home than abroad. There was, however, a discretionary policy and industries with large growth potential or firms in high-tech areas were allowed to borrow abroad.

Rapid growth of household savings was strongly supported by high growth of household incomes. As stated earlier, this sector continued to be a large supplier of funds even after the slowing of growth rate over the 1970s. From an average of 15 per cent of GNP in the early 1970s, it rose to 20 per cent or more in the mid-1970s. Finally, it declined to 15 per cent of GNP in the mid-1980s. Excess savings resulted, due to a declining trend in private sector investment. That Japan's household saving rate is one of the highest in the world was recognised as early as 1960. An exhaustive survey (Horioka, 1985) lists over thirty possible factors that might contribute to Japan's high household savings rate. The four celebrated reasons for the high household savings are: (i) high income growth rate (ii) favourable tax treatment of both small and large savings (iii) an inadequate social security system and (iv) the high prices of land and houses. Bequest has been a strong motive in Japanese society (Hayashi *et al.*, 1987). However, there are disagreements on saving motives. For instance, Yoshitomi (1989) has argued that expensive land and houses can explain high household saving rates only if the demand for owner-occupied housing is price-inelastic. He demonstrated evidence of price elasticity in the demand for land and houses. Such high rates of savings and investment were instrumental in the rapid industrialisation of the war-ravaged economy. When reconstruction began, the industrial sector in Japan was in a worse shape than in West Germany and other war-torn European economies.

Over the years a pattern of industrial growth evolved. First, preference was accorded to basic industries like iron and steel, heavy and chemical industries and power generation. They had a pre-war base and contributed to the upgrading of the industrial structure. In addition, due to lower imported raw material content, chemical industries had greater domestic value-added. The government supported the growth of all three sectors financially. Conversely, inefficient industries like coal, non-ferrous metals, paper and pulp were ruthlessly eliminated. There was another set of industries which were considered unsuitable and in which Japan did not want to become competitive in the future. It included cotton textiles, bicycles, and sewing machines. These were discouraged because strategists saw them as those fit for economies at an early stage of industrialisation, like China and India. Under official guidance, firms had to release resources – that is, labour and materials – for more efficient sectors that buttressed growth.

After the basic industries, two groups were sequentially provided with official stimulus. The first included shipbuilding, trucks and buses, television and radio, rolling stock and optical equipment. The second group of industries was palpably at a higher technological level and comprised consumer electronics, machinery, precision tools, autos, optics, heavy construction equipment and, later on, computer hardware. Development of these sectors contributed a great deal to Japanese growth efforts, particularly the second list of product lines which comprises what is called the second stage industrialisation products. Growth in these sectors first met the needs of the growing domestic markets and, therefore, was import-substituting. But firms soon had to begin exporting and ensure the competitiveness of their products in the international markets. Consequently, most of these industries succeeded in becoming substantial exporters by the 1960s.

A well-defined technology plan was also adhered to. Since cheap steel was essential for industrial growth, two rationalisation plans were implemented for upgrading the steel industry in the 1950s. The spread of oxygen converters, which used scrap iron as raw material, was a big help. The second rationalisation plan essentially focused on the construction of strip mills to make thin steel plates for producing consumer durables. By the early 1960s, steel mills were producing over 5.5 million tons a year. This volume of output was greater than that of France and England. In terms of the number of hot strip mills, Japan was next to the USA and in oxygen converter capacity it soon reached the leading position in the world. All along this development, a good deal of attention was paid to quality improvements and new product development, like high-quality steel sheets, light-guage steel, seamless electrical pipe and high tensile-strength steel. By the mid-1970s, Japan's steel industry was widely recognised as being the strongest in the world, producing the finest steel. This was not merely due to the locational advantages of its coastal steel mills. Technological progress had been phenomenal, which in turn had halved the unit cost of production in several plants.

Cheap sources of energy were essential for efficient industrialisation. Therefore, to reduce energy prices, steam-powered, high-capacity power plants were installed. Fall in the unit price of oil brought the costs down further. This almost started an energy revolution which benefited the industrial sector a great deal, and which continued until the oil crisis of 1973 (Kosai, 1986). The flip-side of this development was that the reliance of the economy on oil grew inordinately. Modernisation and technological upgrading in the manufacturing sector in general continued to proceed. Typical was the development of such consumer durables as automobiles and electric machinery and appliances. A series of technological advances finally resulted in the mass production of automobiles. This was not without snags, but after they were overcome, it contributed a great deal to mass production. Similar technological upgrading took place in the motorcycle industry. After meeting the explosive domestic demand, a large part of the international motorcycle market was captured by Japan. The car industry is known for strong backward linkages. It provided strong stimulus to steel and machine tool industries. It also supported a wide range of small subcontracting firms, because the large car firms had adopted the just-in-time system. Several of the technological advances were linked and fed on each other. For instance, when the steel industry was able to introduce the automatic, continuous-process stamping machines, mass production in electric machinery, washing machines and refrigerators became possible. In short, rapid industrial growth was constantly underpinned by technological upgradation. The two together changed the industrial scene out of recognition.

Japan succeeded in absorbing Western technology because of two major reasons. First, in the beginning, Japan relied on foreign engineers who were subsequently replaced by those trained in the domestic universities. These engineers studied foreign technical treaties and actual imported machinery. They copied what they saw, often adding improvements and modifications of their own. Thus, they were innovative imitators. Secondly, a good deal of research and development (R&D) took place before actual application and absorption of modern technology. The scale of R&D expanded after the Second World War. In two decades, it became immensely sophisticated, which in turn had a great deal of impact over the industrial sector and, therefore, industrial value-added. A symbolic representation of Japanese technological advancement was the *Shinkansen*, or the bullet train, that began to operate in 1964. This is generally considered the time when the Meiji dream of catching up with the West was attained and Japan had reached by and large the same stage of industrialisation as the West. Its growth was fast-paced because it had a lot of catching up to do.

During Japan's early growth phase, enormous investment was made in education, particularly engineering education. Japanese corporations are now reaping the benefits of this investment. Technical literacy is more widely diffused throughout Japanese business than elsewhere in the industrial world. Japan had 5000 technical workers per million people in 1990.

The comparable figure for the USA was 3500, for West Germany 2500, and no other country came close (*The Economist*, 1991). Another characteristic of Japanese technological advancement was that it was made without breaking through the boundaries of existing technologies. A large proportion of innovations came through fusion of different types of technologies rather than by technological breakthroughs (Kodama, 1991). By the mid-1980s Japan had become a frontrunner in industrial technology. Scientific and technological researchers, both academic and industrial, had begun to pay more attention to what was happening in Japan. Japan's strength lay in the mass-market technologies, including video cameras, semiconductors, advanced colour televisions and computer displays, semiconductor-manufacturing equipment, computer-controlled machine tools and, since the late 1980s, luxury cars. Although all these are important areas of strength, they are medium value-added technologies. There are, however, several very high value-added products in which Japan does not lead: for instance, satellites, supercomputers, aero engines, and jet aircraft (Emmott, 1992). Japan also has weaknesses in biotechnology, chemical engineering and pharmaceuticals.

Although Japan's GDP growth rate in real terms for 1955–65 was admirable at 8.0 per cent, the following decade was even better in terms of growth. It enhanced Japan's international status. In 1963, Japan acceded to Article VIII of the International Monetary Fund and, in recognition of its status as an advanced country, it was made a member of the Organisation for Economic Co-operation and Development (OECD) in 1964. The latter half of the 1960s was a period of phenomenal growth performance. Kosai called it 'a time of record-setting long-term prosperity'. The real growth rate over the period 1955–60 was 9.0 per cent, which rose marginally to 9.7 per cent for the 1960–65 period and further to an unprecedented 13.1 per cent for the 1965–70 period. The last part of the upswing of this business cycle lasted for 57 months, from the autumn of 1965 to the summer of 1970. It was christened the '*Izanagi*' boom[3]. This was the period when investment was calling for investment and was instrumental in creating new processes and industries. It made growth autonomous and self-propelled. By the time the *Izanagi* boom ended, Japan was fully established as a respectable – if somewhat envied – member of the community of mature industrial economies.

The Japanese economy adopted an outward-orientated stance from the beginning because after the mini-boom of the Korean war, when its current account was helped by American procurement orders, it was faced with a difficult situation. Overseas assets were lost due to the war. Japan needed foreign exchange to sustain the recovery which was beginning to get under way. Ironically, the world economy was showing signs of a down-turn at this time. Under these circumstances there was little choice but to turn to exporting in an aggressive manner and, to this end, be as competitive in the international markets as possible. In this venture, Japan received US help in two ways: first, because of its special relationship with the USA, it found American markets welcoming its exports; second, the USA was championing the cause of free trade in the world. It succeeded in trade and exchange regime liberalisation, which, in turn, helped Japan expand its export markets.

International trade, following the regulations and discipline of the General Agreement on Tariffs and Trade (GATT), expanded at an unprecedented pace. The 1950s and 1960s are widely considered the halcyon period of world trade. The two countries that made the most of this free trading environment and rapid trade expansion were Japan and Germany. Japanese exports started from a tiny base of $ 2 billion in 1955, doubled to $ 4.1 billion in 1960 and catapulted to $ 19.3 billion in 1970. This means an average growth of 16.9 per cent for the 1960s. Import growth kept pace with export growth, soaring from $ 2.2 billion in 1955 to $ 4.5 billion in 1960 and further to $ 18.9 billion in 1970 (Table 3.4). Import growth rate averaged 15.0 per cent for the 1960s (Kojima, 1977). Japanese export growth was twice as rapid as world trade during this period, which resulted in a doubling of its share of world trade, from 3.2 per cent in 1960 to 6.2 per cent in 1970.

Table 3.4 Foreign Trade Indicators, 1960–91

Year	Exports (in $ m)	% change over preceding year	Imports (in $ m)	% change over preceding year	Volume index (1985=100)		Gold and foreign exchange reserves (in $ m)	Exchange rate (¥/$)
					Exports	Imports		
1960	4 055	+17.3	4 491	+24.8			1 824	358
1965	8 452	+26.7	8 169	+2.9			2 107	360
1967	10 442	+6.8	11 663	+22.5			2 005	362
1968	12 972	+24.2	12 987	+11.4			2 891	358
1969	15 990	+23.3	15 024	+15.7			3 496	358
1970	19 318	+20.8	18 881	+25.7			4 399	358
1971	24 019	+24.3	19 712	+4.4			15 235	315
1972	28 591	+19.0	23 471	+19.1			18 365	301
1973	36 930	+29.2	38 314	+63.2			12 246	280
1974	55 536	+50.4	62 110	+62.1	45.8	79.6	13 518	300
1975	55 753	+0.4	57 863	-6.8	45.4	69.8	12 815	305
1976	67 225	+20.6	64 799	+12.0	54.8	76.8	16 604	293
1977	80 495	+19.7	70 809	+9.3	59.2	78.6	22 848	240
1978	97 543	+21.2	79 343	+12.1	59.3	83.4	33 019	195
1979	103 032	+5.6	110 672	+39.5	60.0	94.0	20 327	240
1980	129 807	+26.0	140 528	+27.0	70.6	91.2	25 232	204
1981	152 030	+17.1	143 290	+2.0	78.0	89.9	28 403	220
1982	138 831	-8.7	131 931	-7.9	76.3	89.4	23 262	235
1983	146 927	+3.8	126 393	-4.2	82.3	90.1	24 496	232
1984	170 114	+15.8	136 503	+8.0	95.6	99.6	26 313	252
1985	175 638	+3.2	129 539	-5.1	100.0	100.0	26 510	200
1986	209 151	+19.1	126 408	-2.4	99.4	109.5	42 239	160

Table 3.4   Continued

Year	Exports (in $ m)	% change over preceding year	Imports (in $ m)	% change over preceding year	Volume index (1985=100)		Gold and foreign exchange reserves (in $ m)	Exchange rate (¥/$)
					Exports	Imports		
1987	229 221	+9.6	149 515	+18.3	99.7	119.7	81 479	122
1988	264 917	+15.6	187 354	+25.3	104.8	139.7	97 662	126
1989	275 175	+3.9	210 847	+12.5	108.8	150.6	84 895	143
1990	286 948	+4.3	234 799	+11.4	114.8	159.3	77 053	135
1991	314 948	+9.6	236 737	+0.8	118.2	164.0	6 880	125

Source: Bank of Japan, Economic Statistics Annual 1991, Tokyo: Research and Statics Department, March 1992.

The silver lining had to have a cloud. Producers in the importing countries found the loss of their own markets disconcerting. Japanese exports also chipped away their shares in the third country markets. Dumping and unfair trade charges became rampant. United States textile and steel producers were among the first to accuse. The USA was Japan's biggest market in several products. When the Japanese economy was tiny, its export expansion was, if anything, admired. However, by 1970 it had grown into a large economy exporting large volumes of manufactured goods and importing massive amounts of raw materials. Japan's trade expansion was far more rapid than that of other industrial economies. By the early 1970s, West Europeans were also disaffected and Japan began to be seen as an economy that was de-stabilising the world economy. The accusation took a pungent edge because, at 358 yen to the dollar, the yen was undervalued and Japan's domestic markets had protectionist tariffs, quota restrictions (QRs), exchange controls, capital controls, administrative guidance and were reputed to be the most difficult to break into for foreign exporters. Japan's distribution system worked as a barrier in its own right. Certainly, consumers around the world benefited from good quality products at internationally competitive prices and international welfare and household welfare in the importing countries were raised. However, as we have seen above, the volume of Japanese exports rose too fast for firms to adjust production and for economies to adjust structurally, so both micro and macroeconomic adjustments were rendered difficult. Hindsight reveals that in some product lines the importing countries had lost comparative advantage, therefore, they could not compete with Japanese products in their own markets. Yet, largely for non-economic reasons, they did not wish to give up on those product lines and turn to areas where they did have comparative advantage. Consequently, the drumbeats of protectionist lobbies in the industrial countries went on becoming increasingly strident.

Comparative advantage is a dynamic phenomenon. In a growing economy, it is always in a state of flux. Japan's comparative advantage shifted from unskilled, labour-intensive products in the 1960s to skilled, labour-intensive products later and then to high-technology products. Balassa and Noland (1988) computed the indices of revealed comparative advantage (RCA) of a range of products for the period 1967–83 to demonstrate changes in international specialisation. The RCA is defined as the ratio of a country's share in the exports of a particular commodity to that country's share in total merchandise exports. For any particular industry, a value > 1 reflects comparative advantage while < 1 stands for comparative disadvantage. In the mid-1960s, Japan's comparative advantage was in products like textiles, apparel, rubber and plastic products, leather and leather products, clay and miscellaneous light manufactured products. They were unskilled, labour-intensive products. Japan also had some comparative advantage in human capital-intensive products like non-electrical machinery, electrical machinery, transportation equipment, instruments, and so on. By the early 1980s, the unskilled, labour-intensive products had shifted from a position of comparative advantage to one of comparative disadvantage. Skill-intensive and high-tech products began to record high points on the RCA index. Japan increased its comparative advantage in twelve out of nineteen high-tech product categories considered by Balassa and Noland. It also did well in several R&D and science-based industries. It did better in industries in which research is product-specific and management of research activities is important (Kodama, 1991). This transformation in comparative advantage is clearly visible in Japan's exports. Japanese firms constantly moved up-market, and in thirty years became world leaders in industries as complex as automobiles.

For the first time in 1965, a small surplus was recorded on the current account as well as the trade balance. However, by 1967, it had disappeared (Table 3.2). The Nixon 'shockoo' of 1971 abruptly discontinued the dollar convertibility into gold. For a considerable time before the Nixon shock, the exchange rate in force was believed to have been undervalued relative to the yen's purchasing power parity (ppp). The fixed exchange rate regime ended and floating exchange rates began. The Bretton Woods exchange rate of the yen was no longer valid and the yen appreciated, fluctuating between 280 to 310 to the dollar. Despite currency appreciation, Japan recorded large current account and trade balance surpluses. This was essentially due to the poor export performance of other industrial countries, particularly the USA. This resulted in large amounts of dollars and foreign exchange flowing into Japan, and its foreign exchange reserves jumped from $ 2 billion in 1965 to over $ 15 billion in 1971 (Table 3.3). The surpluses in the current account and balance of trade took everyone by surprise, including the Japanese. The current account moved into the red in 1973 because of several factors. First, the oil-price hike was a serious shock to the Japanese economy. Second, progress was being made in import liberalisation and import had recorded a large increase in 1973. Third, the adverse impact of the yen appreciation was felt after a time-lag. Foreign exchange reserves declined after touching the high-mark of $ 18 billion in 1972, and economic growth languished. The oil shock dealt a severe blow to the Japanese economy because its energy sector was based entirely on the availability of cheap oil. It sent the Japanese economy into an inflationary tailspin. However, Japan was not the lone sufferer as the whole of the industrialised world went into a deep recession in the mid-1970s. Japan, unlike the other industrial economies, had only one year of poor growth. After recording GNP growth of 2.9 per cent in real terms in 1975, it improved this to 4.2 per cent in 1976 and sustained it around this level during the rest of the decade (Table 3.5).

There are two noteworthy, if not remarkable, features of the Japanese economy of this period that must not elude our attention: first, remarkable as the high rate of growth was, the wealth that was created was well diffused in society and unemployment was maintained at a low ebb. Income distribution, measured by the Gini coefficient, demonstrated one of the highest degrees of equality found among industrial nations (*The Economist* Intelligence Unit, 1991). This became possible because of various forms of protection provided to labour during the US occupation as well as because rapid gains in productivity were rewarded with commensurate wage increases. The latter worked to provide a social consensus in favour of economic growth.

Table 3.5   Gross National Product, 1955–91

| Year | Gross National Product (billions of yen) | Percentage change over the preceding year | |
		In nominal terms	In real terms
1955	8 399		
1960	15 998	21.3	13.1
1965	32 773	11.3	5.8
1970	73 188	17.9	10.2
1975	148 169	10.6	2.9
1976	166 417	12.3	4.2
1977	185 530	11.5	4.8
1978	204 475	10.2	5.0
1979	221 825	8.5	5.6
1980	240 099	8.2	3.5
1981	257 417	7.2	3.4
1982	270 669	5.1	3.4
1983	282 078	4.2	2.8
1984	301 048	6.7	4.3
1985	321 556	6.8	5.2
1986	335 838	4.4	2.6
1987	350 479	4.4	4.3
1988	373 731	6.6	6.2
1989	399 046	6.8	4.8
1990	428 668	7.4	5.2
1991	456 113	6.4	4.4

Source: Ministry of Finance, *Financial Statistic of Japan 1992*, Tokyo.

Secondly, although by the early 1970s the Japanese economy had grown to be the second largest in the world and it had earned the appellation of economic 'superpower', a fundamental change took place at this time, namely, the economy left behind its high-growth era and became a moderate-growth economy. Although the oil crisis created massive economic disruption, the economy did not return to its high-growth path even after its adverse influence was dissipated. The single most important reason for Japan settling to moderate growth was that the technology gap between Japan and the industrial economies was bridged. When it existed, Japan had become adept at importing and adapting technology, in the process benefiting from fast productivity gains. This process made private sector investment highly profitable (Lincoln, 1988). When Japan caught up with the industrial nations, this process ceased to work and the Japanese economy found itself in a new era. Between 1974 and 1985, the economy suffered no recession, yet its average annual growth rate in real terms was as low as 4.3 per cent. This was less than half of the average for the preceding twelve years. However, Japan continued to outperform the other industrial economies, albeit with a smaller margin than that in the past.

As in other industrial countries, the service sector in Japan had enlarged at the expense of the primary and secondary sectors, more at the expense of the former. This expansion of the service sector was rapid between 1955 and 1970. When it began to slow in the early 1970s, it triggered a debate among the Japanese economists regarding shifting of the industrial structure towards 'knowledge-intensive industries'. The Ministry of International Trade and Industry (MITI) published a report spelling out the new direction that industry should take. The knowledge-intensive industries that it recommended were information services, computer software, systems engineering and telecommunications (MITI, 1971). Subsequently this list was expanded to include construction services, entertainment-related services, technical counselling and the like. MITI took a great deal of initiative in supporting industrial expansion in high-tech services and provided 'seed money' to firms for R&D, until this sector picked up its own momentum. It considered support and development of the high-tech services sector *a fortiori* important because it reduced the dependence of the industrial sector on oil as well as making it more technology-intensive.

The service sector began expanding faster than in the past and its share of total economic activity, whether measured in terms of the value added to GNP, or in terms of sales or the number of businesses established, or in terms of the labour force employed, rose considerably. These industries accounted for more than half of GNP in the early 1990s (Fujii, 1992). Since the growth of the service sector in general is increasingly tied to growth in business and professional services, and in manufacturing, this sector in Japan has remained increasingly sensitive to activity in the manufacturing sector. The Japanese economy is given a good deal of credit for turning towards the development of the services sector at the appropriate juncture in its growth process.

When the yen left its fixed parity, or its Bretton Woods rate, after the Nixon shock and began to appreciate in 1971, it soon acquired a high place in the demonology of Western economic and financial analysts – although for no fault of its own. If one juxtaposes the current account and trade balance deficits and surpluses in Table 3.2 with the value of the yen, one cannot fail to observe a pattern. Whenever the current account plunged into deficit, the yen depreciated with it (see statistics for 1973, 1974 and 1980). The Japanese were accused of currency value manipulation for trade revival. In support of this accusation, it can be seen that Japan did keep coming out of the red faster and further than other OECD countries. To buttress this conspiracy theory, the yen remained rather weak during the period 1982–84 when the economy was recording strong trade balance and current account surpluses. The sharp gyrations in the value of the yen and their clear relationship with Japan's current account were hardly the result of deliberate policy.

The culprit was Japan's unusual trade structure which, during the 1970s, was dominated by imports of oil and raw materials. Unlike most industrialised countries, Japan depended 100 per cent on imported oil and raw materials accounted for 75 per cent of its imports, compared with about 40 per cent in France and West Germany and a little higher in the USA. Manufactured goods accounted for almost the whole (98 per cent) of Japanese exports, against 90 per cent for France and West Germany and 70 per cent for the USA (*The Economist* Newspaper Ltd, 1983). Therefore, any changes in the price of oil or raw materials had a relatively larger effect on Japan's terms of trade. Following the two oil-price hikes, the adverse terms of trade movement for Japan was much higher – by about three times – than other major OECD economies. That led to a deeper swing of the current account into the red. During the 1970s, the yen exchange rate was determined by movement in the current account. Therefore, every time the current account dipped into the red, the yen depreciated against other currencies.

A good illustration of this was provided by the late 1970s, when the real effective exchange rate dipped by 25 per cent in two years. Another reason why the current account bounced back into surplus so quickly after each oil crisis was MITI's determination to export their way out of trouble. Exporters responded to rapid domestic sales by aggressive sales overseas. With improvement in exports, the current account came into surplus, the yen began to appreciate and the cycle was complete. As Table 3.2 shows, this process failed to work in the early 1980s because Japan's trade partners were still in recession. After 1982, the yen was weak, and again the current account surplus began to rise, eventually peaking at 4.5 per cent of the GNP.

By 1976, the economy had recovered fully from the first oil shock as well as the recession. Between 1976 and 1981, when the second post-war recession began, Japanese GNP grew at 4.4 per cent in real terms (Table 3.5) while that of Japan's four biggest rivals (the USA, West Germany, France and the UK) grew by an average of 2.5 per cent. In 1982, Japan had the largest manufacturing base in the capitalist world; was the largest producer of memory chips; overtook the USA in production of vehicles; was the second-largest producer of steel; and overwhelmingly dominated world markets in motorcycles, engines, cameras, calculators, television, photocopiers and several other product lines. The industries in which it could not compete with the Western firms were: aircraft, drugs and pharmaceuticals, biotechnology, and nuclear power.

Although in terms of inflation and unemployment, the world-wide recession of the early 1980s left Japan in a better shape than other industrial nations, the Japanese economy was faced with a dilemma. It had grown so large that its export expansion, which was faster than world trade, was resented and resisted by other industrial economies. Economic growth in Japan had become closely tied to exports at a time when world trade had lost steam. In 1980, the volume of world trade rose by 5 per cent against Japan's export volume growth of 17 per cent. The very next year the volume of world trade expanded by 2 per cent while that in Japan rose by 11 per cent (Table 3.4). Retaliation and retribution were swift. In 1982, for the first time in the post-war period, the value of Japanese exports declined by 8.7 per cent and the volume contracted by 2.2 per cent (Table 3.3). Voluntary export restraints (VERs), orderly marketing arrangements (OMAs) and other ingenious protectionist measures put Japanese exports on a tight leash. Japan could have stimulated domestic demand so that the economy could run on its own steam, but this was not done. The rate of domestic capital formation also dipped after 1981.

Was this the end of the *Asahi* phase? Hardly. Notwithstanding the economic doldrums, Japan was far from heading for a sustained down-turn, and unmistakenly had several elements of sound economic health. For instance, its efficacious manufacturing base and technological powers were as strong as in the high-growth era. In 1982, output per man-hour in Japan was 47 per cent above its level in 1975. For the USA the proportion was 21 per cent, France 34 per cent, Germany 24 per cent and for Britain 18 per cent (*The Economist* Newspaper Ltd, 1983). Another important feature, high-productivity growth, was also intact and in 1982 its industrial production was 50 per cent above its level in 1975. The comparable proportion for the USA was 17 per cent, West Germany 8 per cent and Britain 5 per cent (*The Economist* Newspaper Ltd, 1983). By the early 1980s, Japan had become a highly efficient, productive and, therefore, prosperous economy. It was inventive and innovative in ways that seemed marvellous and exemplary. The Japanese economy began to loom large in the international economic and financial news.

THE *ENDAKA* PHASE

The Plaza accord of September 1985 was the largest and the most successful exercise of macroeconomic co-ordination ever attempted in the international economy. It was made among the Group of Five (G-5) countries to bring their exchange rates into line with economic fundamentals. In keeping with the objectives of the accord, the yen appreciated by 92 per cent against the dollar from 1985–8. Its nominal effective exchange rate appreciated by 29 per cent against the trade-weighted currency basket. Did this create an *endaka*, or high yen, recession? In the first post-appreciation year (1986) the negative effects were strong and the economy showed clear signs of deceleration. The nominal and real economic growth rates dived to 4.4 per cent and 2.6 per cent, respectively (Table 4.5). Plant and equipment investment rose only one-quarter of its 1985 increase, and gross domestic capital formation stagnated. The economy had absorbed the deflationary impact of the high yen by mid-1986 and the bottom of the *endaka* recession was reached in the third quarter of 1986. Thereafter, economic activity displayed a gradual and sustained recovery led by domestic demand. An extraordinary rebound in capital spending was the other propelling factor. This upswing of the business cycle continued unabated until 1991.[4] In 1990, when the other major economies were sliding into recession, Japanese economists and banking circles were worrying about possible overheating – and with reason, since the economy demonstrated remarkable vigor in the face of recession abroad and high interest rates at home, and grew at an astonishing annual rate of 11.2 per cent in the first quarter of 1991 (Chandler, 1991). This exceeded even the *Izanagi* boom, to become the most enduring upswing of the business cycle in the post-war period. The boom soon came to be named after *Izanami*, wife of the god *Izanagi*, and co-creator of the Japanese archipelago – an appropriate choice since it was partly created by domestic demand and led by personal spending, both of which are largely controlled by non-working wives and mothers (Kazutomo, 1990).

During Japan's high growth era, manufacturing output, labour productivity and export achievements were the building blocks of spectacular economic growth. Down to the first quinquennium of the 1980s, net exports were responsible for almost 40 per cent of real GNP growth. Currency appreciation changed this scenario. In the second half of the 1980s, unlike the first, external demand made negative contributions to real GNP growth: –1.4 per cent in 1986; –1.0 per cent in 1987; –1.7 per cent in 1988 and –0.7 per cent in 1989 (Economic Planning Agency, various issues). Domestic demand gained strength in 1986 and became stronger thereafter, leading to accelerated growth in 1987 as well as to import expansion. The domestic economy changed completely during the post-appreciation period, from a supply-oriented to a demand-oriented economy. For the first time excess demand was implanted in the system. As domestic sales activity expanded with increasing domestic demand, the population structure became domestic-demand-oriented rather than export-oriented. Firms began to aim at achieving scale economies through expansion of sales volumes in the domestic market rather than in export markets. The Bank of Japan estimated the total demand conditions in each industry using inducement coefficients derived from the input–output tables, and found that manufacturing industries' demand slackened after the yen appreciation on account of weakened export demand and that growth in non-manufacturing industries' demand gained momentum reflecting a firm domestic demand, specially from the household sector (The Bank of Japan, 1987).

As stated earlier, the extraordinary rebound in capital spending by industry underpinned much of the post-appreciation surge in Japan's economic growth. In the immediate aftermath of the yen appreciation, investment in plant and equipment fell, but soon rebounded to 14.3 per cent in 1988, 15.5 per cent in 1989 and 13.6 per cent in 1990, making this the decade's highest period of investment increase. This investment was directed at high-tech industries, and was supported by a flood of technological innovations. Part of these outlays were also devoted to shifting capacity offshore. The industrial restructuring took place in an environment of declining interest rates and monetary relaxation. There was a monotonic fall in the official discount rate (ODR) and during 1987 and 1988 this remained as low as 2.5 per cent, the lowest level during the post-war period. The three-month gensaki rate also fell from 7.4 per cent in 1985 to 4.2 per cent in 1989. Lower interest rates helped in overcoming the initial deflationary impact of yen appreciation and softened its negative impact on the business enterprises.

The new economic strength as reflected in import volume growth has already been dealt with. Japan's large domestic market was now available to the exports of other industrial economies, stabilising the international economy. This so-called locomotive role was, until recently, performed only by the US economy. While imports first increased in the context of a stronger yen, the fact that their growth continued even in 1989, when the yen had weakened to 143 to the dollar, indicated that import expansion had taken root as a stable trend in the economy.

The increased manufactured-goods imports included semi-finished goods used by processing industries as well as durable and non-durable consumer goods. This shift away from imports of raw materials was first noticed in a small way in 1980 when the upgrading of technological levels and progress in industrialisation had created substantial supply capacity in the Asian newly industrialising economies (ANIEs). The appreciation of the yen brought this shift to light and accelerated it. Several domestic suppliers of semi-finished goods were forced out of market. In short, Japanese trade shifted its axis from vertical to horizontal specialisation.

The yen appreciation had a wealth effect through a terms-of-trade gain estimated to have amounted to ¥12 trillion annually in 1986 and 1987 (The Bank of Japan, 1988). Domestic demand increased in 1986 due to the increase in the real purchasing power and real income of the household sector, despite slower economic growth.

Somewhat paradoxically, the trade surplus and the nominal current account surplus co-existed with the appreciated yen for some time. This seeming incongruity could be explained by the following factors.

- Terms-of-trade improvement leading to real income effect.
- Continued growth in demand in the other industrialised countries.
- Several areas of Japanese exports consisted of strong non-price competitive products, their sales volumes did not

decline even after dollar prices were readjusted for these export products.

- Wide differences in the starting-bases of exports and imports.
- The pass-through coefficient of Japanese export prices was low, therefore full impact of currency appreciation was not felt by importers.
- Oil and raw material prices were bearish and the yen appreciation magnified this decline for Japan.
- Low interest rates and falling unit labour costs helped.[5]
- Intra-company exports were not affected by the yen appreciation.

Currency appreciation polarized the Japanese firms into those benefiting from the strong domestic demand and those suffering from the deflationary impact created by the adjustment in import and export volumes. Profits improved for the former category of firms while they suffered a decline in the latter group. In general, the price-stabilising effect of yen appreciation had a favourable impact on corporate finances. Some of the exporters brought down their fixed costs and succeeded in re-establishing an improved profit structure, allowing them to be profitable without large increases in sales.

The economy began to slow down in the latter half of 1991; demand and production began to contract and the rate of investment recorded a decline. Serious jolts were created by the emergence and burst of 'the bubbles', steep rises in stock and land prices, well above the level consistent with economic fundamentals, followed by correspondingly sharp falls. GDP fell in both the second and third quarters of 1992 – a textbook definition of recession. The economy would seem to be shifting from expansion to adjustment, meaning stock adjustment and the adjustment in plant and equipment that occurs after a period of high growth (Economic Planning Agency, 1992). Such recessionary stock adjustment periods have followed the Jimmu, Iwato and Izanagi booms. All three recorded falling investment rates in their final phases. Thus, the current recession has resulted from autonomous endogenous factors.

TRADE LIBERALISATION AND FINANCIAL DEREGULATION

Japan has long taken a protectionist stance, with history of tariffs, quota restrictions (QRs) and non-tariff barriers (NTBs). Together, these have firmly controlled imports and managed to captivate the domestic market for domestic producers. Initially, all imports (both agricultural and manufacturing) were protected from foreign competition on balance-of-payments and infant-industry grounds. Agricultural imports were restricted by stringent QRs while manufactured products were largely protected by tariffs. One of the consequences of this was that when Japan became a contracting party (CP) of the GATT in 1955, 14 industrial countries invoked Article XXXV, withholding most-favored nation (MFN) treatment. Several British and French colonies, after becoming independent followed the metropolitan powers and withheld their application of the agreement to Japan, bringing to 30 the number of countries that invoked Article XXXV.

Although trade liberalisation began in 1960, it progressed at a snail's pace. It was believed that after the 1965 trade balance surplus was attained, rapid liberalisation will follow. But policy-makers considered this an inadequate signal. Besides, the economic community was convinced that the protectionist policy has served Japan well, leading it to export expansion almost twice as rapid as world trade. It was widely agreed, therefore, that it should not be abandoned until export surplus became a steady economic trend. Hesitation on this count was not given up until 1969, a fact which rankled Japan's trade partners. Joining the Kennedy Round of multilateral trade negotiations (MTNs) was the first firm step towards trade liberalisation. Japan benefited considerably from the 'free ride', that is, other countries' general tariff reduction during the MTNs. After Kennedy Round, Japan began to record large trade surpluses, partly attributed to the Round. Complying with the Kennedy Round recommendations, Japan brought average tariff levels on durable manufactured goods down to 12.7 per cent in 1972, compared with 8.8 per cent in the EC and 8.2 per cent in the US. On semi-manufactured goods, Japanese tariffs averaged 6.3 per cent, compared with 5.6 per cent in the US and 4.8 per cent in the EC.[6] However, tariffs on finished consumer goods remained high even after the Kennedy Round.

Japan incurred the ire of its trade partners because of NTBs such as a steep tax on luxury goods, large cars and high-quality whisky, government procurement practices that were based on non-competitive selection of supplying firms, thus excluding foreign suppliers. Technicalities such as custom valuation, industrial standards and safety regulations, the anti-dumping restrictions and countervailing duties also irritated the trade partners. All these inconveniences deterred exports to Japan. It was also apprehended that exports were perceived to be obstructed by strong 'administrative guidance' or government pressure without the backing of statutes. In the case of large thermo-electric generators, for example, importers were advised to import one 'prototype' and then meet domestic demand by manufacturing copies at home. Administrative guidance and buying cartels effectively work like quotas. Price changes by exporters did not affect imports in these cases because they failed to affect imports that were barred by quotas. Other practices led to higher domestic prices for imported products, effectively working like tariffs. These imports, however, were sensitive to price changes by exporters (Lawrence, 1991). For instance, if an imported product is sold by a firm having monopoly over its distribution, its profit mark-up will be higher than the mark-up for competitive distribution. These informal market practices managed to decelerate imports considerably.

Japan had to pay the price of its protectionist stance. Many of its large export markets frequently resorted to OMAs and VERs. By the mid-1970s, some 264 products were under VERs imposed at the request of importing countries, and reported to the GATT by the Japanese government (Kojima, 1977). Some restraints such as VERs on steel exports to the US, had been imposed without government intervention. VERs were often put in place jointly by the importing country and Japan after sharp increases in Japanese exports in some product category, and after Japan was convinced that an accusation of market disruption was about to be made, or that the importing country would erect trade barriers. VERs were less damaging to Japan than possible trade barriers, and allowed for some discretion in determining export volume ceilings. In addition, VERs improved its terms of trade.

The issue of insufficiently open markets remained contentious and Japan was frequently accused of being mercantilistic. In the early 1980s, the EC sought redress through the GATT and the US forced Japan to engage in extensive bilateral negotiations. In 1985, the US started negotiations with Japan on opening its telecommunications, electronics, forest products, medical equipment and pharmaceuticals markets and sought more and wide-ranging changes in Japanese markets, and through the so-called Structural Impediments Initiative (SII).

Several studies have examined why Japan's imports-to-GNP ratio is abnormally low (Balassa 1986; Bergsten and Cline 1988; Lawrence 1987; Noland 1990; Saxonhouse 1983). Some of these focused on manufactured imports alone. The structures of their models varied widely and depended upon the assumptions made and the methodology followed. In addition, there were serious divergences in the definitions of the variables. But they all believed that countries located far from their trading partners tended to trade less because of higher transport costs. Notwithstanding, they each took a different approach to calculating the transport cost. Some inferred that Japan's import behaviour is not significantly different from that of other OECD countries when all the relevant explanatory variables are taken into account. Others reached the opposite conclusion. A recently completed OECD study concluded that while Japan's merchandise imports were well explained, a significant negative factor lowering the manufactured imports was found, due either to Japan's comparative advantage or to trade barriers (Barbone, 1988). Juxtaposing these results, we see that these empirical studies are inconclusive.

From time to time Japan has taken measures to fend off criticism from its trade partners. In 1982, three extensive lists of measures were prepared to dismantle tariff and non-tariff measures, and quota restrictions. Japan also has an excellent record of implementing the Tokyo Round recommendations. Japan's trade structure underwent a dramatic market-driven change after the post-Plaza yen appreciation. Imports recorded a sharp surge from $ 129 billion in 1986 to $ 237 billion in 1991. In terms of volume, the index showed a jump from 100.0 to 164.0, 64 per cent rise over six years. Traditionally, imports constituted a smaller share of Japan's domestic consumption of manufactured goods than in other industrial countries. After the yen appreciation, this was no longer the case. Imports of manufactured goods increased from $ 40.16 billion to $ 106.11 billion between 1985 and 1989. In terms of volume, they grew by 102.1 per cent. In addition, the SII negotiations with the US were not only wide-ranging but also addressed some deep changes in traditional market practices, effectively obstructing imports. The resulting changes benefited all Japan's trade partners, developed and developing. Thus viewed, a good deal of adjustment was made to liberalise the markets during the 1980s.

The highly regulated financial markets of the 1950s and the 1960s had served the economy well. Interest rates were controlled by the monetary authorities, while financial authorities exercised control over financial institutions and emphasised functional separation. For example, banks and securities companies had to maintain separate identities, somewhat along the lines of the US Glass-Steagall Act (the Japanese equivalent was known as Article 65). Clear lines were drawn between banks lending to large corporations, and the financial institutions dedicated to small business. Loans from financial institutions to firms financed plant and equipment expenditure according to the priority of the government. Thus finance was channelled to sectors considered important for growth. Firms generally remained highly leveraged. The moderate growth rates of the 1970s created pressure to deregulate the tightly-controlled financial system by reducing the dependence of firms on banks. Also, when the government planned to start floating bonds to finance deficits, control over interest rates appeared to be an

obstruction. The current account surpluses created external
pressure to deregulate external transactions so that more surpluses could flow to capital scarcity regions of the world. In
response to these developments, the financial system was
diversified and more financial instruments were developed.
Also, interest rates began to be more market-influenced.
Sweeping deregulatory measures were not adopted
overnight, however, and the Ministry of Finance remained
committed to gradualism. Deregulation accelerated after
1985, however. Likewise, deregulation in external transactions began in 1980 with revision of the Foreign Exchange
and Foreign Trade Control Law, entailing drastic liberalisation of all foreign exchange transactions. Similar deregulatory
measures began to unfold more rapidly after 1984 and eventually helped Japan become a financial superpower.
International financial liberalisation was important for any
reasons, not least because it forced the pace of domestic
liberalisation.

UNIQUE PRACTICES AND INSTITUTIONS?

One way of explaining growth is to examine trends in the
principal factors of production, namely labor, capital and productivity growth (the latter encompassing a variety of elements). Denison and Chung's extensive empirical work on
the macro-explanations of post-war growth in Japan concluded that of the 8.77 per cent average annual rise in real
national income between 1950–70, productivity gains contributed 4.82 per cent, capital 2.10 per cent and labour 1.85
per cent. There are myriad explanations for the a high contribution of productivity gains. Some cite certain unique, cul-
turally-derived, characteristics of Japanese society, while
others point to mere superior working out of market forces,
and to 'situational' responses and motivations which have
led to Japan's miraculous emergence as a first-rate economic
power. Still others think that it was an extraordinary combi-
nation of the two. The aforementioned unique cultural factors
are easily listed: strong Confucian influences, the life-long

employment system and seniority wage system, enterprise unionism, domestic savings (as described earlier) system, the multi-tier distribution system, the Keiretsu system, subcontracting, the business-government relationship, and the role of the Ministry of International Trade and Industry (MITI) are all thought of as inherently 'Japanese'. All or some coalesced to create the economic 'miracle'. But did all of these practices and institutions make unique contributions to Japan's development? Did they help economic development on neo-classical economic lines? Or were all, or some of them, irrelevant to its post-war evolution?

Confucianism, with its inherent striving for chowa or harmony, its respect for elders and hierarchical superiors, and its emphasis on the group rather than the individual, is said to have fostered amicable relationships between business and government and between managers and workers. The first of these co-operative relationships, as we have seen, dates back to the post-Meiji era when large-scale government investment meant that appropriate scale economies could be reaped and modern technology imported. During the post-war reconstruction phase, government assisted numerous industries in procuring and transporting raw materials and by protecting their domestic markets. High tariffs and QRs created large rents for business. Under these circumstances, firms were not averse to making minor sacrifices at the behest of the government, such as giving up sales, and therefore Confucian harmony could be attained anywhere.

Life-time employment and cordial manager-worker relationships also have an economic rationale. When Japan was industrialising in the 1950s and 1960s, master/apprentice relationships still existed, binding the skilled worker to the firm during a period of skilled labor shortage. However, the majority of other workers and women employees had no employment security. Trade unions, other than company unions, did develop but lacked power because the labor force was divided into long-term, potentially long-term and casual workers, and because of the large volumes of unskilled and semi-skilled workers. Rapid productivity gains benefited the workforce, and living standards improved steadily, taking the wind out of the sails of the trade union movement. The old customs of non-monetary incentives as well as monetary rewards kept the worker/manager relationship non-confrontational (Hirono, 1988).

Japan's seniority pay system in fact began to change in the 1970s, and firms have increasingly started paying according to merit.

Certain carefully-planned patterns of industrial organisation and economic behavior have enormously strengthened Japan's economic base. Far from deeply-entrenched traditions, these have grown up over the past 30 years and include:

- Instigation of a microelectronic-based industrial revolution and laser control of production processes. This reduced the need for production-line workers, increased flexibility in manufacturing, reduced costs and gave Japan a competitive edge over other countries. Japan could apply the new manufacturing technology because it produced more electrical engineers than any other OECD country (Vogel, 1986).
- Rapid expansion of R&D investment in terms of men and money for the development of new electronics-related areas and new materials and products in order to develop new business areas. After the *endaka*, these were spurred only further economic restructuring and fear of losing international economic competitiveness due to the yen's strength against other major currencies. Throughout the 1980s, Japan had the largest industrial robot population in the world. In 1990, this stood at 274 210 compared with 41 304 in the US, 28 240 in Germany and 12 500 in Italy. France and the UK came next with 8551 and 6418 robots respectively.[7] According to a US National Science Foundation study, Japan had achieved parity in semiconductor technology, silicon product technology and high-definition television by 1989 and was pulling ahead in superconductivity research.[8] This commitment to R&D reinforced a well-established industrial base and further buttressed the economic superstructure compared to that of other competing economies.

- *Sub-contracting.* Because of difficulties in diversification, Japanese firms tended to specialise narrowly and therefore were generally smaller than their Western counterparts. However, by supplying parts or sub-assemblies, they became vertically integrated in the system, bringing the benefits of specialisation without the drawbacks of excessive size.
- *The relatively lower importance of shareholders' rights in Japan compared to other major industrial economies.* In joint-stock companies, there is always a potential for conflict between the shareholders who own assets, and the company as a group of people having their own objectives. In Japan, shareholders take the back seat because stocks are traditionally held for capital gains and not for earnings from dividends. Institutional investors hold stocks to cement other relations with a company, such as managing its pensions, lending in times of need and acting as large buyers or suppliers. This has three important consequences. Firstly, firms are free to plough back a higher proportion of their earnings. Secondly, short-term profit fluctuations concern them less and thirdly, it is nearly impossible to buy and sell firms on the stock market. Consequently growth and diversification in Japan is more gradual than in other major industrial economies where firms often tend to expand and diversify by buying competitors, or even firms in entirely different industries. In Japan, therefore, firms tend to focus on incremental improvements in their own production and profits (*The Economist* Newspaper Ltd, 1983).
- The kanban system or zero defect movement, which has made Japanese products extremely competitive in world markets. Under the kanban system programmes and schemes for improvements in work methods were established in various industries to suit their specific needs. Larger firms constantly encourage and assist their subcontractors in improving work processes, and reducing unit cost of production. Also, the government has devised schemes to help small business enterprises adopt the kanban system.

To return to the questions posed at the beginning of this section: if by 'unique' we mean a distinctive characteristic or practice, then the above can be seen as unique practices and institutions conceived as perceptive, rational and pragmatic situational responses, immensely facilitating the successful post-war operation of the economy on neo-classical economic lines. But if by unique we mean unequalled, or matchless then the term can no longer apply. Several of these practices and institutions have been used in Western, east Asian or south-east Asian economies in one form or another, and with varying degrees of success. Their unique 'Japaneseness' is hard to vindicate. However, two vitally important Japanese institutions have remained by and large 'matchless', with only scant resemblance to their roles and structures found elsewhere. These are the MITI and the keiretsu, Japan's unique, closely-tied structure of industrial and financial corporations.

Noted scholars such as Edward Chen (1979) and Hugh Patrick (1977) have credited private individuals and enterprises for Japanese economic growth. The latter have, in their view, exploited the opportunities provided by free markets while the government created an environment of growth. But these claims are unconvincing particularly in the face of MITI's role. MITI has long been considered the most effective economic bureaucracy in the world – the domain of Japan's brightest and best administrators. For a long time, it had absolute control over sangyo seisaku (industrial policy), although large enterprises are now known to challenge this. MITI considered its primary duty was to create 'those powerful interests in the economy that favor the shift of energy and resources into new industrial and economic activities', and it was convinced that market forces alone would never succeed in producing those shifts. It used familiar tools to implement its industrial policy – discriminatory tariffs, preferential commodity taxes, import and foreign exchange restrictions and discretionary foreign currency allocation for protection, and for growth, the low-interest financing of targeted industries through government financial organs, subsidies, special amortisation benefits, duty draw-backs on capital equipment, the licensing of imported technology, and the provision of industrial parks and infrastructure facilities for business (Johnson, 1982). MITI worked closely with big business and perfected *ikusei*, a system of 'nurturing' new industrial sectors, including the following steps:

● Formulating basic industrial policies based on a close examination of trends.
● Promoting the selected sectors and financing them through cheap Japan Development Bank loans and, when needed, foreign currency allocations.
● Facilitating technology imports.
● Granting accelerated depreciation allowances for strategic industries.
● Creating cartels to regulate competition and co-ordinate investment.

MITI's Industrial Structure Council, a joint government-industry advisory body, co-ordinated *ikeusei*.

In common with many 'late starters', the Japanese state took responsibility for development upon itself. MITI and other economic ministries turned Japan into a developmental state. In Chalmers Johnson's terms, Japan is a plan-rational state as opposed to a market-rational state such as the US. In the former, government industrial policy takes precedence, while in the latter such a thing may not even exist. The Japanese system depends upon the existence of a widely agreed set of universal social goals, in this case growth; growth with stability and catching up with the West. When such a consensus exists, the plan-rational system can well outperform the market-rational system, as Japan outperformed all the other OECD economies. To be sure, MITI was the fount of much wisdom on economic growth and industrialisation, and played a role of unique significance, but it should not be considered the sole source of bright ideas. Sony and Honda succeeded despite having tenuous ties with MITI.

And there is a tendency to see Japan's economic model as over-deterministic because MITI seems to be behind virtually every significant event. Was there no scope left for private initiatives? But Messrs Chen and Patrick were not completely wrong. Any casual observer will see that a vigorous private economy did and does exist in Japan, that market forces operate almost completely freely, with firms picking up on signals from MITI and often growing in the direction indicated. MITI has, if anything, practised market-conforming rather than market-smothering intervention.

Rapid growth provoked 'excessive competition' in Japan which tended to work in favor of large firms, because they could capitalise on their scale economies and internalise important externalities. Their finances were in generally sound shape, and hence, firms formerly affiliated to the pre-war *zaibatsu* were re-integrated as *keiretsu*. There were six of these latter groups. Unlike *zaibatsu* they are essentially horizontally-integrated, oligopolistic groups. *Keiretsu* are a loose federation of independent firms, clustered around a bank and a general trading company. Cross share holding is common among the members of a *keiretsu*. The group members are given priority funds by their core bank. Trading companies such as Mitsubishi and Mitsui are flush with funds and have hundreds of subsidiaries (Fujigane and Ennis, 1990). The *keiretsu* system evolved out of the old *zaibatsu* system for strong economic reasons. The stability of long-term inter-firm relationships promoted by the system contributes to free flows of information, tightly coordinated production schedules, wide dissemination of technology and meaningful long-term strategic planning. The *keiretsu* did appear to be a closed organisational system but it has allowed Japan to produce quality goods at lower prices, and enhanced its competitiveness in the international markets.[9]

CORPORATE STRATEGY AND STRUCTURE

The foregoing exposition is likely to lead one to believe that the striking performance of the Japanese economy was essentially due to macroeconomic reasons. However, the role of business corporations, or the *kaisha*, was no less in Japan's competitiveness and acquisition of a domineering position in a respectable array of industries. In several industries, they rose like the phoenix from the debris of the war to hold leading or important positions. In several industries they are now hard to compete with for their Western counterparts. In several major sectors like automobiles, steel, electrical appliances, electronics, construction equipment, photography, semiconductors, and mainframe computers, Japanese firms are the market leaders or among the largest in the world. They are not limited to the manufacturing sector but lead in service sectors such as banking, insurance, telecommunications and airlines.

Japanese firms operate in a hierarchical and disciplined manner under their *kairetsu* arrangement. Many of them, certainly the successful ones, have a growth bias which has a marked imprint over their behaviour pattern. They display a strong commitment to pursue growth unfalteringly and are known to create capacity ahead of demand. Prices are not set at the level the market can bear but at the lowest level to fit the available production capacity. Costs are programmed to come down to support the pricing policies, and investments constantly rise in keeping with the projected demand (Abegglen and Stalk, 1985). When the market response is strong, the *kaisha* adopt 'doubling strategies' which enable them to double capacity and output in a short span of two to four years. The *kaisha* with a strong growth bias are also known to step up output and investment when the market is weak. In this case product variety is increased, prices are cut and distribution is expanded. Some Western companies, such as Apple Computers and IBM, also behave like a *kaisha* with a growth bias.

Invariably, *kaisha* define their goals in terms of volume and market shares, so that fixed investment cost (like labour) can be met without any problem. But it also reflects their belief in scale economies and an intense desire to outperform rivals. Indeed, there are variations in responses to a competitor's initiatives. Some *kaisha*, while driving for volume, may not aim at market dominance. Others may try to differentiate themselves by matching competitors' product. However, competitor's initiatives hardly ever go without response.

Once a comparative and competitive advantage is located, it is exploited to the fullest. Initially, low-cost manufacturing was used as a competitive tool. Low wages allowed *kaisha* to be keenly competitive in textiles and shipbuilding. Since the wages grew to international levels, new weapons such as product line variety, high quality, and technological innovation, were found. A strong belief in R&D and in the most modern facilities and equipment has helped *kaisha* sharpen their competitiveness. With this emphasis on R&D, over the years *kaisha* have succeeded in creating technology-based comparative advantage (Porter, 1990). This turn of event was natural because most top managers were technically trained, and therefore had the advantage of having a technically-orientated perspective. Consequently, as alluded to in another context, investment in the key, leading-edge technologies has been on the rise since the early 1980s. Due to this mode of operation, the successful *kaisha* were able to develop major positions in international markets since the mid-1960s, in products ranging from ball-bearings, forklifts and machine tools to a large array of high-tech products such as computer hardware, robots and unmanned production systems.

THE INTERNATIONAL ROLE

The Perception Gap

When Japan acquired the appellation of economic 'super-power' in the early 1970s, it was confounded, nonplussed and did not recognise its position and power in the world economy. Perhaps because of the rapidity of growth, Japan could not adjust to its new status right away. Although Japan did not consider itself a powerful nation, to the rest of the world its new-found economic status was a stark reminder of its economic prowess. This created a perception gap, which was to endure. Refusing to recognise its place in the international community, Japan remained wrapped-up in itself, paying attention only to matters that affected it directly and judging them entirely in terms of their impact on Japan (Okita, 1990). In 1978, Japan's per capita income was close to that of the USA. Its current account surplus was $ 16.5 billion, while the US deficit stood at the same level. Japan's economy was growing, and so was its significance in the international economy. Yet the perception gap persisted. Japan remained economically strong but internationally passive. Japanese society had single-mindedly devoted its energy to developing economically and becoming the most competitive in the world. It seemed that like the Venetians and the Dutch of the medieval period, the Japanese envisioned becoming only a one-dimensional economic power. As Japan become more economically successful, this notion strengthened.

As set forth earlier, the Japanese economy entered a new phase of maturity characterised by moderate growth rates over the 1970s. Over the 1980s, its new GDP growth rate averaged at 4.4 per cent. Forecasting exercises put future growth rates at the same or lower levels. According to one such exercise, it will grow at the rate of 4.5 per cent over the period 1990–2000 and at 3.7 per cent over 2000–2010 (Japan Center of Economic Research, 1992). In 1990, world GDP was $ 23 trillion. If the future exchange rates for all countries *vis-à-vis* the US dollar are taken as being determined by their purchasing power parities, the forecast GDP of the world for the year 2000 comes to $ 44.4 trillion and for the year 2010 to $ 91.3 trillion. (Another forecast [Sekiguchi, 1991] which stopped at the year 2000, estimated it at $ 41.7 trillion, not very far from the first forecast.) The 2010 GDP of the world is four times the 1990 GDP, and may appear inexplicably inflated. However, if one looks back, world GDP rose from $ 3.7 trillion to $ 23 trillion over the 1970–90 period. The forecast exercise takes the world GDP as rising in real terms by a factor of 1.8 and the global wholesale prices in dollar terms rising by a factor of 2.2; therefore, the nominal GDP over the 1990–2010 period will increase by a factor of 4.

In the years 2000 and 2010, the USA will continue to be the leading economic power, with Japan coming closer to it. In 1990, Japan's GDP was 12.8 per cent of the world GDP, in

2000 it is forecast to be 16.7 per cent and in 2010 17.5 per cent
– meaning the importance of Japanese economy will continue
to grow. Despite some possibility of labour shortage and con-
tinuing economic friction, Japan's economy is expected to
continue on its growth path. The per capita GDP of Japan
was forecast to be $ 57 786 in the year 2000, the highest in the
world. This forecast was made with the yen/dollar exchange
rate of 120.90. Japan's external surplus has been projected to
decline due to currency appreciation against the major currencies, domestic wage-hikes and further growth in manufactured imports due to the opening of domestic markets and
the rising strength of the yen. Standardised manufactured
imports will rise more than other manufactured imports and
the Asia-Pacific economies will be their most likely source.
Also, labour shortage and the yen's appreciation will force
the domestic economy to shift further from the traded goods
to the non-traded goods sectors and to resort to off-shore production – this happened perceptibly after *endaka*. Imports of
agricultural products and foods will rise with the decrease in
domestic production.

Notwithstanding the fact that the external surplus may
dip, as the forecasting exercise revealed, Japan's GDP will be
absolutely and relatively larger in the foreseeable future. It
has to see and perceive that the world of the future will be
led not so much by military might as by economic and technological power. Economic power can potentially sway the
world and have lasting influence on several areas of international life. In the post-cold war world, when the international
economy is measuring the peace dividend, economic principles will have a greater say in the world than ever in the past.
Japanese society has to begin to believe that the language of
economic principles is the language of rational and optimal
resource allocation, profits and of living standards (Fujii,
1989). It transcends national boundaries, cultural differences
and race relations. Therefore, in the increasingly interdependent world of tomorrow, Japan will have an enormous role to
play. Its internationally-minded opinion leaders like Okita
(1990) and Morita (1993) have exhorted Japan to take its
commensurate place on the international stage and perform

like a global actor. Being stage-shy for too long may not help Japan retain its superpower status. It is never too late for Japan to change its perception of itself.

The USA is, and will be continue to be, the dominant economic and strategic power. However, its relative economic decline *vis-à-vis* Japan and the large European economies means erosion of its 'rule-making' authority or, in somewhat coarse language, the end of *Pax* Americana. This assigns Japan an opportunity to play an increasing role in the Asia-Pacific and international economic affairs. To be sure, Japan is not destined to attain a hegemonic status. For that matter, no single nation could attain the pre-eminence attained by the USA in the post-war period. However, time is ripe for Japan to assume Asia-Pacific economic leadership and be one of the leading lights of the multipolar or pluricentric world of today.

Japan's Role in the Asia-Pacific

Japan has been playing a role of increasing significance in the growth, and industrialisation of the Asian newly-industrialising economics (ANIEs) as well as helping the ASEAN growing fast. The economic structure that has developed in the Asia-Pacific in the recent past worked as follows. Capital and intermediate products were received from Japan by these two groups of countries transfer of Japanese technology to them. The output of these countries was exported largely to the USA and to Japan, the EC and the other countries of the Asia-Pacific region. Thus, the USA played the role of a significant export absorber for these two groups while Japan became an important supplier. In the first half of the 1980s, these economies recorded strong export-driven growth, which was largely due to Japanese-aided supply-side developments, particularly in capital accumulation and technology transfer (Watanabe, 1988). To a great extent this growth depended on the USA for import demand; in this, it was assisted by US deficits. This pattern is evidently unsustainable, because the US deficit has declined.

Takenaka (1991) developed an econometric model of the global economy to see the effects of a 2 per cent drop in US

GNP on economic growth in the Asia-Pacific region. Since these economies have a large dependence on the US market, the deflationary effect on them will be large. Korea and Malaysia will experience a contraction of 4.6 per cent and 4.4 per cent, respectively; Singapore GNP will contract by 3.4 per cent and Thailand by 2.6 per cent; similarly, Indonesia and Japan will experience a deflation of 1.4 per cent and 1 per cent, respectively. As opposed to this, a 2 per cent expansion of the Japanese economy will have a substantial impact on these economies. But Japan cannot pick up the slack and compensate totally for a decline in US demand – although the expansionary fiscal policy followed by Japan since 1987 has helped inflate demand.

The degree to which Japanese markets will be able to replicate the role of US markets for the Asia-Pacific countries will essentially depend on the success of structural adjustment measures affecting consumer goods markets, and the removal of whatever NTBs that still persists. A reference needs to be made again to post-*endaka* import escalation, particularly the rise in manufactured imports. Japanese imports from the ANIEs doubled over 1986–8. This trend was assisted by changes in the exchange rates of the Asia-Pacific countries after the *endaka*. Although the extent of change varied from country to country, the general direction was as follows: (a) relatively mild appreciation against the US dollar; and (b) significant depreciation against the yen. The second change helped bring about the horizontal division of labour between Japan and the Asia-Pacific countries.

New patterns of outsourcing and original equipment manufacturing (OEM) with the ANIEs increased, and so did intra-industry trade. It may take time to establish similar relationships between Japan and the ASEAN countries but this is already under way (Noguchi, 1988). Though these trends will affect the basic nature of the impact of Japan's economic policies and business cycles on the Asia-Pacific countries, they are also of vital importance for Japan's future. Although market forces are responsible for these trends, there are certain non-market developments that are still forcing Japan to make retrograde motion. For instance, Korean steel products were held off by Japan and as recently as June 1989 Korea announced the imposition of VERs on shipments of knitwear to Japan. Another example is protection of the agriculture sector, where Japan has enormous comparative disadvantage. This protection has continued despite vocal opposition from the *keidanren*, Japan's federation of economic organisations. If Japan wishes to be the trade policy leader for the region, dispelling these impediments is a small cost.

Since Japan has had a special relationship with the USA and it has also been Japan's largest trade partner, Japan is highly susceptible to bilateral political and economic leverage from the USA. In the past, in response to US demands for greater access to Japanese beef and chicken markets, Japanese negotiators acceded too easily. This had a trade diversion effect and adversely affected the exports of countries like Australia and Thailand. This was also a case of clear compromise of Article 1 of the GATT. At first sight, Japan's move appeared correct, but it turned out to be an abrogation of the international trade discipline as well as being injurious to the regional economies. As a future regional leader, this should be a lesson to Japan, something never to be repeated.

The past deep-seated rancour in the Asia-Pacific region against Japan has faded away. In April 1992, the *Nihon Keizai Shimbun* conducted an opinion survey among the corporate managers and academics of China, South Korea, Taiwan, Hong Kong, Singapore, Malaysia, Thailand, Indonesia, the Philippines and Australia.[10] According to 70 per cent of respondents, Japan should play the role of regional leader in the Asia-Pacific region. On the question of what form Japan's regional leadership should take, investment in the region topped the list with 26.7 per cent, followed by market opening and greater provision of technical assistance, including technology transfer.

International Economic Leadership

Growing into an economic superpower has generated special patterns of relationships with the rest of the world economy as well as new perspectives for the Japanese. They need to locate a leadership role within the pluralist structure of world economic power, while representing the broader global interests of the Asia-Pacific region. Japan's international economic interaction has expanded over the years and has diversified in every field. Its relationship – both macroeconomic and microeconomic – with the other industrialised economies has deepened considerably. Under the stable post-war system governed by GATT and the International Monetary Fund (IMF), Japan established strong ties with other economic aspects. The deepening interdependence has enhanced the influence of the Japanese economy on other economies, and vice versa. For instance, Japan's fiscal and monetary policies will have a pervasive effect on other industrial environments in other economies. Analogously, changes in the other countries will imminently affect Japan. As the international financial and capital markets are becoming increasingly integrated through deregulation of domestic markets they will influence each other through exchange rates and interest rates as well as capital movements. Thus, deepening of interdependence has made macroeconomic policy co-ordination under collective economic management all the more important, if not indispensable. Japan needs to become a partner in this collective management exercise. In this respect, the Plaza and the Louvre accords show that Japan has made steady headway. In the future, Japan's role in co-ordinated intervention in exchange markets will have to continue.

The domain of international public goods includes, among other things, economic assistance, refugee relief, maintaining and lubricating the systems of free trade, international investment and international finance. The supply of these goods in the international system is not assured by any government body and is, therefore, not so well institutionalised. The supply is undertaken or regulated by either supranational organisations or by countries willing and capable of assuming the burden. If Japan sees itself as one of the principal supporters of the collective management system, it will have to assume actively the burden of providing international public goods, as well as working for the maintenance of a stable international economic system. This will not only ensure

Japan's future prosperity but also stable growth of the international economy (Murakani and Kosai, 1986). The relationship will be symbiotic. Furthermore, active involvement in the global collective management system will mean making a commitment to harmonise national economic strategy with international interests, which in turn may call for reforms and adjustment of the domestic systems, somewhat on the lines of the Maekawa committee recommendations.

The four domains of public goods into which Japan can step forthwith or step up its on-going involvement are as follows.

- During the high-growth era, Japan benefited immensely from free trade. Now that the GATT discipline has eroded considerably and the Uruguay Round has been floundering after collapsing once, Japan's support for the GATT in general as an institution will rejuvenate free trade. Although it is too late, it would have been ideal for Japan to play the same role in the Uruguay Round as the USA did during the Kennedy Round. Now, with the USA backtracking and turning protectionistic, Japan needs to move forward and support the free-trade system in the manner in which the USA supported it during the 1950 and 1960s.
- Japan could enhance mutually beneficial direct investment, particularly in the developing economies. This will promote the transfer of production and skills and put Japanese economic and industrial vitality to work in the world at large.
- Since Japanese industries are well known for their prowess in applied research, science and technology-related exchanges at various levels – for example, student researchers, technologists and business leaders – need to be stepped up.
- In the late 1980s, Japan became the largest donor country in the world. It can further its involvement with the developing economies by lending support to their fragile trade structure and make their former slogan of 'trade not aid' meaningful. This endeavour will also integrate the developing economies better into the international economies.

Problem-ridden developing economies can be helped in their debt-related and structural adjustments-related endeavours through the two Bretton Woods institutions. A great deal of scope exists for enlarging this channel of support to developing economies.

CONCLUSION

The USA rendered assistance in reconstructuring and rehabilitating the Japanese economy after the Second World War, and it applied several reform measures. The Dodge plan was formulated to stabilise the economy. Japan experienced its first boomlet during the Korean war, and during the same decade two more booms followed. Japan's savings and investment rates were much higher than those in other industrial countries, with household saving rates being particularly high and meeting the large investment needs of the corporate sector. The economy was determined not to rely too much on external finances for growth. Large dosages of investment renewed the old capital stock and created new capital stock, which, in turn, raised labour productivity as well as the efficiency of capital.

When planning industrialisation, the priority was accorded to basic industries like iron and steel, and heavy and chemical industries which had some pre-war base. Industries that were considered unsuitable were eliminated. Modernisation and technological upgradation in the manufacturing sector continued constantly. Next, the development of consumer durables such as automobiles, electrical appliances and electronics was emphasised. A well-developed basic sector, like steel, helped in the growth of the consumer-durable industries. Japan successfully absorbed Western technology, first with the help of Western engineers and then through the efforts of its well-trained, technology-conscious managers and labour force. A great deal of attention was paid to R&D. Technological advancement showed through in industrial value-added. Japan took the export-led growth out of sheer necessity. It was one of the two countries that benefited the most from the liberalisation of international trade under the aegis of the GATT, and its exports grew at a staggering pace. By the mid-1960s, Japan had had a decade-and-a-half of brisk growth and in recognition of its status as an advanced economy, it was made a member of the OECD in 1964. The following five years turned out to be a period of record-setting growth.

The economy became exceedingly competitive in several product lines and a successful, if somewhat aggressive, exporter. The importing countries found the loss of their own markets and the third country markets disconcerting. Charges of dumping and unfair trade practice became frequent, and VERs, OMAs and other protectionist measures began to be applied against Japanese exports. Japan's own record of market liberalisation was poor. By the early 1970s, it had grown into the second-largest economy in the world, exporting large volumes of a wide array of products. The 1973–4 oil-price hike had a massive adverse effect on the oil-based Japanese economy. Its era of high growth ended and one of moderate growth began. This was not entirely due to the oil shock. The economy was, however, faced with a dilemma. It had grown so large that its export expansion, which was faster than world trade, was constantly being resented and restricted by other industrial economies. Economic growth in Japan had become closely tied to exports at a time when world trade had lost steam. This is not to say that the economy had lost its vitality – its efficacious manufacturing base and technological prowess were as strong as they were in the high-growth era and it survived the two recessions, of the mid-1970s and the early 1980s, much better than did the other industrial countries.

Japan's current account surplus was rising from the early 1980s, peaking at 4.5 per cent of GNP. The undervalued yen was squarely blamed for this by the other industrial economies and the Plaza accord attempted to bring the surpluses down by appreciating the yen in an internationally co-ordinated manner with the other SDR currencies. The yen appreciation created a year-long *endaka* recession in Japan, but the economy was pulled out of it by domestic demand

and a very high rate of investment. It entered an upswing of the business cycle which became the longest-lasting boom in Japan's post-war economic history. *Endaka* changed both the production structure and the trade structure. The economy became orientated through domestic demand instead of export-orientated. Its imports increased enormously, particularly the imports of manufacturers, and the axis of trade structure changed from vertical to horizontal. The restructuring of the economy was helped by low interest rates, which assisted in softening the deflationary effect of the currency appreciation.

Although liberalisation of the trade regime began in 1960, it was done in a very slow manner which rankled Japan's trade partners. Joining the Kennedy Round was the first firm-footed step. Yet several NTBs continued to obstruct imports. From time to time Japan took measures to dismantle trade barriers, such as offering to implement three lists of such measures in the early 1980s. It also has an excellent record for implementing the Tokyo Round recommendations. The post-Plaza yen appreciation also gave a tremendous boost to imports. In addition, the SII negotiations with the USA were not only wide-ranging but also addressed some deep changes in traditional market practices. Similarly, Japan's highly regulated financial markets were to a great extent liberalised in the 1980s.

It was widely believed that there existed some culturally derived unique characteristics of the Japanese society that were responsible for high productivity gains in the economy. However, there are few such practices which cannot be explained by superior working of market forces and 'situational' responses and motivations. Perhaps two exceptions to this could be the two important institutions, the MITI and the *keiretsu*. *Kaisha*, or business corporations, played a significant role in making the economy competitive in a respectable array of industries. The striking performance of the economy cannot entirely be attributed to macroeconomic factors. The successful *kaisha* were able to develop major positions in the international markets from the mid-1960s in products ranging from ball-bearings, forklifts and machine tools to a large array of high-tech products.

Although Japan acquired the appellation of economic 'superpower' in the early 1970s, it did not consider itself a powerful nation and refused to take its rightful place in the international economy. It remained wrapped up in itself, paying attention only to matters that affected it directly and judging them entirely in terms of their impact on Japan. The rest of the world expected it to play a role commensurate with its economic status in the internal arena. Its absolute and relative strengths in the international economy are growing and in twenty years it is projected to be a larger economic power, although the USA will continue to be the largest economy and geopolitical power. Two significant roles await Japan:

- regional economic leadership role in the Asia-Pacific region;
- international leadership role within the pluralist structure of the world economy, which will entail being ready to bear the burden of providing international public goods.

4 Market-led Integration

THE FLYING-GEESE PARADIGM

Akamatsu's (1962) simile of *ganko keitai*, or the wild geese flying pattern, has been often used to explain the linkage between industrial growth and the changing trade pattern of a developing economy as well as to explain the growth and trade nexus of the Asia-Pacific economies. In the former case, it shows the standard process of an industry in a developing economy beginning at the stage when the product is being imported and the output of the industry essentially substitutes for imports, at the next stage the economy becomes self-sufficient in that product. The last stage is when this industry grows and turns to exports. In the latter case, which is germane here, Japan is seen as the leading goose economy of the Asia-Pacific region, while the other economies form the rest of the V-formation of the flying geese pattern. They receive a stimulus from the leading economy in the same manner as the following birds do from the birds ahead in the V-formation.

Detailed mathematical calculations of the aerodynamics of the flock by P. Lissaman and C. Shollenberger, at the California Institute of Technology, estimated that a bird could fly as much as 70 per cent further by joining in a V-formation and placing itself in the rising air currents streaming off the wings of its neighbours. Like the birds that get more lift and make better headway by making a V-formation, economies also seem to grow better in the presence of one or more lead economies in the vicinity. In the Asia-Pacific region, the leader-follower relationship has worked in the following manner: Japan is the undisputable leader, followed by Australia and New Zealand, the four ANIEs (South Korea, Taiwan, Hong Kong and Singapore), the ASEAN-4 (Indonesia, Malaysia, the Philippines and Thailand) and China. The V-formation of countries, like that of geese, becomes integrated into a compact whole. The integrating forces in the case of economies are the links established by

131

means of trade, investment, economic assistance and technology transfer. Through these channels, the economies react with one another. The economic synergy that is created provides impetus for mutual growth. Like the flock, the group of economies advances faster with relatively less efforts. The fast growth of the Japanese economy into the second-largest economy in the world in terms of GDP, followed by more rapid growth in the four ANIEs, created a swirling pool of economic change in the Asia-Pacific region and soon other economies were drawn into it. This is evident from the growth in their GDPs relative to the GDP of the world – in 1970 this group of twelve economies accounted for 10.4 per cent of world GDP, in 1990 their share had soared to 19.3 per cent. By 2000, they will account for 29.0 per cent of world GDP (Japan Center for Economic Research 1992).

Since the classical period, it is well known that increasing trade, roughly along the lines of comparative advantage, increases productivity, is mutually advantageous for the trading partners, and in the process integrates their economies. Another explanation of trade to come later was based on the Heckscher-Ohlinian principle, which linked trade patterns with factor endowments. This has relevance to the Asia-Pacific region because economies in the region are at differing stages of development and the stage of development can be taken for a determinant of the factor composition of a country's trade in the region. In a dynamic Heckscher-Ohlinian context, one can say that a country will trade commodities that are less capital intensive, or have a lower K/L ratio with partners higher on the development ladder. Conversely, it will trade commodities that are high in capital-intensity with countries that are lower on the development ladder than itself. The development ladder in the region has already been spelled out in the paragraph above, when talking about the wild geese formation. Other factors than factor endowments can also promote trade: for instance, some resources can be location-specific and, given time and investment may not be reproduced elsewhere in the trading partner countries. These resources are called the Ricardo goods and could include special quality minerals or other natural or man-made factors. Trade based on Ricardo goods is possible even among countries trading in similar K/L ratio goods and is an important source of trade among countries that are, by and large, on the same tier of development.

Yet another explanation of the integration of economies through trade is given by Vernon's (1966) product life cycle theory. It is based on the premise that production technology for a new product does not become contemporaneously available everywhere. The country that pioneers it is not only ahead, but also has proprietary rights over it. This leads to trade in what is called the product-cycle goods. Since this trade is based on a certain knowledge, it spreads over time, and other countries invest in the profitable idea to be able to exploit the new technology. This apart, factor proportions change in the pioneer country and may well change away from the production of the product pioneered by it. This change generally benefits those countries that follow the pioneer and are ready to exploit the technology which the pioneer is phasing out. This explanation is closely related to the dynamically based Heckscher-Ohlinian goods explanation. Although the product life cycle is a one-sector theory, it can be rationally broadened to a multi-sector analysis and be applied to an industrial sector as a whole. In addition, if variables like scale economies and cost advantage due to learning by doing are taken into account, it is easy to see the rationale for trade among countries that are, by and large, at the same level of economic development. This explanation, at its present stage, is not highly relevant to the Asia-Pacific region.

An index of K/L ratios for the Asia-Pacific economies (excluding China) was prepared to rank them according to their comparative advantage in producing more or less capital-intensive goods (Campbell, 1986). This index indicated which country or country groups can be expected to export particular classes of Heckscher-Ohlinian goods. A great deal of variation existed in the region in terms of K/L ratio, the index ranging from 340 for Japan to 15 for Indonesia. As expected, the economies at the upper end, with Japan, were Australia (339), Singapore (272), New Zealand (233), and Hong Kong (174). These economies, being industrialised, have high K/L ratios. Hong Kong and Singapore seem to have exceptionally high K/L ratios because, first, their route to development was somewhat different from other developing economies; and, second, the services sector dominated their economies, resulting in high K/L ratios. The index was in the middle range for Taiwan (91), South Korea (78) and Malaysia (77). The remaining countries were congregated at the lower end. One must take the index with caution, because it is based on the statistics of the mid-1980s. Since then Taiwan, Korea, Malaysia and Thailand have made considerable strides in industrialisation. If the index is recomputed with the data series of the early 1990s, the K/L ratios of the last-named country group will be much higher. The economies at the upper end of the index spectrum were comparatively more efficient in producing and exporting highly capital-intensive goods, whereas those at the other end of the spectrum had comparative advantage in labour-intensive products.

As alluded to earlier, the product-cycle goods movement is based on technological know-how, which needs certain preconditions to spread in the region. The transferable technology will move easily to economies that have relatively better-trained manpower and industrial infrastructure. In the Asia-Pacific region, Japan is the unrivalled technological leader and Australia and New Zealand are quite advanced in this respect. After this group come South Korea and Taiwan, two economies capable of participating well in the product-cycle process. A good deal of footloose technology moved from Japan to these countries, with highly encouraging results, and Japan has established itself as the largest initiator of the product-cycle process in the region. After South Korea and Taiwan, the two close follower countries were Hong Kong and Singapore. Their readiness in terms of human resources and infrastructure was also high. They met the necessary conditions and, therefore, were recipients and beneficiaries of the movements of the product-cycle goods. In a similar manner, the other economies closely following them were Malaysia, Thailand, China and the Philippines. The product life cycle has operated well in the region over the 1980s and beyond.

No matter what is taken as the premise of comparative advantage, let it not be overlooked that comparative advantage is a dynamic concept. Initially natural resource-based products and low K/L ratio products were important for many economies in the region, but their share in total exports declined dramatically. (Indonesia is an exception to this because of its oil exports.) Similarly, initially labour-intensive goods were important for Japan and the ANIEs, but their share in total exports declined very sharply at early stages of industrialisation. They increased their export shares of both human-capital-intensive and technology-intensive exports, as did Australia and New Zealand, albeit to a lesser extent (Krause, 1987). Japan and the ANIEs, by the late 1980s, became successful in exporting high-tech and knowledge-intensive products. Among the ASEAN-4, the Philippines and Thailand emerged for the first time in the 1970s as significant exporters of labour-intensive products. An interesting trend in intra-trade had emerged by the early 1980s: ANIEs that exported manufactured goods found the USA and the ASEAN-4 markets most attractive. The other Asia-Pacific countries that had natural resource-based or labour-intensive products still as a considerable part of their exports found Japan and the ANIEs attractive markets.

With changing comparative advantage, the product-cycle has moved in industries like textiles and steel from one sub-group of economies to another in the region – in textiles it moved from Japan to the ANIEs and further to ASEAN and China; in steel it moved from Japan to the ANIEs. In automobiles and electronics it is moving identically, from Japan, to the ANIEs and then to ASEAN. These movements have worked as a catalyst for deepening interdependence in the Asia-Pacific region. There were two prime movers in the movement of the product cycle: first, indigenous enterprises in the developing countries spotted the opportunity to acquire new products, and therefore technology, to catch up with the leading countries; secondly, the multinational enterprise in the leading country felt the loss of comparative advantage and spotted the most appropriate developing economy for the transfer of industrial technology and the product. Who will make the first move, the receiving indigenous enterprise or the multinational firm in the leading country? This will depend on both the industry in question and the receiving enterprises in the developing economy. It was observed that in the case of mature industries like textiles and steel, the initiative was taken by the enterprises in the developing economies or the receiving enterprises. However, in industries having relatively advanced technologies, say, electronics or fine chemicals, where new products emerge more frequently, the prime movers of the product cycle were the multinational firms in the leading country.

INCREASING INTERDEPENDENCE

With growth, there have been numerous, significant changes in the trade and industrial structure of the Asia-Pacific economies which, in turn, have created economic forces that led to clear economic co-operation and integration of these economies centring around Japan. As seen in Table 4.1, in 1991 it was the most important export partner of two regional economies and second-most important export partner of five. On the import side, for six regional economies it was the most important trade partner, while for two it was the second-most important partner. In each case, substantial proportions of imports and exports came from or went to Japan. For Indonesia and Australia, almost one-third of total exports went to Japan, whereas for South Korea, Taiwan, Malaysia and Thailand, almost one-third of imports came from there.

The macro-level trade statistics demonstrate that the long-term average growth rate of intra-trade in the Asia-Pacific region was higher than those in the two large economic blocs, the EU and NAFTA. In terms of volume, it was $ 300 billion in 1990, larger than that in NAFTA but about one-third that of the EU intra-trade volume (Table 4.2). Similarly, long-term average growth rates of intra-trade in manufactures were higher for the Asia-Pacific region than that for the two large trading blocs (Table 4.3). In terms of volume, intra-trade in

Table 4.1 Trade Partnerships of the Asia-Pacific Economies with Japan

	Exports				Imports			
	1990		1991		1990		1991	
	Rank	% Share	Rank	% Share	Rank	% Share	Rank	% Share
North-east Asia								
Korea	2nd	19.5	2nd	18.1	1st	26.1	1st	27.5
Taiwan	3rd	12.4	3rd	12.4	1st	29.8	1st	29.8
Hong Kong	4th	5.8	4th	5.5	2nd	15.9	2nd	16.3
China	2nd	14.4	2nd	14.4	2nd	14.7	2nd	16.7
South-east Asia								
Indonesia	1st	42.4	1st	36.9	1st	24.9	1st	24.4
Malaysia	3rd	15.2	3rd	15.8	1st	24.9	1st	26.9
Philippines	2nd	19.8	2nd	19.9	2nd	18.5	2nd	19.3
Singapore	2nd	8.6	3nd	8.5	1st	17.6	1st	19.5
Thailand	2nd	17.1	2nd	18.3	1st	30.7	1st	29.0
Australia & New Zealand								
Australia	1st	26.1	1st	27.9	2nd	18.8	2nd	17.5
New Zealand	2nd	15.8	2nd	15.9	3rd	15.4	3rd	15.5

Source: International Economic Databank, Australia National University, IMF Direction of Trade Statistics, June 1992.

Table 4.2 Intra-Trade within the Asia-Pacific Region and the EU and NAFTA Blocs

Year	NAFTA			Asia-Pacific			EU		
	Volume of intra-trade (US $B)	Annual growth rates (%)	Selected average growth rates (%)	Volume of intra-trade (US $B)	Annual growth rates (%)	Selected average growth rates(%)	Volume of intra-trade (US $B)	Annual growth rates (%)	Selected average growth rates (%)
1965	11.9			6.0			32.8		
1966	14.1	18.6		6.9	14.3		36.0	9.9	
1967	15.7	11.3		7.6	10.8		37.8	5.0	
1968	18.6	18.3		8.6	12.8		42.9	13.7	
1969	21.1	13.4		10.5	22.5		52.6	22.5	
1970	22.0	4.5		12.1	15.5		61.8	17.4	
1971	24.8	12.7		13.7	13.3		71.4	15.6	
1972	29.6	19.3		16.8	22.7		88.6	24.1	
1973	36.8	24.5		28.6	69.6		123.0	38.7	
1974	48.2	30.8		40.5	41.6		155.0	26.0	
1975	49.7	3.3		39.4	2.7		162.0	4.5	
1976	56.9	14.4		47.0	19.4		185.0	14.2	
1977	61.5	8.0		54.3	15.4		211.0	14.1	
1978	69.7	13.3		68.8	26.8		260.0	23.2	
1979	84.7	21.6		88.4	28.4		339.0	30.4	
1980	101.0	19.2	15.1 (1965–80)	109.9	24.3	22.5 (1965–80)	384.0	13.3	18.9 (1965–80)
1981	115.0	13.9		120.2	9.3		334.0	-13.0	
1982	99.8	-13.2		117.5	-2.2		330.0	-1.2	
1983	113.0	13.2		119.4	1.6		326.0	-1.2	

Table 4.2 Continued

Year	NAFTA			Asia-Pacific			EU		
	Volume of intra-trade (US $B)	Annual growth rates (%)	Selected average growth rates (%)	Volume of intra-trade (US $B)	Annual growth rates (%)	Selected average growth rates (%)	Volume of intra-trade (US $B)	Annual growth rates (%)	Selected average growth rates (%)
1984	136.0	20.4		136.4	14.2		330.0	1.2	
1985	140.0	2.9		137.2	0.6		352.0	6.7	
1986	127.0	-9.3		142.8	4.1		450.0	27.8	
1987	155.0	22.0		182.0	27.5		559.0	24.2	
1988	182.0	17.4		236.5	29.9		626.0	12.0	
1989	200.00	9.9		272.2	15.1		674.0	7.7	
1990	219.0	9.5	8.4 (1981–90)	300.3	10.3	11.8 (1981–90)	820.0	21.7	11.6 (1981–90)

Source: International Economic Data Bank, Australian National University, Canberra.

manufactures was about one-third that of the EU intra-trade volume but much larger than that in NAFTA.

Analysis of matrices of various economic transactions in the Asia-Pacific region gives clearer evidence of increasing interdependence in the region towards the end of the 1980s. Even during the first half of the 1980s, when the growth of world trade slowed, trade within the region increased steadily at an average annual rate of 6.8 per cent. During the latter half of the decade it tripled to 22.1 per cent (Table 4.4). Also during the latter half of the 1980s, exports from ANIEs to other ANIEs grew by 44.7 per cent per year compared to 26.6 per cent during the first half. Likewise, exports from ANIEs to ASEAN grew by 31.7 per cent per year during the latter half of the 1980s, compared to 10.4 per cent during the first half. Table 4.4 also shows evidence of large increases in trade from ASEAN and China to other parts of the Asia-Pacific region. Exports from Australia and New Zealand recorded similar increases, albeit in an uneven manner. Japan's exports to the region, although started from a large base, went up by 8.4 per cent over the first half of the decade but this rate doubled to 16.5 per cent over the second half.

The direction of exports also changed confirming the increasing intra-regional integration hypothesis (Table 4.5). Between 1980 and 1986, the intra-regional trade of Japan, the ANIEs and the ASEAN countries declined somewhat, from 33.1 per cent to 30.1 per cent. But it increased considerably over the period 1986–90 to reach 39.6 per cent of the total trade. This increase was at the expense of the USA and Canada: the proportion of exports from these countries to them fell by 8.2 per cent over the period 1986–90. The same point needs to be repeated for Australia and New Zealand, whose exports to the region fell during the 1980–86 period but rose from 43.3 per cent to 51.5 per cent over the 1986–90 period. In this case, the increase in trade with the Asia-Pacific region was at the expense of both North America and the EU. A significant development was the growth of the ANIEs and the ASEAN countries as important markets for the regional exporters. The proportion of exports directed towards the

Table 4.3 Intra-Trade in Manufactures within the Asia-Pacific Region, the EU and the NAFTA Blocs

Year	NAFTA			Asia-Pacific			EU		
	Volume of intra-trade in manufactures (US $B)	Annual growth rates (%)	Selected average growth rates (%)	Volume of intra-trade in manufactures (US $B)	Annual growth rates (%)	Selected average growth rates (%)	Volume of intra-trade in manufactures (US $B)	Annual growth rates (%)	Selected average growth rates (%)
1965	7.4			2.9			22.6		
1966	9.3	26.6		3.3	14.5		25.2	11.4	
1967	10.9	16.6		3.7	11.3		26.5	5.3	
1968	13.0	19.6		4.4	20.2		30.4	14.6	
1969	15.1	16.4		5.4	22.3		37.9	24.6	
1970	15.5	2.6		6.4	18.5		44.9	18.5	
1971	17.9	15.0		7.4	16.6		52.5	16.9	
1972	21.0	17.8		9.2	23.5		65.1	24.0	
1973	25.8	22.7		15.4	67.8		88.9	36.6	
1974	32.6	26.2		21.2	37.6		110.0	23.7	
1975	34.4	5.7		20.8	-2.1		115.0	4.5	
1976	39.8	15.8		24.9	19.7		134.0	16.5	
1977	42.8	7.4		28.5	14.7		152.0	13.4	
1978	48.8	13.9		39.9	39.9		189.0	24.3	
1979	57.4	17.8		48.7	22.2		244.0	29.1	
1980	65.0	13.2	15.2 (1965–80)	60.0	23.0	21.7 (1965–80)	271.0	11.1	19.1 (1965–80)
1981	77.5	19.3		68.5	14.3		229.6	-15.3	
1982	64.7	-16.5		64.3	-6.1		228.7	-0.4	

Table 4.3 Continued

Year	NAFTA			Asia-Pacific			EU		
	Volume of intra-trade in manufactures (US $B)	Annual growth rates (%)	Selected average growth rates (%)	Volume of intra-trade in manufactures (US $B)	Annual growth rates (%)	Selected average growth rates (%)	Volume of intra-trade in manufactures (US $B)	Annual growth rates (%)	Selected average growth rates (%)
1983	75.0	15.8		67.9	5.6		224.5	-1.8	
1984	94.9	26.5		80.4	18.4		226.9	1.0	
1985	100.8	6.3		83.4	3.7		246.2	8.5	
1986	96.6	-4.2		95.6	14.7		366.4	36.7	
1987	118.7	22.9		125.7	31.4		428.3	27.3	
1988	141.6	19.3		170.2	35.4		485.8	13.4	
1989	156.2	10.3		197.3	15.9		525.8	8.2	
1990	167.6	7.3		219.9	11.4		646.1	22.9	
			10.8 (1981–90)			14.4 (1981–90)			13.7 (1981–90)

Source: International Economic Data Bank, Australian National University, Canberra.

Table 4.4 Export Value Matrix for 1980, 1986 and 1990

				Japan, ANIEs ASEAN & China		Japan, ANIEs & ASEAN		Japan	
		Value of exports ($ m.)	Average rate of growth (%)[a]	Value of exports ($ m.)	Average rate of growth (%)[a]	Value of exports ($ m.)	Average rate of growth (%)[a]	Value of exports ($ m.)	Average rate of growth (%)[a]
Japan, ANIEs, ASEAN & China	1980			84 945		77 891		29 065	
	1986			125 930	6.8	107 193	5.5	32 022	1.6
	1990			280 296	22.1	251 217	23.7	62 375	18.1
Japan, ANIEs & ASEAN	1980	56 848		75 364		68 310		25 033	
	1986	151 718	17.8	109 193	6.4	90 456	4.8	26 943	1.2
	1990	195 138	6.5	238 747	21.6	209 668	23.4	52 609	18.2
Japan	1980	34 359		28 467		23 358			
	1986	87 587	16.9	46 311	8.4	36 375	7.7		
	1990	97 858	2.8	85 277	16.5	79 132	21.4		
China	1980	1 120		9 581		9 581		4 032	
	1986	2 940	17.5	16 737	9.7	16 737	9.7	5 079	3.9
	1990	7 962	28.3	41 549	25.5	41 549	25.5	9 766	17.8
ANIEs	1980	10 520		9 592		8 340		3 948	
	1986	49 615	29.5	29 720	20.7	22 169	17.7	11 797	20.0
	1990	68 102	8.2	83 294	29.4	62 962	29.8	25 812	21.6
ASEAN	1980	11 969		37 305		36 612		21 085	
	1986	14 516	3.3	33 162	-1.9	31 913	-2.3	15 146	-5.4
	1990	29 178	19.1	70 176	20.6	67 574	20.6	26 797	15.3
Australia & New Zealand	1980	3 879		17 871		16 914		13 854	
	1986	3 811	-0.3	12 338	-6.0	11 066	-6.8	6 928	-10.9
	1990	4 921	6.6	20 053	12.9	19 098	14.6	10 206	10.2

Table 4.4 Continued

		China		ANIEs		ASEAN		Australia & New Zealand	
		Value of exports	Average rate of growth (%)[a]	Value of exports	Average rate of growth (%)[a]	Value of exports	Average rate of growth (%)[a]	Value of exports	Average rate of growth (%)[a]
		($ m.)		($ m.)		($ m.)		($ m.)	
Japan, ANIEs ASEAN & China	1980	7 054		19 092		29 734		7 179	
	1986	18 737	17.7	45 323	15.5	29 849	0.1	10 675	6.8
	1990	29 079	11.6	107 306	24.0	81 535	28.6	16 060	10.8
Japan ANIEs & ASEAN	1980	7 054		14 739		28 538		6 925	
	1986	18 737	17.7	35 547	15.8	27 967	0.3	10 438	7.1
	1990	29 079	11.6	79 454	22.3	77 604	29.1	15 396	10.2
Japan	1980	5 109		10 177		13 181		4 087	
	1986	9 936	11.7	25 674	16.7	10 701	-3.4	6 386	7.7
	1990	6 145	11.3	46 066	15.7	33 066	32.6	8 136	6.2
China	1980			4 353		1 196		254	
	1986			9 776	14.4	1 882	7.8	237	-1.1
	1990			27 852	29.9	3 931	20.2	664	29.4
ANIEs	1980	1 252		1 050		3 342		796	
	1986	7 551	34.9	4 313	26.6	6 059	10.4	2 386	20.1
	1990	20 332	28.1	18 905	44.7	18 245	31.7	4 157	14.9
ASEAN	1980	693		3 512		12 015		2 042	
	1986	1 250	10.3	5 560	8.0	11 207	-1.2	1 666	3.3
	1990	2 602	20.1	14 483	27.0	26 293	23.8	3 104	16.8
Australia & New Zealand	1980	957		953		2 108		1 755	
	1986	1 272	4.9	2 440	17.0	1 698	-3.5	1 961	1.9
	1990	955	-6.9	4 537	16.8	4 355	26.5	1 954	-0.1

Source: MITI 1992 a statistics gleaned from Table 2.1.
[a] The first growth rate is for the 1980–86 period the second rate is for the 1986–90 period.

Table 4.5 Direction of Exports for 1980, 1986 and 1990 (%)

		Japan, ANIEs ASEAN & China	Japan, ANIEs ASEAN & China	Japan	China	ANIEs	ASEAN	Australia & New Zealand
Japan, ANIEs ASEAN & China 1980		33.1	11.3	2.7	2.7	7.4	11.6	2.8
1986		30.1	7.6	4.5	4.5	10.8	7.1	2.5
1990		39.6	8.8	4.1	4.1	15.2	11.5	2.3
Japan 1980	26.3	21.8		3.9	3.9	7.8	10.1	3.1
1986	41.6	22.0		4.7	4.7	12.2	5.1	3.0
1990	34.0	29.6		2.1	2.1	16.0	11.5	2.8
China 1980	6.2	52.8	22.2	0.0	0.0	24.0	6.6	1.4
1986	9.4	53.4	16.2	0.0	0.0	31.2	6.0	0.8
1990	11.5	59.8	14.1	0.0	0.0	40.1	5.7	1.0
ANIEs 1980	28.3	25.8	10.6	3.4	3.4	2.8	9.0	2.1
1986	45.1	27.0	10.7	6.9	6.9	3.9	5.5	2.2
1990	32.6	39.8	12.3	9.7	9.7	9.0	8.7	2.0
ASEAN 1980	16.8	52.5	29.6	1.0	1.0	4.9	16.9	2.9
1986	21.7	49.7	22.7	1.9	1.9	8.3	16.8	2.5
1990	20.7	49.8	19.0	1.8	1.8	10.3	18.6	2.2
Australia & New Zealand 1980	14.1	65.1	50.5	3.5	3.5	3.5	7.7	6.4
1986	13.4	43.3	24.3	4.5	4.5	8.6	6.0	6.9
1990	12.6	51.5	26.2	2.5	2.5	11.7	11.2	5.0

Source: MITI, 1992 a, Statistics gleaned from Table 2.2.

ANIEs and ASEAN rose enormously. In 1990, each group imported more from the region than did Japan.

The degree of export dependence in general in the Asia-Pacific region, measured by the value of the exports/GNP ratio, increased from 10.1 per cent in 1986 to 12.1 per cent in 1990. The degree of dependence for intra-regional exports increased more, from 6.5 per cent to 7.9 per cent over the same period. This implies that the increase in exports directed within the region made up 1.4 per cent of the total increase of 2.0 per cent in total export dependence (MITI, 1992a). This further establishes the increasing interdependence in commodity trade in the region.

As the above statistics convincingly show, with growing industrialisation and rising income levels, trade has been growing in the region, including the intra-trade. The export composition has changed towards higher technology and, therefore, high-value-added goods. This transformation was more pronounced over the latter half of the 1980s. Throughout the decade, the share of machinery has increased in Japan's trade with the region, particularly in its trade with the ANIEs and the ASEAN. Japan's exports of capital goods and intermediate goods to these two groups increased considerably, as did its imports of semi-finished goods, parts and machine tools, and finished electric and electronic equipments and audio-visual equipment. A work-sharing structure in manufacturing processes has developed rapidly. Use of Japanese capital goods was common in these countries, Japanese firms tending to help all along the way in the process of transfer of technology which, in turn, helped in the production of high-value-added products in the region. The output was used by Japanese firms as well as exported to the USA and the EC. As we shall see, a work-sharing pattern evolved between the Japanese firms and those in the Asia-Pacific region. It increased Japan's intra-industry trade, particularly with the ANIEs and the ASEAN countries. This kind of trade led to a mature manner of economic integration. Whereas some intra-industry trade had existed between Japan and the ANIEs in the 1970s, it rose considerably during the 1980s and the index of intra-industry trade soared from

26.9 in 1984 to 35.4 in 1990, declining marginally to 34.6 in 1991 (Table 4.6). Intra-industry trade with the ASEAN countries started from a low level, but it rose steadily during the 1980s, with the index rising from 4.8 in 1980 to 7.0 in 1984 and further to 19.6 in 1991. Japan's intra-industry trade, with the south-east Asian countries as indicated by the index, doubled over the 1980–91 period.

Using the 'gravity'-type model, developed by Tinbergen (1962), trade flow equations were estimated for several years between 1965 and 1985 for trade between the Asia-Pacific countries. Good data series were available for ten industries: chemicals, plastics, textiles, iron and steel, non-electrical machinery, electrical machinery, clothing, footwear, transport equipment and precision instruments. The results from estimating equations lent support to the following conclusions.

• Intra-industry specialisation has been rising in the region for the majority of bilateral trade flows, albeit at varying rates. It appeared to be the lowest when trade with China was involved. Relative resource endowment of China was such that it was difficult to integrate it into the industrial division of labour with industrially more advanced

Table 4.6   Index numbers of Japan's Intra-Industry Trade with South-east Asia

Year	South-east Asia	ANIEs	ASEAN
1970	14.6	16.4	5.5
1975	14.5	23.2	4.3
1980	15.7	26.3	4.8
1981	16.0	25.9	5.4
1982	16.1	27.0	5.2
1983	17.4	26.4	5.9
1984	18.8	26.9	7.0
1985	20.1	28.4	6.8
1986	21.3	26.2	8.7
1987	23.1	28.4	9.1
1988	26.5	32.6	11.5
1989	28.7	35.3	13.4
1990	28.5	35.4	14.7
1991	29.9	34.6	19.6

Source: MITI, 1992b.

neighbouring countries such as Japan and the ANIEs. Its trade with the other regional economies was more on inter-industry lines. It was conspicuously so with the advanced countries of the region, namely, Japan, Australia and New Zealand.

- A relatively high level of intra-industry specialisation existed between Japan, the ANIEs and the ASEAN on the one hand, and Australia and New Zealand on the other. The coefficients showed a surprisingly high degree of intra-trade between Japan and the ASEAN members. This resulted from Japanese-dominated joint ventures trading with companies in Japan, not necessarily parent companies, in both directions and in the same industries (Langhammer, 1989).

Trade in services, an important indicator of deepening economic interdependence, has expanded faster in the Asia-Pacific region than in the rest of the world. Its rate of expansion over 1980–6 was 11.1 per cent for the region, against 10.5 per cent for the world. For the 1986–90 period, the corresponding averages were 19.4 per cent and 13.5 per cent. In 1990, services trade reached $ 288.1 million, which was half of the total world trade in services (MITI, 1992a).

The expansion is particularly striking in east and southeast Asia, where Japan, the ANIEs and ASEAN economies have expansion rates reaching 20 per cent. Japan and ANIEs have recorded striking growth in air transport and telecommunications. Air cargo arriving in the region increased at an average annual rate of 16 per cent over the 1984–9 period. Large growths have taken place in air cargo arriving in China (average increase 37 per cent), in the ANIEs, (average increase 23 per cent) and in the ASEAN countries (average increase 19 per cent). Particularly noteworthy was the increase in air cargo between the four ANIEs (average increase 28 per cent). Movements of air cargo between the ANIEs and the ASEAN had the same average rate of increase. The maritime cargo movement within the region was close to 40 per cent of the total maritime cargo transport world-wide. Of this, a substantial proportion (65 per cent) moved on routes within the region. The maritime cargo movement in the region grew at an average rate of 40 per cent per annum during the 1980s. The communication volume on international telephones in the region surpassed 1570 million calls in 1989, averaging a growth rate of 20 per cent over the 1980s (MITI, 1992a). This indicates rapid progress in the movement of information. Increases in this mode of communications were the most striking for the ASEAN and the ANIEs countries.

EXPORT-LED INDUSTRIALISATION AND INTEGRATION

The foregoing exposition imparts an inkling of the process of industrialisation and the changing structure of comparative advantage. As indicated by the sequential flying geese scenario, Japan, Australia and New Zealand were the leading economies of the region, followed by the ANIEs, which – by and large – completed the import substitution (IS) phase of industrialisation in the 1950s and entered the export-led growth path in the early 1960s. The ANIEs were followed by the ASEAN-4 and China, at an interval of a decade in each case, in terms of the phases of industrialisation. The four ANIEs started exporting manufactured products to mature industrial economies in the 1960s, followed by the ASEAN-4 a decade later, and then China in the 1980s, exporting to the same markets. Over the 1970s, the ANIEs succeeded in achieving a great deal of expansion in their manufactured exports which changed the composition of their merchandise exports out of recognition: between 1968 and 1979 their share in world manufactured exports increased from 2.1 per cent to 5.4 per cent. Since Japan's growth rate of manufactured exports over this period was far below those of the ANIEs, it helped them catch up with Japan. The manufactured exports from the ASEAN-4 were small, but their growth rate was as rapid as those in the ANIEs. Therefore, the proportion of manufacturers in total exports increased substantially in three of them, the exception being Indonesia. The other three of the ASEAN-4 could no longer be called monocultural or primary commodity exporters by the end of the 1970s. The

ANIEs' export expansion in textiles and electrical and electronic machinery was remarkable and, at this stage of industrialisation, these products came to command a central importance in their total exports. The same product group was also important for the ASEAN-4, but their exports were not as large as those of the ANIEs.

It is hardly counter-intuitive that at an early stage Japan began to lose comparative advantage in textiles, a labour-intensive commodity, and the ANIEs and the ASEAN-4 began to improve their comparative advantage. However, Japan retained comparative advantage in upstream textiles, which included synthetic and regenerated fibres, and continued to capture a significant part of the world market. Its eventual loss of comparative advantage in upstream textiles was slow, but when it occurred, the ANIEs and the ASEAN-4 were quick to take over this segment of the world market. This picture emerged from the indices of the revealed comparative advantage (RCA) for these commodities computed by Watanabe and Kajiwara (1983). Electrical and electronic machinery repeated the same story: that is Japan first losing its comparative advantage, then the ANIEs picking up fast and capturing large world market shares – again, the RCA index confirmed the story. Close on the heels of the ANIEs were the ASEAN-4, whose growth rates in the production of electrical and electronic products were even higher than those for the ANIEs. The change in the structure of comparative advantage subsequently became visible in the capital-intensive industries, such as steel, as well. In the early 1980s, Japan had a large part of world market share and high RCA index value, while the ANIEs and the ASEAN-4 did not count for much. However, with respect to iron and steel primary products, Japan's RCA index number had begun to dip, while those of the ANIEs and ASEAN-4 had begun to rise as early as the early 1980s. This continual waxing and waning of comparative advantage among the regional economies kept a dynamic process of catching-up unfolding, integrating the regional economies in the process. This process continued to refine the structure of comparative advantage in the regional economies, made them increasingly sophisticated and gave substance to the term 'growth pole'. It should be noted that this process of industrialisation would not have been feasible if these economies had not embraced the strategy of export-led industrialisation: it would have been a non-starter under the IS strategy.

This process of industrialisation led to interesting changes from complementary to competitive relationships between countries and country groups in the region. It began with a complementary relationship between Japan and the ANIEs on one side and the ANIEs and ASEAN-4 on the other. Soon competition developed in several areas between the two sets of partners. It became pronounced after the ANIEs began their heavy industrialisation. Australia and New Zealand did not figure in this relationship because they had a different and mature industrial base. Their economic interaction began first with Japan and, after the mid-1970s, with the ANIEs, but relatively less with the ASEAN-4. Australia, for geopolitical reasons, tried to cultivate a low-ebb relationship with China. The ASEAN-4 and China have had a competing relationship: they competed with each other in Japan, the USA and EC markets also. This competition was limited to primary and labour-intensive goods. Little competition was experienced among the manufactured products exported by the ASEAN-4 and China. As the process of industrialisation in the region progressed, Japan established itself as the principal supplier of capital goods, intermediate goods, industrial raw materials and heavy industrial products. The ANIEs had a weak capital industry sector until late. With upgradation in their industrial structure and improvement in supply capabilities, Japan began to import from them low-price, light manufactures and semi-processed goods instead of producing these domestically. The yen appreciation of 1985 changed in one sweep comparative advantage in the Japanese industrial sector and a whole range of intermediate-range technology industries could no longer compete with cheaper imports from the ANIEs. The yen appreciation of 1971 had also had the same effect, albeit to a smaller extent.

An examination of the international input–output tables reveals an interesting phenomenon on the lines noted above.

Although the ANIEs, and to a lesser degree the ASEAN-4, have substantially increased their exports of consumer goods, they still could not supply many of the intermediate and capital goods. Therefore they had to depend on imports from Japan or other industrial economies. The input–output tables show the clear role of Japan in providing the ANIEs and the ASEAN-4 with the intermediate inputs needed for their manufacturing output. Although the ANIEs' heavy industrialisation will reduce the complementarity, in future, they cannot progress too far in many product lines together because of market limitations. Also, heavy industrialisation in the ANIEs and the ASEAN-4 will promote Japan's exports of intermediate and capital goods through the inducement effect (Yamazawa, 1987). The three country-groups competed with each other in several light industrial product groups in both North American and EC markets. Although Japan retained much larger shares in these products, the ANIEs and ASEAN-4 managed to expand their shares considerably.[1] This shows how, due to economic differences among various sub-sets of regional economies, the industrial structure in the Asia-Pacific region has come to have both competitive and complementary elements. The process of export-led industrialisation made economic interaction and market integration more intense and logical. This process facilitated growth in one economy to stimulate growth in the other regional economies – that is, the flying geese formation did operate.

MACROECONOMIC AND MICROECONOMIC INTEGRATION

As we have seen regional economies were increasingly interacting with each other, and this interaction grew considerably over the 1980s, becoming particularly intense from the middle of the decade. The industrial structure and production of the ANIEs was such that they had to rely for technology and intermediate and capital-goods on Japan. This sub-group had a strong manufactured goods and machinery sector. During its export-led growth process, this sector developed in such a manner that the ANIEs' economies came to specialise in the production and assembly of final products: they did not manufacture their own components, intermediate goods and capital goods. With its proven records of product quality and servicing expertise, Japan established itself as the major source of these vitally necessary goods. Japan's exports of these goods to the ANIEs tended to be inelastic with respect to changes in the real exchange rate. These lines of Japanese exports are the so-called L-curve goods – that is, products having non-price competitiveness. This one feature of their industrial structure closely integrated the ANIEs with the Japanese economy. Traditionally, they depended on the US market for their exports of manufactured products. However, their success in penetrating the Japanese markets was limited, because Japan itself was highly competitive in many similar sectors. In addition, Japan's distribution system, which worked on the basis of long-term, good customer relationships, made market penetration difficult (Park and Park, 1991).

The yen appreciation changed this state of affairs. As the Japanese manufacturing sector lost comparative advantage in several sectors, the ANIEs' market penetration increased. In labour-intensive manufactured goods, such as electrical and general machinery, it increased considerably. Although the ANIEs also increased their exports of TV sets, tape recorders and VCRs, their market share was not large. During the latter half of the 1980s, they began to promote their high-tech industries vigorously by introducing new technology from Japan and investing more capital (Hanazaki, 1989). The ANIEs, over the early 1990s, managed to cut down Japan's lead in manufacturing and have begun to export capital-intensive and technology-intensive products as well. This they did inside the Asia-Pacific region as well as outside. In spite of Japan's high competitiveness in iron and steel, Korea succeeded in penetrating Japanese markets. Due to geographical proximity and historically closer economic ties, Korea and Taiwan were able to penetrate the Japanese markets more than Hong Kong and Singapore. This trend became more pronounced after Japan took measures to expand its imports. Sub-contracting, outsourcing and original equipment manufacturing (OEM) also received a well-deserved stimulus. This promoted what has come to be known as the horizontal division of labour between Japan and the ANIEs, and will further closer economic ties.

In the south-east Asian region, Japan has intensified its efforts at deepening economic cooperation to bolster growth. It has supported efforts to improve infrastructure and the training of skilled workers. The economic rationale was simple: backyardism was gaining ground in Japanese foreign economic policy. By improving technological levels and enhancing supply capacity Japan could further increase its imports, particularly those of manufactured goods, from the Asia-Pacific region. The Japanese private sector was playing a role in these endeavours as well as in efforts related to technological transfer, environment protection and energy efficiency improvement in the south-east Asian region. Support industries were being nurtured and policy dialogues were being promoted (Yamazaki and Clifford, 1992). The MITI stepped up its involvement in the domestic-oriented economic policies of the regional economies. It sent advisory groups to the ASEAN countries to promote their industrialisation on the Japanese prototype. The policy advice essentially focused on export-oriented industrialisation and increasing competitiveness (Nakajima, 1992). Although careful utilisation of market forces was a part of it, *laissez-faire* was not recommended. The strategy worked in the following manner: first, bilateral assistance improved the infrastructure; secondly, the government offered technological advice followed by macroeconomic and industrialisation-related advice; thirdly, the private sector stepped in for joint ventures or other business alliances; fourthly, Japanese firms opened their doors for imports from these off-shore factories.

These plans were based on resources endowments in the regional economies, and division of labour. For instance, Indonesia was seen as having a good deal of potential for textiles, sports shoes and plastics; Thailand in industries related to metals, furniture, die-cast moulds, and so on; and Malaysia in copiers, TV tubes, word processors, answering machines and facsimile devices. The co-ordination policies with the ANIEs differ and they have been discussed in the preceding paragraphs. These developments indicate the emergence of a regional economy which has a special significance for Japan. After the Plaza accord in 1985, Japan's trade surplus with the USA declined steadily until 1990 and recorded minor increases over the period 1990–92. However, its trade surplus increased continuously *vis-à-vis* the Asia-Pacific region. The ANIEs and ASEAN-4 ran chronic deficits with Japan. If, over the coming years, a strong regional economy emerges, it will enhance interdependence among the Asia-Pacific economies and provide Japan with an opportunity to control its trade imbalance with the regional economies. Current account imbalance is never a one-way street. In addition – notwithstanding its industrial prowess – Japan cannot be, and remain, internationally competitive in all industries. It will have to cope with – if not promote – the catching-up of the ANIEs, the ASEAN-4 and then China by rapidly adjusting domestic industrial and economic structure. It has done well on this count so far.

The ANIEs are important in their own right, because by the late 1980s their imports grew larger than those of Japan and their exports were almost as large as that of Japan. Although they travelled their separate economic development paths, the ANIEs and the ASEAN intensified their interdependence. Being at different stages of development and having different patterns of factor endowments helped this process. Trade and investment between the two groups became increasingly important. The interplay between complementarity and competition between the two groups has already been discussed. Since the ANIEs were progressing towards the production and export of capital-intensive goods, they had a natural interest in the ASEAN markets. Also, as the former group grows more competitive in the high-tech industries, it will be interested in transplanting its plant and equipment to the latter group, by selling or through creation of joint ventures.

As alluded to earlier, Australia and New Zealand's economic relations leaned relatively more towards Japan, Hong Kong, Korea and Taiwan. The ASEAN-4 economies likewise leaned towards Japan, the ANIEs and intra-ASEAN. Australia and New Zealand were not of critical importance to the economies of ASEAN-4 or the ANIEs. Although Australia, New Zealand and the ASEAN-4 are primary-orientated economies, some complementarity does exist between the manufacturing sectors of these economies. The manufactured exports of the former were capital-intensive and technology-intensive, whereas those of the latter were largely labour-intensive. The former have started importing labour-intensive products increasingly from the ASEAN-4 and China, and by the early 1990s these imports reached conspicuous proportions.

The last link in the chain is China, to which Japan and the ANIEs have increasingly turned. By the late 1980s, most investors had completed their overseas expansion plans in the ASEAN-4. Besides, overheating of these economies was causing concern. It led to increased interest in China by the regional economies and decline in interest in the ASEAN-4. China's eagerness as well as its decision to join APEC promoted its interaction with the other regional economies further.

With the Japanese and the ANIE's firms becoming increasingly Asia-orientated, the process of integration has also continued at the microeconomic level. Large firms established regional procurement and distribution centres linking Japan, the ANIEs and the ASEAN. Several have established comprehensive international distribution systems in different parts of the Asia-Pacific region. Japanese firms dealing in warehousing, transportation, marine transport and retailing were active in different parts of Asia. Capital procurement has also grown pan-Asian over the years, and so has hedging of exchange rate risk operations (Tokunaga, 1992). Large firms, the majority of them Japanese, have created a system of account settlements without the use of forex in the region. Since some of the countries in the region are still subject to exchange rate control, it is not always feasible to take in foreign capital to hedge against foreign exchange risk. What the large firms do is make payments for procurements in the local currency as well as receive payments for the sale of finished goods in the local currency. It is possible to settle accounts without forex at the regional level when each of the factories purchases parts and materials from abroad as well as selling finished products abroad. At the regional level, a large part of such exchanges can be 'married', that is, by forex debits cancelling out forex credits. The portions that cannot be cancelled are generally put to use as a hedge against risk, using the futures exchange markets at Singapore or anywhere else in the international money markets.

Large Japanese corporations have also created distribution systems on Asian and international scales in the region. They first created regional and global information communications systems which, in turn, became instrumental in the flow of parts and products between different parts of the Asia-Pacific region and the rest of the world without the need of maintaining inventory reservoirs. With a global distribution network run on these lines, the flow of goods can be precisely managed at all times, which is highly cost-efficient. With the regionally and globally integrated distribution systems established by large corporations, the distribution industry has created, what is called, 'timeless space' (Tokunaga, 1992). Several large Japanese firms have created pan-Asian networks which will be discussed in the next section. Thus viewed, economic ties strengthened in the region at both the macro-level and the micro-level.

AN INTEGRATED PRODUCTION ZONE

There are in the Asia-Pacific region several cash-rich countries having large reserves. At the end of 1992, Taiwan had the second-largest total reserves (minus gold) in the world. Japan the third-largest, China the fifth-largest and Singapore the seventh-largest. These countries have been flooding the region with investments. Consequently, several nationwide and sub-regional industrial areas have emerged. These large investments have integrated several industrial sectors and propelled the region towards industrial integration. The Asia-Pacific region, therefore, has become more economically cohesive than ever before.

FDI by Japan

In the latter half of the 1970s, Japan's foreign direct investment (FDI) grew at the rate of 9.6 per cent per annum, the
lowest rate among the industrialised economies. However, for
the 1980–7 period its average annual growth rate was 21.6 per
cent, the second-highest among the industrialised economies
(Hyun and Whitmore, 1989). Going by the International
Monetary Fund statistics published in the *International
Financial Statistics*, total outflow was $ 19.5 billion in 1987, and
rose to $ 34.2 billion the next year, which was twice the
outflow of the USA and almost equal to that of the UK, which
had invested the highest amount ($ 37.3 billion) that year. In
1989, with an outflow of $ 44.2 billion, Japan became the
highest foreign investor in the world. The next year, Japan
continued to be the top FDI economy, with $ 48.1 billion
(Tejima, 1992). It has become conventional wisdom to divide
Japanese FDI into two periods: the new wave and the old
wave, with 1985 being taken as the dividing year. During the
old wave, FDI in Asia was concentrated in resource extrac-
tion, import-substituting manufacturing for the host market
and, to a smaller extent, in production of parts and components for use by the investing firm in Japan. To attain the first
objective, the favoured sites were Australia and the ASEAN-4,
whereas to attain the second and third objectives, the
favoured sites were the ANIEs. The relocation of manufacturing industries occurred largely in the labour-intensive sectors
in which Japan's comparative advantage was slipping
(Ozawa, 1985). The well-known reason behind the new wave,
which in fact comprised a sharp spurt in FDI, was the yen appreciation and rising current account surplus. This implies a
confluence of currency valuation effect and wealth effect. In
addition, the rising current account surpluses exacerbated
trade friction with the USA and the EC. Japanese firms began
to invest in those Asian countries that had current account
deficits. It promoted growth and employment in the host
countries and allowed the investing firms to circumvent the
trade barriers in the USA and the EC. In several sectors the investing firms could make use of the host countries' unfulfilled

Generalised System of Preference (GSP) quota and have a preferential access to the USA and the EC markets. During this period, investing firms became less interested in passive portfolio investments and intensified their purchase of controlling interests in the overseas production facilities.

Exploring the driving forces behind this change, one first comes to the supply-side effects of currency appreciation. The Japanese economy has been experiencing rapid structural changes, shifts which had caused fast rises in labour productivity and upward pressure on wages. In this process, Japan gained comparative advantage in many high-tech, knowledge-intensive areas but at the same time lost comparative advantage for many of the production processes which had been important to the economy in the immediately preceding period. In addition, currency appreciation made several intermediate-technology processes and industries uneconomic to run domestically. To continue to grow and retain market shares, firms had to relocate production to cheaper locations in the region. Japanese firms could relocate the whole, or part, of their production processes abroad and still be competitive, because of their firm specific advantages – such as vertical linkage to the high-tech process in Japan, accumulated product management expertise, production and marketing skills, organisational innovations which minimised the cost of transnational operations and marketing properties such as brand names (Phongpaichit, 1990). The firm-specific advantages were also realised in other manners – for example, technology contracts, brand-name franchising and co-operative production arrangements. The yen appreciated, reduced the prices of overseas assets drastically and, therefore, the cost of investing abroad: in yen terms it was reduced by half, and in those countries of the Asia-Pacific region whose currencies were pegged to the dollar, Japan's cost of investment came down substantially.

A unique feature of Japanese FDI was that, unlike other industrial countries, a significant proportion of it was made by small and medium-sized industrial enterprises. The reason simply was that in the Japanese economy small and medium-size enterprises were more active and important than in other industrialised economies. This was true in qualitative as well as quantitative terms. Since FDI entails a package transfer of capital, technology and managerial resources, apparently the small and medium-sized firms cannot compete with the large firms in terms of transferable factors. Therefore, they needed to be more creative to succeed in their overseas ventures. With regard to the factors of production, most firms in host economies in the Asia-Pacific region are similar to the small and medium-sized firms in Japan. This similarity implied that the small and medium-sized firms related to the host economies better and, therefore, were more welcome. Also, due to the high social cost of collapse of these firms, the Japanese government subsidised FDI by these firms through the Japan Overseas Development Corporation.

Compared to the 1970s, the importance of Asia declined in relative terms in the early 1980s. This was essentially due to an increase in the proportion of FDI to North America and the EC. This does not imply that flows to Asia stagnated in absolute terms: in 1985, total FDI in Asia was $ 1.9 billion, and between 1986 and 1989, it grew from $ 2.3 billion to $ 8.2 billion – that is, by three-and-a-half times. Investment in the ANIEs fell by over $ 1 billion in 1990, which reduced total flows to Asia by about the same amount, but the volume going to the ASEAN countries recorded a healthy increase in 1990 as well: over the period 1987–90 the amount of FDI going to this subgroup more than tripled (Table 4.7).

Table 4.7   Japan's Foreign Direct Investment in Asia, 1985–91 ($ m)

Year	Asia	Of which to ANIEs:	Of which to ASEAN:	Proportion of Total FDI (%)
1985	1413	717	596	9.2
1986	2327	1531	553	10.4
1987	4868	2581	1030	14.6
1988	5569	3264	1967	11.9
1989	8238	4902	2782	12.2
1990	7054	3354	3241	12.4
1991	5936	2203	3083	14.6

Source: Research Institute of Overseas Investment, *EXIM Review*, Tokyo, various issues.

As set forth in Table 4.8, during the 1985–8, the ANIEs were the greater recipients of the two country-groups. Hong Kong and Singapore were the largest recipients. (Among the ASEAN-4, Indonesia was an exception and it continued to receive large investments in oil exploration and mining sectors.) This was a reversal of the situation in the early 1980s, when the ASEAN group received larger investment than the ANIEs. Again, Indonesia had attracted large investments because of its large natural resources, low-labour cost and large domestic market potential. Towards the end of the decade, as their currencies appreciated and wages rose, the growth rate of FDI in the ANIEs stagnated while that in the ASEAN increased considerably (Table 4.8). By 1991, FDI flows in the latter group were 40 per cent higher than those towards the former. Japanese corporations felt particularly welcome in Malaysia because they were given near *carte blanche* to invest in and export to, with little consideration about bilateral economic relationships getting seriously out of joint. Malaysia's 'Look East' policy flattered Japan and it became a microcosm of precisely the sort of relationship that Japan would like to have with its Asia-Pacific neighbours (Vatikiotis, 1992). However, it was Thailand that benefited the most from Japanese FDI, by transforming its economic policy structure and by integrating its economy with the international economy, particularly with that of Japan. The investing firms found Thailand attractive for non-economic reasons as well. Both the societies had several common traits – for example, they are homogeneous, of Buddhist background and share a tradition of constitutional monarchy. In 1988 something of a Thailand rush began among the Japanese firms because they found the country closer to them emotionally and easier to access economically. Thailand is most aptly suited to become the fifth region of Asia in the near-term. The Philippines lagged behind because of its confused macroeconomic stance, lacklustre economic performance and unwelcoming policies towards FDI. Large increases in Japanese investment in services such as hotels, retailing, restaurants, leisure activities and the like are on the cards for the ASEAN region for the 1990s (*Financial Review, 1992*).

Table 4.8 Japanese Foreign Direct Investment in the Asia-Pacific Region by Country and Industry ($ m.)

Fiscal Year	Korea							Taiwan						
	1985	1986	1987	1988	1989	1990	1991	1985	1986	1987	1988	1989	1990	1991
Foodstuffs	2	4	32	14	11	11	4	1	2	12	7	27	18	6
Textiles	1	7	4	18	5	7	2	2	2	3		9	5	6
Lumber and pulp	1		2	2	1			1			3	3		3
Chemicals	3	7	14	35	41	28	57	4	13	27	24	47	40	37
Iron and steel/non-ferrous metals	2	4	18	5	15	13	12	3	25	26	28	57	48	15
Machinery	4	10	33	25	19	11	12	6	13	22	23	29	36	21
Electric/electronic	5	69	93	84	66	22	14	9	84	75	75	78	62	60
Transport equipment	12	21	31	52	68	36	34	66	72	55	19	12	13	2
Others	7	21	20	19	25	19	22	17	62	35	83	40	53	35
Manufacturing total	37	143	247	254	251	147	157	109	273	255	262	302	275	185
Agriculture and forestry														
Fisheries														
Mining														

Table 4.8 Continued

Fiscal Year	Hong Kong							Singapore						
	1985	1986	1987	1988	1989	1990	1991	1985	1986	1987	1988	1989	1990	1991
Foodstuffs	6	3	21	14	11	11	12		2	7	1	438	3	8
Textiles		1	3	6	16	4	3				2	2	101	15
Lumber and pulp				1	1	1					42	4	24	
Chemicals	1	1	5	1	7		5	6	11	146	16	42	52	45
Iron and steel/non-ferrous metals		4	8	9	10	9		6	6	14	4	13	10	7
Machinery	1	12	16	8	18	4	50	59	19	14	70	30	11	14
Electric/electronic	5	12	34	40	26	70	14	12	37	75		91	54	54
Transport equipment			1				1	4	8	1				
Others	1	19	20	6	27	15	36	4	19	11	38	58	15	34
Manufacturing total	14	52	108	85	116	114	121	92	104	269	173	678	270	177
Agriculture and forestry						2	3				1		1	
Fisheries					3							1		
Mining				1									4	

Table 4.8 Continued

Fiscal Year	Indonesia							Thailand						
	1985	1986	1987	1988	1989	1990	1991	1985	1986	1987	1988	1989	1990	1991
Foodstuffs	1		19	12	3	10	14	8	2	13	23	30	49	86
Textiles	2	4	3	63	17	65	57		3	8	30	41	88	54
Lumber and pulp	1	3	7	143	32	15	10	1	3	1	13	10	10	3
Chemicals	7	1	24	30	26	241	314	4		15	23	55	51	58
Iron and steel/non-ferrous metals	10	2	193	3	20	13	21	1	11	28	108	134	57	40
Machinery		2	2	5	2	8	21		36	13	136	181	59	77
Electric/electronic	10	5	4	14	15	5	83	4	22	91	208	243	177	203
Transport equipment	28		12	16	27	170	26	1	3	13	24	17	118	18
Others	7	9	30	12	24	9	33	6	7	28	61	78	105	56
Manufacturing total	66	26	294	298	166	536	579	25	87	210	626	789	714	595
Agriculture and forestry			8	6	1	2	1		2	4	11	12	17	18
Fisheries	6	3	4		8	12	9		1		2	3		
Mining	300	208	224	229	177	171	201						1	

Table 4.8 Continued

Fiscal Year	Indonesia							Thailand						
	1985	1986	1987	1988	1989	1990	1991	1985	1986	1987	1988	1989	1990	1991
Resources development total	306	211	236	235	186	185	211	0	3	4	13	17	18	18
Construction	5	2			1	11	2	6	9	4	16	47	23	44
Commerce	5	1	1	3		18	3	10	14	5	15	56	60	34
Finance and insurance	1	3		27	211	84	283	7	4	6	9	13	49	32
Services	25	7	13	18	57	233	23		4	3	57	150	127	33
Transportation						2	3			1	13	28	21	11
Real estate			1	4	3	36	89		2	1	50	159	110	24
Other					7				1					
Commerce and services total	36	13	15	52	279	384	403	23	34	20	160	453	390	178
Branches										16	60	16	32	16
Real-estate														
Total	**408**	**250**	**545**	**585**	**631**	**1105**	**1193**	**48**	**124**	**250**	**859**	**1275**	**1154**	**807**

Table 4.8 Continued

Fiscal Year	Malaysia							Philippines						
	1985	1986	1987	1988	1989	1990	1991	1985	1986	1987	1988	1989	1990	1991
Foodstuffs	1	10	4	1		2	7	11		30	5	1	4	2
Textiles	1			6	1	3	7			1	1	1	1	2
Lumber and pulp			1	7	8	23	16			3	15			2
Chemicals	3	6	5	21	50	96	41	6		4	4	10	13	6
Iron and steel/non-ferrous metals	9	6	11	23	45	52	94							40
Machinery	2	2		37	26	81	26				5	9	8	4
Electric/electronic	2	30	26	229	273	261	284		1	14	29	55	138	29
Transport equipment	4	3	85	4	3	11	27	23	13		16	13	19	64
Others	11	7	16	18	65	53	110	2	1	3	14	36	9	9
Manufacturing total	33	64	148	346	471	582	612	42	15	51	89	127	196	158
Agriculture and forestry		1			4	3	2					3	8	1
Fisheries					1		10				1			1
Mining	28		1		25	6	32	17	1	15	4	4	30	4

Table 4.8 Continued

Fiscal Year	Malaysia							Philippines						
	1985	1986	1987	1988	1989	1990	1991	1985	1986	1987	1988	1989	1990	1991
Resources development total	0	29	1	0	30	9	44	17	1	15	5	7	38	6
Construction	4	2	1	2	71	5	22				1	4	6	2
Commerce	37	24	6	14	25	11	5		1	3		6	1	3
Finance and insurance	2	34	1	1	40	22	58				33	1	1	
Services	1	1	5	17	10	33	72	1	3	3	2	24	7	23
Transportation				3		6						1		
Real estate		4		4	26	51	56				2	32	9	11
Other			1			5								
Commerce and services total	44	65	14	41	172	133	224	1	4	6	38	68	24	39
Branches	2					1		1	1		2			
Real estate														
Total	79	158	163	387	673	725	880	61	21	72	134	202	258	203

Table 4.8 Continued

Fiscal Year	China							Australia						
	1985	1986	1987	1988	1989	1990	1991	1985	1986	1987	1988	1989	1990	1991
Foodstuffs	4	4	4	16	13	9	19		1	8	44	60	115	39
Textiles	1	1	4	16	11	21	70			2	2		1	
Lumber and pulp	1	1	1	4	2	1	1			6	2	3		
Chemicals	5	5	5	9	11	12	11	2	1	1	31	33	5	1
Iron and steel/non-ferrous metals	3	2	7	10	6	14	11	1	1				27	48
Machinery	2	3	2	12	42	50	29	2	4	12	1	16	11	10
Electric/electronic	3	4	43	101	80	22	124	2	4	9	1	10	37	2
Transport equipment				5	1	1	9	1	103	208	123	27	160	239
Others	3	3	4	30	40	31	35	4	9	7	6	11	5	4
Manufacturing total	22	23	70	203	206	161	309	12	123	253	210	160	361	343
Agriculture and forestry	1	1	2	3		1	2	2	3	57	29	25	64	20
Fisheries	3		16	15	6	5	3		2	3	1	4	2	2
Mining	3	1			4	20	1	23	193	56	156	487	703	269

Table 4.8 Continued

Fiscal Year	China							Australia						
	1985	1986	1987	1988	1989	1990	1991	1985	1986	1987	1988	1989	1990	1991
Resources development total	4	2	18	18	10	26	6	25	198	116	186	516	769	291
Construction	1				4	7			8		13	3	1	116
Commerce	3	21	5	7	9	3	7	58	77	109	92	296	326	204
Finance and insurance		1			10	2	11	244	92	208	363	545	200	72
Services	55	102	79	65	174	137	188	70	251	103	242	991	585	264
Transportation	4	1			15	1	1			5	3	1	19	3
Real estate	11	14	61	2	9	9	16	56	127	411	1 270	1 622	1 333	1 255
Other		9	993					3	5	16		108	2	255
Commerce and services total	74	148	1138	74	221	159	223	431	560	852	1983	3566	2466	1914
Branches		53		1	1	3	41		0	1	34	14	73	2
Real-estate														
Total	100	226	1226	296	438	349	579	468	881	1222	2413	4256	3669	2550

Table 4.8 Continued

Fiscal Year	New Zealand						
	1985	1986	1987	1988	1989	1990	1991
Foodstuffs					5		11
Textiles							
Lumber and pulp		1			7	20	50
Chemicals					9		
Iron and steel/non-ferrous metals							
Machinery							
Electrical/electronic		1	5	2			
Transport equipment		25	30	24		1	
Others			2	2	1		
Manufacturing total	0	27	37	28	22	21	61
Agriculture and forestry		1	2	12	1	11	124
Fisheries							
Mining	1		1		1	1	

Table 4.8 Continued

Fiscal Year		1985	1986	1987	1988	1989	1990	1991
	New Zealand							
Resources development total		1	1	3	12	1	11	124
Construction				12				2
Commerce		22	5	22	20	7	30	7
Finance and insurance								
Services			8	17	16	28	30	14
Transportation			50		26			1
Real estate			2	30	12	43	139	27
Other				9				
Commerce and services total		22	65	81	74	78	199	51
Branches								
Real estate					3			
Total		**23**	**93**	**121**	**117**	**101**	**231**	**236**

Source: The Export Import Bank of Japan.

Australia has had a tradition of having Japanese investment in mining, which has continued. The newest development was sharp increases in investment in finance and insurance and real estate after 1987, making Australia the largest recipient of Japanese capital in the region (Table 4.8). In 1987, it absorbed $ 1.2 billion, which increased to $ 4.3 billion in 1989. However, there was a decline thereafter because of a downward trend in both the above-named services. Japan also had substantial investment in the Australian automobile sector, which continued. Unlike Australia, New Zealand attracted a scant amount of investment in the manufacturing and real estate sectors.

During the 1980s, China began to attract a great deal of Japanese FDI (Table 4.8). Although the increase was slow, there was a spurt in 1987, when it received $ 1.2 billion. This, however, was an exceptional year. The Tiananmen Square incident of 1989 sent a wave of revulsion against China in the international community and Japan's FDI flows declined. However, the acceleration of economic reforms led to a re-evaluation of China as a destination for investment. Land and labour costs in China, say in the Shengzhen Special Economic Zone (SEZ), were 40 per cent lower than those in the ASEAN region, say in Batam island. The corporate tax rate in the SEZs was as low as that in Hong Kong and per capita income in China was approaching $ 1000 (Nomura Research Institute, 1993). This made China an attractive market, particularly for consumer durables. To facilitate more FDI, the Chinese government expanded the list of industries open for investment by foreigners to include the service sector, and regions open to foreign investment were extended beyond the coastal regions to major cities along the border. In 1991, foreign investment projects in China included many mega-projects – for instance, a consortium consisting of six major Japanese trading companies was investing $ 4 billion in a large-scale petrochemical plant in Liaoning.

Electronics and electrical goods, chemicals and ferrous and non-ferrous metals were among the subsectors that attracted large amounts of Japanese FDI, with electronics and electrical goods topping the list in the manufacturing sector.

In the non-manufacturing sectors, retailing and other services and finance and insurance accounted for a dominant part of FDI. Real estate and commerce were also substantial sectors. A large part of the expansion in finance and insurance-related FDI took place in Hong Kong and Singapore. Deregulation and liberalisation in Japanese financial markets and the demand by Japanese affiliate banks and their subsidiaries in the region were responsible for expansion in finance and insurance-related investments. Expanding Japanese FDI had a good deal of impact over the region. Japanese firms formed regional networks in Asia, in which an affiliate produced labour-intensive components in one country and assembled final goods in another, while other affiliates in yet another country produced relatively capital-intensive and technology-intensive components, and some affiliates worked as the regional headquarters. Financing, procurement of spare parts and regional marketing were controlled by the regional headquarters, whereas the Japanese headquarters were generally responsible for capital investment (both financial and physical) and key components which were not available in the region (Tejima, 1992). Such networks served both the Asian and Japanese markets along with the markets in the host economy. They were frequently used as bases for exports to third countries, including North America and the EC.

Several of Japan's mega-firms in areas like automobiles and consumer electronics started using pan-regional networks for producing parts and components through an international division of labour stretching across the Asia-Pacific region. The carmakers have developed sophisticated systems in their Asian operations. Whereas production is centralised at strategic bases, the labour for parts manufacture is divided among different companies. For instance, Toyota's joint venture in Thailand supplies engines to its plants in Malaysia and New Zealand. Another automaker was producing steering parts in Malaysia and transmissions in the Philippines for its central production facility in Japan. Mitsubishi operated a joint venture firm called Proton in Malaysia. Proton produces Malaysia's national car, the Sega, which managed to find a niche in the EC – particularly the UK – markets (Kubo, 1992). Sony has production facilities for audio, TV, and video players and recorders and parts, two each in Taiwan, Korea and Thailand, three in Malaysia and one in Singapore. In 1990, a new semi-conductor factory went on stream in Thailand, and two factories in Malaysia that manufactured floppy discs and videos. Sony International of Singapore (SONICS) is Sony's regional general headquarters and is connected to factories in the region by its own communications network. At the end of 1991, Asia Matsushita Electronics Singapore (AMES) managed twenty-two of its group factories and trading companies in the region from its Singapore headquarters. Similarly, the operational headquarters of Fujikura controlled fifteen affiliated companies in the ANIEs and the ASEAN regions from Singapore.

The energy stimulating the spread of manufacturing processes throughout Asia also exists in the recipient economies. It must not be taken for a unidirectional process. In the early 1990s, the ASEAN-4 and China were actively attracting export-orientated investment from Japan and the ANIEs. Consequently, production facilities were dispersing throughout the Asia-Pacific region. Other than the manufacturing giants, the large general trading companies called the *sogo shosha* have also expanded their operations in the region considerably. Many of them have set up their regional and sub-regional headquarters in various parts of the region, Singapore being the most favoured locale. Large investors have begun to see Asia-Pacific economies as partners in the international division of labour and have launched localisation, or *genchi shugi*, operations to assimilate with the regional economies better.

For the small and medium-scale Japanese firms that invested abroad, the Asia-Pacific was the favoured region: almost 40 per cent of the total number of cases were concentrated in the region during the late 1980s. This was largely because the region helped them in minimising cost and maintain a competitive edge. If investment in manufacturing is singled out, the concentration in the Asia-Pacific region was even more pronounced: over 60 per cent of the total number of FDI cases in manufacturing were concentrated in the region. As usual, there has been a marked shift from the ANIEs to the ASEAN as favoured location, with China's attraction for the small and medium-sized firms increasing. Their favoured sectors were machinery, miscellaneous goods, textiles and metals, in that order (Adachi, 1992). In manufacturing, more than half of the small and medium-sized firms are sub-contractors. When the parent companies move their facilities off-shore and they wish to increase the local content of their products, the sub-contracting firms have little choice but to invest with the parent firm or forgo the business. This must not be taken to mean that firms do not invest of their own accord: according to a survey (Adachi, 1992), 35 per cent of the small and medium-sized firms invested on their own initiative; 25 per cent moved in on their parent firms' request; and the remaining 40 per cent claimed that their investment decision coincided with that of their parent firms. This last answer has been taken to mean pressure from the parent firm. There are firms whose off-shore operations cover more than one country of the region. Such firms divide different functions like product development, materials procurement, assembly operations and so forth into different locations and form a global network. This network helps them in optimising the locational advantage. For instance, there were TV and transistor firms that kept their product development activities in Japan, shifted assembly operations to joint ventures in China's SEZs and imported parts and dies from Hong Kong and Taiwan.

FDI by Korea

Korea was not very active in FDI in the 1970s because domestic firms lacked capital and there was a chronic deficit in the balance of payment. FDI picked up in the 1980s because manufacturing and overseas construction grew substantially as a result of an upsurge in exports. During the pre-1986 period, Korean overseas investment was dominated by large corporations' investment in construction projects abroad, whereas during the post-1986 period a rapid increase was made by small and medium-sized firms. A noteworthy upswing resulted from the domestic and external environmental changes. Domestically, the appreciation of the Korean won – brought about by a sustained surplus in the balance of payments during the period 1986–8 and steep wage-hikes triggered by labour disputes following the democratic upheavals – weakened the comparative advantage of labour-intensive industries. It forced them to the ASEAN countries, to look for lower wages. Externally, the favourable inducement policies of the ASEAN countries and protectionist stance of the industrial economies encouraged firms to shift production bases abroad. In 1987, the government introduced a formal proposal which eased regulations and improved incentives for FDI. Consequently, Korea's overseas investment by small and medium-sized enterprises surged. However, as seen in Table 4.9 below, Korea is still a small foreign investor. The largest amount of FDI went into manufacturing. Over the period 1986–91 it increased eightfold, from $ 73 million to $ 599 million. In 1991, 53 per cent of total FDI was in this sector. Fabricated metal products, basic metals and textiles and apparel were the principal activities attracting investment. Retailing and commercial investments were the next largest category, accounting for 21 per cent of the total FDI in 1991.

In the recent past, the areas of concentration were ASEAN and North America, the two regions accounting for 79 per cent of the total FDI in 1991. Although there has hardly been

Table 4.9   Korean Foreign Direct Investment 1986–91 ($ m.)

Year	Total		In ASEAN		FDI in ASEAN as proportion of total (%)
	Amount	*No. of cases*	*Amount*	*No. of cases*	
1986	183.9	52	6.9	14	3.7
1987	410.5	92	132.3	18	32.2
1988	223.8	176	42.2	70	18.9
1989	569.6	269	129.6	129	22.8
1990	959.3	339	300.5	189	31.3
1991	1125.4	453	431.3	272	38.3

Source: The Bank of Korea.

any trend (Table 4.9), the volume and proportion both increased substantially during the period 1989–91. In 1991, the Korean government revised the foreign exchange regulatory system to cope efficiently with the trend towards the globalisation of financial markets and the continued process of liberalisation and internationalisation of the Korean economy. The Foreign Exchange Management Act was also revised to streamline outdated rules that hampered Korean companies' overseas investment and to provide greater freedom in offshore financing.

Korean FDI crossed the $ 1 billion mark in 1991, of which $ 431 million, or 38 per cent, went to the ASEAN countries. In terms of volume, it was close to that made in North America, although the number of cases were far more than those in North America, at 272 for the ASEAN against 88 in the USA and Canada. This can be explained by the fact that small and medium-sized enterprises in light industries made investment in the ASEAN, whereas big corporations in capital-intensive industries – such as automobiles, iron and steel and consumer electronics – invested in North America for the purpose of tariff jumping (Korean Development Bank, 1992). The 1991 level of FDI was more than double the 1989 level. It was the first year when Korean companies' investment exceeded the inward investment. A trend was set in motion, in which Korean companies were destined to become an international force more than just exporters. The surge showed up in the Asia-Pacific region. Korea exported to the region the labour-intensive, low-wage industries that were once the backbone of the Korean export economy. China emerged as a major destination for investment because it offered distinct advantages like proximity, low-wages, labour-discipline and high productivity. Availability of a large number of ethnic Koreans, mostly in north-eastern China, provided a back-up supply of mid-level managerial manpower. Small and medium-sized Korean firms have been increasingly supplying FDI. In 1991, their share rose to 77 per cent of total Korean FDI (Hoon, 1992). In 1991, total stock of Korean FDI was $ 3.4 million for 1673 cases. The ratio of FDI stock to GNP was 1.20 per cent, very low when compared to 7.71 per cent for the USA and 6.79 for Japan.

FDI by Taiwan

With an economic growth averaging 8.7 per cent a year for nearly three decades and booming industry and export sectors, Taiwan (its official name is the Republic of China) has become a successful little industrialising country. The export boom of the 1980s has spilled over into the 1990s, adding huge sums to Taiwan's coffers. Since the mid-1980s, its trade surpluses have hovered above $ 10 billion annually. Due to the central bank's repeated purchasing of foreign currency to keep the new Taiwanese dollar from appreciating, the forex reserves ballooned. In addition, Taiwan earned a whopping $ 5 billion annually in interest income. It is little wonder that it has the second-largest forex reserves in the world. Moving off-shore for the manufacture of labour-intensive products was not following the trend for Taiwan, but an economic imperative. During the latter half of the 1980s, a severe labour shortage hit Taiwan and the wages soared. Also, the currency appreciated by more than 50 per cent against the dollar. Taiwan emerged as the largest source of FDI, after Japan, in the region. By the end of 1991, its total stock of FDI was $ 4.96 billion, of which 41 per cent or $ 2.05 billion was invested in the Asia-Pacific region. The favourite destinations for Taiwanese FDI were Malaysia, Thailand and Indonesia. In each of these, Taiwan was either the largest new investor or the second-largest after Japan (*Far Eastern Economic Review*, 1991). Taiwan also invested in the region to secure supplies of raw materials and diversify markets. As seen in Table 4.10, FDI data are incomplete. A reasonable statistical picture, however, does emerge for the 1987–90 period. Total annual flows grew from a mere $ 0.5 billion to $ 4.7 billion over this period, a ninefold increase. However, 1991 turned out to be a year of steep decline, particularly in Thailand and the Philippines. The latter received virtually no new investment. This was essentially because Taiwan legalised FDI to the mainland in 1991. Similar to the pattern in Korea, the FDI share from Taiwan's small and medium-sized firms has increased considerably, rising to over two-thirds of the total number of cases.

Table 4.10   Taiwanese Foreign Direct Investment, 1986–91 ($ m.)

Year	Total in Asia		In ASEAN-4		In China	
	Amount	No. of cases	Amount	No. of cases	Amount	No. of cases
1986	92	44	92	44		
1987	500	265	400	185	100	80
1988	2698	959	2178	522	520	437
1989	2430	1197	1993	645	437	552
1990	4690	1783	3903	666	984	1117
1991	N/A	N/A	1775	217	N/A	N/A

Source: The Ministry of Economic Affairs, Government of the Republic of China, 'Investment Commission Report', Taipei, 1991.

Before 1987, Taiwanese citizens who visited mainland China were subject to criminal prosecution. However, in 1987 Taiwan adopted a flexible policy towards China and it soon began to emerge as another favourite location for FDI. As mentioned earlier, low-priced land and lower wages than ASEAN made China an attractive alternative location. Similarity in culture and language was another motivation. However, the average size of investment in China was far lower than that for the ASEAN: it was $ 0.93 million for the former in 1990, but $ 4.54 million for the latter (Chiu and Chung, 1992). The reason was that investors in the ASEAN were mostly medium-size to large-size firms, whereas FDI on the mainland was dominated by small and medium-sized firms. It was the labour-intensive and processing industries that moved to the mainland. After investment was legalised in 1991, Taiwanese firms began scouting for Western partners to carry out joint ventures on the mainland. Such tie-ups are expected to provide Taiwanese investors with access to state-of-the-art technology and much-needed market channels (Shapiro, 1991). This amounts to an expansion of the pan-Asian industrialisation concept.

With political barriers gone, FDI flows towards the mainland are expected to overtake those towards the ASEAN region. As regards geographical distribution, a high concentration was observed in Guangdong and Fujian provinces. The three top industrial sectors were electrical and electronic components, vehicles and shoes. These and other FDI projects have given an impetus to semi-finished materials, parts and raw materials producing industries in the mainland (Chiu and Chung, 1992).

FDI by Australia

Australia is not a net-investor. It has, in fact, been a large net absorber. Its inward FDI from the OECD countries is seven to eight times larger than its outward FDI. In whatever little FDI it makes, New Zealand has a predominant share.

Geographical and historical links between Australia and New Zealand have been strong. That apart, the two are tied to each other by two trade and economic co-operation agreements. Therefore, in the Asia-Pacific region, New Zealand has historically attracted an overwhelming proportion of Australian FDI (Table 4.11), while paltry sums have gone to the ASEAN region. That being said, it must not be overlooked that the principal destinations of the Australian FDI were the OECD countries, not the Asia-Pacific region. The OECD has traditionally accounted for 90 per cent or more of Australian FDI flows.

PERIPHERAL INTERMEDIATION AND TECHNOLOGICAL INTERDEPENDENCE

Australia and New Zealand are technologically advanced economies because they have continually received trans-

Table 4.11   Australian Foreign Direct Investment, 1986–91 ($ m.)

Year	Total	In New Zealand	In ASEAN
1986	4 862	2	111
1987	12 870	1 550	252
1988	16 179	1 319	−108
1989	12 791	565	797
1990	4 890	1 433	739
1991	3 410	−276	−287

Source: Australian Bureau of Statistics. *International Investment Position of Australia*, Canberra, June 1992.

plants of leading-edge technology from the other OECD countries along with their FDI inflows. Although they managed to keep abreast, they did not interact much technologically with the regional economies. Australia needs to shed its little-house-on-the-prairie image and begin to export technology to the regional economies, because its technological capabilities are of a high order. The process of industrialisation in the region, as detailed in the preceding sections, has greatly influenced the technological development of the regional economies. As stated earlier, one of the characteristic processes of industrialisation in the region was an increasingly inter-regional nature of production and a horizontal divisional of labour, or the so-called 'peripheral intermediation' (Mirza, 1986). In this process, production in a given country predominantly utilised inputs from the other regional economies. This was a process – as we saw – based on rapid growth in exports and imports of intermediate inputs, machine components and capital goods which made technology a pan-regional phenomenon.

It was natural that some technological dualism would occur under these circumstances. Components, parts and sub-assemblies produced in different countries had to be of precise specifications so that they would fit into the wider whole of the final product or production process. Therefore, highly sophisticated and automated techniques were required to be adopted in countries where labour was abundant and where the general technological level was not very high. This pattern of industrialisation enabled the industrialising developing country to acquire and operate imported high-tech equipment and to control imported production processes, without offering it an opportunity to innovate like Japan. The scope for top-down adaption of technology in the short-term was also limited. The countries of the region which participated in this process of industrialisation focused their attention on internationally standardised high-tech industries such as electronics and computers, and on the need to provide a skilled labour force and technicians to operate the related high-tech production processes (Morris-Suzuki, 1992).

The process of regional industrialisation where large and multinational firms located different parts of their production processes in different parts of the region created functional specialisation, with different Asia-Pacific economies concentrating on the manufacture of particular intermediate goods, components or sub-assemblies. This specialisation of production processes was reflected in a growing specialisation of technology. In sum, this division of labour created a new inter-regional division of knowledge. The probability of large regional firms and multinationals locating R&D operation in the Asia-Pacific region therefore considerably increased. A growing number of regional and multinational firms have established their training and research facilities in the region. This included giants like Nestlé and Ciba-Geigy. The ability of an economy to enhance R&D involvement will depend on its level of technological education, the quality of communications infrastructure and its technology policy. Korea, Taiwan and Singapore are highly suited for the establishment of R&D and training facilities because their technological development has reached a relatively higher stage. After the industrialised countries of the region, Korea and Taiwan have the best industrial research capabilities. They invested close to 2 per cent of GNP in R&D, while Singapore invested over 1 per cent. In all the three countries, educational and communications facilities are of a superior quality and their industrialisation had involved peripheral intermediation (Nelson, 1990). Unlike these three, Thailand, Malaysia and Indonesia, despite rapid industrialisation, possessed few attributes likely to encourage the growth of R&D and training facilities (Morris-Suzuki, 1992). Technological advancement has relatively lagged in this group of economies.

ECONOMIC ASSISTANCE

There was a tradition of French bilateral economic assistance concentrating on Africa, British on the Commonwealth countries and the Japanese on the Asia-Pacific region. Until 1988, policy-makers in Japan firmly believed that Japanese economic assistance must adhere to the above paradigm and retain its regional forms. This conviction was based both on strong emotional identification with the region and pragmatic criteria. The former was born of historical and cultural links, whereas the latter was created by similarity in economic philosophy. The early documents of Economic Planning Agency (EPA), the Ministry of International Trade and Industry (MITI) and the Ministry of Foreign Affairs (MFA), when talking about economic assistance to LDCs always used the words *keizai kyoryok*, or economic co-operation. There was no reference to the world *enjo*, or aid. This was not a mere accidental choice of words but a matter of attitude and disposition. The regional economies displayed higher growth potential and tenacious self-help efforts. Their accomplishments and take-off merited the extra attention and resources that Japan provided.

Until the early 1980s, more than 70 per cent of Japanese official development assistance (ODA) went to the Asia-Pacific region. In the mid-1980s, the proportion declined, but it was still more than 65 per cent of the total ODA. The decline was partly caused by Japan's increasing emphasis on multilateral financial institutions like the World Bank, the IMF and the Asian Development Bank (ADB). Since the late 1980s, Japan has consciously expanded its collaboration with the World Bank. In 1992, it accounted for 9.97 per cent of the World Bank's subscribed capital. Since 1970 it contributed $ 12.5 billion in financing the Bank-assisted projects, half of them were in the Asia-Pacific region (*Asian Finance*, 1991). In the ADB, it is the largest shareholder, along with the USA, and plays a domineering role. In 1988, after the announcement of the International Co-operation Initiative, Japan accelerated the expansion of its horizons and globalisation of bilateral assistance efforts.

Since the birth of the Japanese economic assistance programme took place essentially in an environment of *keizai kyoryok*, the private sector has had a greater role to play in economic assistance than in other donor countries. One advantage of private sector involvement was that a link was established between the external economic activities of the donor and recipient economies. If one of the implicit objectives of economic assistance is to help the recipient develop as an open market economy and a full-blooded partner in international trade and investment, elements of commercialism in the assistance package need not be abhorred – if anything, they need to be encouraged, so long as gains are shared by the two sides. If the economic assistance takes place in a private sector framework, exchange of vital commercial inputs like technology, managerial skills and access to markets can be done in an optimal manner. Ozawa (1989) insists that a commercially motivated and market-mediated economic assistance package has greater chances of turning into a dynamic positive-sum game than one in which economic assistance is based on mere altruistic consideration. Besides, the economies of recipient developing countries will not become vigorous without developing the potential of their private sectors. A dynamic private sector is a necessary condition of economic growth. The thinking of economic planners has changed its course with a bang, from Marx to markets. Additionally, in the ultimate analysis, ODA alone cannot sufficiently meet the development needs of the developing economies. When it joins hands with private sector efforts, the economic co-operation programme is rendered more comprehensive.

The private sector slant of the Japanese assistance efforts has persisted over the years. The policy objective of the plan made public in 1987 was to tie together economic assistance, private capital and trade. Its slogan was '*sanmi-ittai*' or 'three sides, one body'. Sometimes this private sector involvement creates confusion regarding Japan's definition of economic assistance and opens it to the charge that it is trying to promote its exports under the guise of economic assistance and that its motives are more commercial than altruistic. The fact that it did so in the early period of its economic assistance programme enhances such a suspicion (Orr, 1989). But it strains credulity to believe that an extremely successful exporter like Japan would need a $ 10 billion economic assistance programme to promote its exports (Das, 1993).

By 1989, Japan had overtaken the USA and become the largest bilateral donor in the world. As Table 4.12 shows, the

Table 4.12   Japan's ODA Distribution in the Asia-Pacific Region, 1980–90 ($ m.)

	1980	1985	1986	1987	1988	1989	1990
Asia	1383 (70.5)[a]	1732 (67.8)	2494 (64.8)	3416 (65.1)	4039 (62.8)	4240 (62.5)	4117 (59.3)
North-east Asia	82 (4.2)	392 (15.3)	490 (12.7)	557 (11.0)	730 (11.4)	919 (13.6)	835 (12.0)
South-east Asia	861 (44.0)	962 (37.6)	1169 (30.4)	1866 (35.6)	2197 (34.2)	2226 (32.8)	2379 (34.3)

Source: Ministry of Finance, *Japan's ODA 1991*, Tokyo, March 1992.
[a] Figures in parentheses represent the share in total ODA.

Asia-Pacific region continued to receive an overwhelming – albeit declining – share of Japanese bilateral ODA. Due to increased flows to sub-Saharan Africa, Latin America and the LDCs and to the multilateral financial institutions, the share of the Asia-Pacific region declined from 68 per cent of the total ODA in 1985 to 59 per cent in 1990. However, in absolute terms the bilateral flows to the region soared, increasing three-fold over the 1980–90 period (Table 4.12). In fact, the rate of increase during the latter half of the 1980s was much faster – between 1985 and 1990 ODA increased from $ 1.7 billion to $ 4.1 billion, a two-and-a-half times increase. The north-eastern region which comprised the ANIEs and China received far less than the south-eastern region which comprised the ASEAN countries. Virtually all of the disbursement to the north-eastern region went to China. Hong Kong did not receive any Japanese economic assistance and Taiwan stopped receiving it in 1972. Korea had dropped off the list of the top ten recipients after 1981, and ODA to Korea was terminated in 1990 because it had graduated from being a recipient to being a donor country. These countries did continue to receive Japan's technical co-operation and assistance. Over the 1980s, the three top recipients of Japanese bilateral assistance were Indonesia, China and the Philippines, in that order. As the ASEAN countries develop and begin to catch up with the ANIEs, the pattern of ODA to those countries will also shift towards developmental loans and technical co-operation (Yasutomo, 1986).

I have discussed earlier how Japan's ODA was followed by private sector investment in a methodological manner. Although Japan's Overseas Economic Co-operation Fund (OECF) has supplied finances largely for the development of infrastructure in the recipient economies since 1966, along with the EXIM Bank of Japan it also carried out equity investment to assist industrial projects in the developing economies. Another organisation called the Japan International Development Organisation (JAIDO) was established jointly by the OECF and large Japanese corporations in 1989, with the latter contributing two-thirds of the financial resources, for making equity investments in industrial co-operation-related projects. JAIDO was the brain child of *Keidanren*, or the Federation of Economic Organisations, which expected JAIDO to begin reinforcing the ODA-related efforts in the short term. The OECF made equity investment through another corporation, called the Japan ASEAN Investment Company (JAIC), which has been operating since 1981. The JAIC has 137 member corporations which own its shares. By 1990, the JAIC had floated five investment funds, the smallest being Y7 bn. and the largest Y71.6 bn., for investment in industrial projects in the ASEAN region. Institutions like the JAIDO and the JAIC establish an invaluable link between the ODA and private sector investment and pragmatically accelerate Japan's ODI and FDI flows into viable industrial projects. Due to active involvement of private sector criteria like market considerations, economic viability and return on investment are given adequate considerations. The *Keidanren* had plans for launching an identical institution for enhancing investment activities in China. This pattern of economic assistance, and on such a significant dimensions, has made the regional economic bond stronger.

Korea and Taiwan have both turned into donor countries. In 1991, the former disbursed $ 70 million and the latter $ 121 million. The amounts are too tiny to matter and did not go to Asia-Pacific countries. The same was the case with China, which disbursed $ 120 million in 1991 (OECD, 1992).

CONCLUSION

The economies of the Asia-Pacific region seem to be behaving like the flying geese, where the ones that are behind in terms of economic development benefit from those that are ahead, and in the process the growth of the group quickens. Japan is the undisputed economic leader of the flying geese formation, while China is the last bird. The leader-follower relationship in the region has worked well. Market-led regional economic co-operation may proceed by way of trade motivated by Heckcher-Ohlinian factors or by the product-cycle dynamism. Since the regional economies were at varying levels of economic development, there was a wide-range in their K/L ratio and therefore the Heckcher-Ohlinian theory operated smoothly. Also, product life cycle has operated well in a large range of products. Trade statistics for the twelve Asia-Pacific economies demonstrated that the long-term average growth rate of intra-trade was higher than those in the other two large economic blocs, the EC and the NAFTA. An analysis of trade matrix of the regional economies also provided unambiguous evidence of increasing interdependence in the region. The direction of exports changed, conforming the increasing intra-regional trade hypothesis. With growing industrialisation, trade expansion has led to expansion in intra-industry trade. Some intra-industry trade existed in the 1970s, and increased considerably over the 1980s. In addition, trade in services expanded faster in the region than in the rest of the world.

Computations of revealed comparative advantage (RCA) showed that in several product lines, with structural transformation of its economy, Japan kept losing comparative advantage while the ANIEs, the ASEAN-4 and later China kept catching up. This process led to interesting changes, from complementary to competitive relationships between countries and country-groups in the region. The industrial structure of the ANIEs was such that they had to rely on Japan for technology and intermediate and capital goods. This one feature of their economies closely integrated their economies with that of Japan. Their success in penetrating the Japanese markets was limited; they depended more on the US markets for their exports. After the yen appreciation, the ANIEs' penetration of Japanese markets increased substantially, particularly in the manufactured goods.

Japan has tried to bolster growth in ASEAN by improving infrastructure and skills and enhancing supply capabilities. Advisory groups were sent by the MITI to improve domestic macroeconomic and industrial policies. To be sure, careful utilisation of market forces was part of the advice, but *laissez faire* was seldom promoted. Similar moves were made at the microeconomic or firm level. These developments portend to the emergence of a regional economy.

Japan, Korea and Taiwan have made large investments in the regional economies, leading to the emergence of several nationwide and sub-regional industrial areas. These large dosages of investment integrated several industrial sectors and propelled the region towards industrial integration. Japanese firms played a leading role. There were both supply-side forces and demand-side forces that drove the Japanese firms to make investment in the region. It was not merely the large corporations – the small and medium-sized firms participated in full swing in Japanese FDI expansion in the region. Initially Japanese FDI in the ANIEs was higher than that in the ASEAN region. In the mid-1980s the situation reversed. In the late 1980s and early 1990, as the currencies in the ANIEs appreciated and wages soared, the growth of FDI in the ANIEs stagnated while that in ASEAN increased considerably. Malaysia and Thailand became favourite countries for FDI. Also, interest in China gradually increased. Several of Japan's mega-firms in areas like automobiles and consumer electronics started using pan-regional networks for producing parts and components through an international division of labour stretching across the Asia-Pacific region. Also, the large general trading companies – *sogo shosha* – have expanded their operations in the region significantly.

During the latter half of the 1980s, Korea emerged as an investor of significance in the region. This upswing was the result of domestic and external economic changes. The largest amount of investment went into the manufacturing sector in the ASEAN region. In 1991, Korea's total FDI crossed the $ 1 billion mark. It was the first year when Korean companies' investment exceeded inward investment. This surge showed up in the Asia-Pacific region. China in particular emerged as a major destination because it offered distinct advantages. Taiwan was another cash-rich economy of the region, investing large dosages of FDI in the region. One of the reasons why it succeeded in becoming the second-largest investor in the region was its large forex reserves. By the end of 1991, its total stock of FDI was $ 4.96 billion, of which $ 2.05 billion was in the Asia-Pacific region. After 1987, when political obstacles were removed, China began to receive a substantial part of Taiwanese FDI.

One of the characteristics of the industrialisation in the region was 'peripheral intermediation', that is, an increasingly inter-regional nature of production and a horizontal division of labour. This process was based on rapid growth in exports and imports of intermediate inputs, machine components and capital goods and made technology a pan-regional phenomenon. Also, countries in the region created a functional specialisation in the manufacture of particular intermediate goods, components and sub-assemblies. This kind of division of labour in the region created an inter-regional division of knowledge.

The accepted and traditional concentration of Japanese bilateral assistance was the Asia-Pacific region. Although this concentration began to decline in the mid-1980s because of Japan's attempts to globalise its disbursements and play a more active role in the multilateral financial institutions, in absolute terms bilateral flows to the Asia-Pacific region soared, increasing threefold over the 1980–90 period. The ANIEs' share in Japan's ODA is relatively much less than that of the ASEAN, while China turned into a major recipient. The private sector has had a great deal of involvement in Japan's economic assistance efforts, which in turn made regional economic bonds stronger.

5 The Undercurrents of Integration

Institutional regional integration on the line of Viner's theory of customs union and Mundell's theory of monetary union are not the only modes of integration of neigbouring economies. It is absolutely feasible for neighbouring countries to develop close economic ties in terms of trade links and financial interdependence without having any formal economic integration arrangement. Increase in trade in goods and services and exchange of factors of production may well be totally market-driven, needing little institutional assistance. Intense interaction between spatial units creates functional economic regions or zones. Flow variables, like trade and financial flows, yield a good measure of this genre of regional integration. It corresponds more to Losch and Christaller's concept of nodal regions, which defines economic zones by analysing the interaction and interdependence between them. Implicit in it is the concept of interaction between centres and peripheries.

This concept has a great deal of relevance to the Asia-Pacific region because, although formal economic integration arrangements such as the ASEAN Free Trade Area (AFTA)[1] and the Australia-New Zealand Closer Economic Relations Trade Agreement (ANZCERTA) did emerge in the region, several sub-regional economic zones have emerged in a non-institutionalised manner. They are of functional variety and based on mutually supportive economic relationships. They essentially came into being through the operation of market forces and the strength of brisk regional growth, expanding regional structure and the wealth effect resulting from the confluence of the two. The increased exchange of goods and services among the neighbouring economies is sure to encourage specialisation and more efficient use of human

191

capital and natural resources. In turn, the more productive use of resources will enable the sub-regions to trade more efficiently in global markets, yielding further gains in specialisation and technology acquisition. Consequently, the economic prospects of the sub-regions will improve and foreign investment from the industrialised economies will continue to rise. Although market forces initiated the development of these sub-regional economic zones, they received formal recognition, encouragement and guidance from the governments of the participating countries.

There is another reason why it is imperative for Japan and the four ANIEs to expand their economic activity in the surrounding geographical regions in such a manner that market-led economic zones are created. All five of them are economic over-achievers and have recorded high growth rates in output which, in turn, were caused by high growth rates of productivity. Productivity is the most telling measure of economic performance. The faster the rate of productivity growth, the faster will the economy grow without igniting inflation. In the five countries named above, a circular and cumulative causation developed between economic growth and productivity growth which led to an upward spiral of industrial growth.

The standard one-way causality of growth is characterised by the conventional neo-classical relationship:

$$g = f(N, L, K, T)$$

where growth rate g is considered a function of the static factors of production, land, labour and capital – denoted by N, L, and K respectively – and technology, T. This formulation takes T as exogenously determined. Since it does not determine the growth rate of T, it cannot explain the growth rate of productivity. Therefore, the conventional formulation is inappropriate for the above-named set of countries because productivity has been of vital importance for growth-rate determination in these countries. Technology imports raised productivity in these economies. Productivity was also favourably affected by operating foreign technology on a scale sufficient to minimise unit costs and from learning how to use it efficiently and innovatively. This, in turn, added up to determine the growth rate of output. Growth depended on productivity, and productivity depended on technology which, in turn, depended on investment, because technology is essentially embodied in plant and equipment. The last link in this chain of causation is that investment depended on growth rate. Therefore, to sum up, growth rate depended on productivity and productivity depended on growth. The circle of causation is thus complete and can be represented by the following formulation:

$$p = g\,(x_1, x_2, x_3 \ldots x_n)$$

where *p* is the growth rate of productivity. It is a function of *g* which can be decomposed into various static and dynamic factors of production – that is, other than *N*, *L*, *K*. These factors include technology, scale economies and learning by doing (Amsden, 1989). This is a realistic scenario, and *if* Japan and the ANIEs have to keep their growth and productivity momentum going, they can neither afford to let N and L work as bottlenecks nor thwart scale economies in production. When such a stage in the economic growth process is reached, these economies will logically need to expand in the adjoining geographical regions in search of fresh factors of production as well as new markets. This is exactly what they did by forming sub-regional economic zones with the neighbouring economies.

The principal sub-regional zones that have emerged or are under way are:

- The growth triangle between Malaysia, Singapore and Indonesia
- The baht zone
- Hong Kong and the Guangdong region of China, or the Pearl River delta
- Taiwan and the Fujian region of China
- The Yellow Sea zone, or South Korea and the Shangdong region of China
- The Japan Sea Rim zone.

As stated previously, although these zones were initiated by private sector initiative, the first one was formally established after the Singapore government's endeavours. In the case of the third, fourth and fifth, the participating countries' provided encouragement by eliminating the barriers to trade and investments. China's adoption of an 'open door' policy was a highly favourable development in this regard, as it designated these areas as Special Economic Zones (SEZs). The four ANIEs and Japan worked as effective catalysts in the formation of sub-regional economic zones.

THE GROWTH TRIANGLE

Economic links among the six ASEAN countries were traditionally weak. They were confined to common stands in the General Agreement on Tariffs and Trade (GATT) and the various Asia-Pacific fora, reduction in tariffs in some products through Preferential Tariff Arrangement Scheme (PTAS), the ASEAN Industrial Project Scheme and the Asean Industrial Joint Venture Scheme. All of these were official or government-to-government points of contact. Singapore was the only economy in the ASEAN region that had strong economic relations with Indonesia and Malaysia, particularly with the adjoining Johor state of Malaysia. This was essentially because of the geographical location of Singapore, entrepôt trade and its role as a middleman economy. During the first half of the 1980s, the private sectors in Singapore and Johor had made some progress towards economic collaboration. But during the latter half they made impressive strides in market integration. To strengthen market forces and quicken the pace of economic integration by reducing uncertainties, the 'Growth Triangle' was first proposed in December 1989 by Singapore. It comprised Singapore, Johor and the Indonesian islands of Batan and Bintan. These two islands are part of Indonesia's Rian archipelago. The proposal made good economic sense and was readily accepted because enlightened self-interest prevailed among the three participating economies.

The strengths of the Singapore economy lay in its strategic geographical location, skilled and trained work force, well-developed physical and telecommunications infrastructure, management experience, links with international markets, and strong financial and other service sectors. Its weakness lay in its small territorial size and declining population growth causing labour shortage. Over the years, the importance of entrepôt trade has declined substantially in the Singaporean economy. In its present form, it is a broad-based manufacturing-service economy. Owing to large multinational investments in infrastructure and continuous upgrading of the labour force, the economy has managed to maintain its competitive edge. During the favourable international trade climate, Singapore's exports grew at a rapid rate. The economy continued to diversify and restructure. Official policy was laid down to develop it as a 'total business centre', or a site for operational headquarters for the multinational corporations by making large investments in the services sector.

Singapore's economic success was indeed impressive, but its future growth was being hemmed in by the smallness of its territory and an oppressing labour scarcity. In addition, the cost of doing business had risen sharply with rapid economic growth (Krause *et al.*, 1987). High and rising labour and land costs compounded with an appreciating Singapore dollar, cutting into the profit margins and making Singapore a far from ideal business location. Manufactured exports began to lose their competitiveness and the multinational corporations (MNCs) began to slow down their investments. Although wages and property price rises were dampened by the 1985–6 recession, they soon began to accelerate again. Nominal wages soared by an average of 12 per cent per year in 1989 and 1990 when measured in Singapore dollars, but these hikes worked out to 15 per cent and 21 per cent respectively when denoted in US dollars. To exacerbate this situation, changes in labour productivity fell far short of real wage increases. In 1989 and 1990, they were 4.8 per cent and 3.4 per cent respectively, and in the manufacturing sector they were even lower, at 2.5 per cent and 3.6 per cent respectively

(Yuan, 1991; Kraas, 1992). Both rental and sale prices of factory space and commercial property accelerated substantially over the 1986–90 period. Thus viewed, in the latter half of the 1980s, the cost of doing business in Singapore rose inordinately. Increases in the foreign worker levy and a ceiling on the number of foreign workers who can be employed by each company restricted the availability of fresh foreign workers. Singapore, therefore, has begun to scale down its future projections of growth rate. Thus there was a compelling, if not imperative, need for Singapore to expand its economic activity – particularly in manufacturing – in the adjacent northern and southern areas. The proximity of Johor and Rian islands is an essential element that encouraged investment there. Professionals from Singapore can transact business in these areas and return within a day. It implies easy access and minimal travel and transport costs.

As opposed to this, Malaysia and Indonesia are rich in natural and human resources, and the former is also known for its efficient bureaucracy. The 1985–6 recession and slump in commodity prices persuaded the managers of these economies to adopt an outward-looking economic strategy, that is, one entailing export-led industrialisation. They also began to deregulate and liberalise. Malaysia even started a privatisation programme. The result was a radical increase in foreign investment in the two economies. Being so close to Singapore, they were not oblivious of its economic success and the possibilities of exploiting the spill-over effects of this growth pole. Collaborating with Singapore provided them with the possibilities of making their industrial structure more competitive, as well as plugging them into the international economy. Following economic deregulation in Malaysia, the Johor state government announced the policy of 'twinning' with Singapore in 1988. The Malaysian Institute of Economic Research (MIER) had posited the 'twinning' concept for accelerating Johor's restructuring as an industrialised economy by attracting labour-intensive industries from Singapore (MIER, 1989). Improvement in the Malaysian infrastructure was certainly badly needed for this purpose. 'Twinning' was regarded as highly plausible because Johor had good economic ties with Singapore and 40 per cent of Singapore-Malaysia trade passed through Johor. In addition, both push and pull factors were in operation, the former being represented by the land and labour constraints in Singapore, and the latter by cheap factors of production in Johor, access to the Generalised System of Preferences (GSP) and liberalisation in FDI policies in Malaysia.

Clear complementarities existed between the factor endowments of the three partners. Singapore's well-developed infrastructure, high-tech industrial sector, sophisticated service sector and managerial capabilities of a high order sit well with Johor's semi-skilled labour and Rian's ample supply of cheap land and labour. Comparative advantage arose out of these differences in factor endowment. Differences in relative factor prices clearly reflected the differences in factor endowments. Land prices in Johor and Batan were less than half those in Singapore in 1990. The ratio of wages of skilled labour between Singapore, Johor and Batan was 3:2:1 (Yuan, 1991). To exploit the variation in factor endowments, firms can locate production facilities according to the factor needs of the production process. For instance, in the Growth Triangle high-tech operations can be located in Singapore, medium-technology operations in Johor and labour-intensive or assembly-type operations in Batan or Bintan islands. Thus the Triangle provides wide possibilities for vertical integration and MNCs can consider it for a manufacturing base. As interaction between centre and periphery picks up momentum, the Triangle will expand. This industrial zone contained, by early 1992, the production bases of forty-four MNCs. The Japanese were represented by fifteen large enterprises and had the largest presence (*Nikkei Weekly*, 1992), Japan's status as the largest investor in the Growth Triangle is expected to continue. Singapore was the second-largest investor and Taiwan the third-largest.

The newest trend among MNCs is to avoid scattering their activities geographically and to regionalise them, preferring to focus their off-shore production in a few select regions. Each region has its metropolitan hub which functions as a servicing, co-ordinating and financial nodal point for the regional activities. In the Asia-Pacific region, Hong Kong, Singapore and, to a limited degree, Bangkok have emerged as such modal points. Creation and expansion of the Growth Triangle will add to the nodal value of Singapore (Ng and Wong, 1991). Apart from the MNCs, indigenous transnational enterprises have emerged in the three participating countries. For instance, the Sime Darby and MMC groups of Malaysia; the Keppel and Singapore Technology groups in Singapore; and the Liem Sioe Liong and Lippo groups in Indonesia. As these groups expand and internationalise their activities, their natural preference will be to begin with the neighbouring regions. Investments by indigenous transnationals will provide impetus to the Growth Triangle (Ng and Wong, 1991).

THE BAHT ZONE

With peace settling in the Indochina region, economic growth has picked up momentum. Thailand made steady economic progress over the 1980s and benefited from double-figure growth rates, emerging as the sub-regional economic leader. Since Thailand is currently not only the most successful economy of the Indochina region but also one of the success stories of the south-east Asian region, and it is believed that it will succeed in creating an economic zone in Indochina. Its GDP growth rate in real terms was 10.7 per cent over the period 1987–91. It has created a diversified industrial base for sustained growth and taken several liberalisation measures to transform its financial sector, actively working on its plan to develop a so-called 'baht economic zone', based on its currency. Laos, Cambodia, Myanmar and Vietnam had weak, unstable, inflation-ridden economies with poor financial systems. Their currencies hardly inspired any confidence among people using them. As opposed to this, the Thai baht has been strong and stable. With its minimum exchange risk and easy convertibility into US dollars and the yen, it appeared attractive and inspired confidence among the neighbouring economies (see Map 5.1).

Map 5.1   The Baht Zone

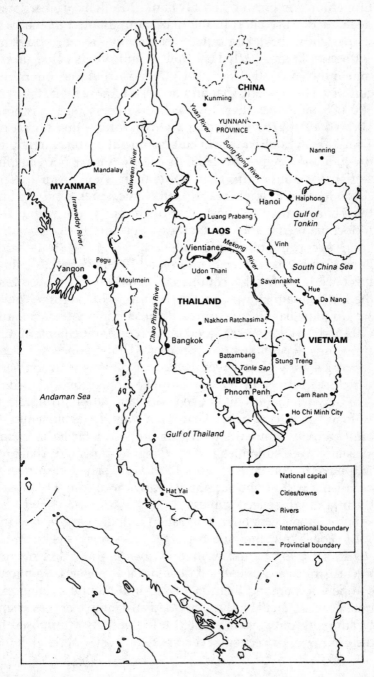

CHINA

Kunming

YUNNAN
PROVINCE

Nanning

Yuan River

Song Hong River

Mandalay

Salween River

MYANMAR

Hanoi   Haiphong

*Gulf of
Tonkin*

Irrawaddy River

Luang Prabang

LAOS

Vientiane   *Mekong River*

Vinh   *South China Sea*

Pegu

Udon Thani

Yangon

Moulmein

Savannakhet

Hue

Chao Phraya River

THAILAND

Da Nang

Nakhon Ratchasima

Bangkok   VIETNAM

Battambang   Stung Treng

Tonle Sap

CAMBODIA

Andaman Sea

Phnom Penh   Cam Ranh

Ho Chi Minh City

Gulf of Thailand

Hat Yai

- ● National capital
- ● Cities/towns
- ⌇ Rivers
- –·– International boundary
- ––– Provincial boundary

To encourage and expand the use of the baht in the Indochina region, the central bank, the Bank of Thailand, decided to raise sharply the maximum amount of the baht which could be taken out of the country to neighbouring countries. Before 1991, Thai traders and others could take a maximum of 200 000 baht ($ 1 = 25.5 baht) in cash out of the country. The Bank of Thailand decided to raise the amount to 500 000 baht. Another key decision in this regard was to allow the baht to be taken to Vietnam for the first time. The Thai baht was already working as a settlement currency in the Indochina region. In 1992, its use as a formal currency for settlement started in Thai trade with Vietnam also. The central bank took these pro-active measures as a part of the Thai strategy to boost investment and trade within the Indochina region and in the process develop a baht economic zone. According to official statistics, in 1991 Thai trade with Laos, Cambodia and Vietnam topped 10 billion baht. Against this backdrop, the Thai commercial banks rapidly moved into the Indochina region and set up branches. In Laos, they have set up joint banking ventures. Similar plans were afoot for Cambodia (Ogasawara, 1992). Active involvement in the Indochina economies will promote Thai trade with these countries as well as opening more avenues for investment which, in turn, will have a salutary impact over the Thai economy. Thailand will, indeed, face competition from other ASEAN countries. For instance, it was up against tough Singaporean competition in Cambodia. Malaysia also has eyes on these economies and their market potential. Thailand will have to continue to work hard at its baht zone strategy because it will not be accomplished without competing with the other regional economies.

Sub-regional economic integration is under way beyond the baht zone. As the sub-regional economies began their structural reforms and economic liberalisation, and moved towards outward-orientated development policies, economic co-operation among them increased in a natural manner. As noted earlier, Thailand has provided an example of the benefit of adopting outward-orientated trade policies as opposed to the policies of protectionism and self-sufficiency popular in the sub-region in the past. The Thai experience, as well as that of the east Asian economies, has encouraged the decentralisation of economies and the use of the market as a guide to policy framework. Cross-border trade has mushroomed and much – if not most – of it is unregulated. In some areas, unofficial trade accounts for more than half of total trade (Asian Development Bank, 1993). Trade in services has also been increasing rapidly. Infrastructure improvement is a necessary but not sufficient condition for expanding sub-regional trade and investment. The sub-region was being assisted by several multilateral organisations and donor countries in this respect in the early 1990s, a wide variety of resources being provided to improve infrastructure and to implement economic reforms. Most of this support was country-specific, designed to strengthen the country's basic economic and social infrastructure and improve the overall economic management. Only the Asian Development Bank (ADB) has a major project for the whole of the sub-region. Its broad aim is to help the sub-regional economies to work together more efficiently as well as to identify specific sub-regional projects suitable for development assistance. The ADB also has plans to work as a catalyst in bringing the regional economies together by lending its institutional support.

During the first quarter of 1993, Thailand established an off-shore banking centre in Bangkok, called the Bangkok International Banking Facility (BIFB), with an objective to promote it as a centre for international finance for the Indochina region. Of the thirty-two foreign banks selected for the facility, eight were based in the USA, eleven were European, eight were Japanese and five were large multinational Asia-based banks. This was a clear and clever move to exploit geographic advantage (Owens, 1993). The new financial centre is expected to take some business away from rivals Singapore and Hong Kong, and can potentially become a financial hub for the Indochina region by the end of the century. The Thai central banking authorities had waited long enough to ensure that local banks are ready to compete before doors are opened for unbridled competition with foreign banks.

THE HONG KONG-GUANGDONG NEXUS

The most outstanding feature of the city economy of Hong Kong has been its tremendous growth over the period 1960–90, when its average annual growth rate in nominal terms was 17.4 per cent and in real terms 9.8 per cent. Its per capita income crossed $ 11 000 in 1990, putting it in the World Bank's category of high-income countries. An economy growing at the rate of 9 per cent per annum doubles its GDP in about eight years. Sustained growth at high level and a strong currency were behind Hong Kong's high income levels. An important feature of the economy was its trade dependence. Being a small, resource-poor economy, it has to import virtually all of its industrial and non-industrial inputs. Given the high import requirement, there had to be a compelling need to export competitively in the world markets. Thus, lack of natural resources turned Hong Kong into an efficiency-conscious exporter and it turned out to be a blessing in disguise. The smallness of the economy *per se* did not prove to be a deterrent, although it imposed the price-taking behaviour. The trade theory shows that the gains from trade accrued to a small economy are larger than those for a large economy (Heller, 1968). The degree of Hong Kong's reliance on imports and its success in exports can be seen in the import/GNP ratio and export/GNP ratio. The import/GNP ratio was 98.9 per cent in 1961, 83.9 per cent in 1981 and 115.6 per cent in 1988. The export/GNP ratio was 65.1 per cent in 1961, 70.9 per cent in 1981 and 114.2 in 1988 (Ho, 1992). Indeed, these ratios were driven upwards by entrepôt trade but even after excluding re-exports, the domestic export ratios for Hong Kong averaged above 50 per cent, high by international standards. Rapid growth in exports was accompanied by even more rapid growth in manufactured exports. Its long-term (1960–90) annual average growth rate in value terms was 17.3 per cent, while it was 11 per cent in quantum terms (Ho, 1992). The growth of manufacturing production, together with the development of the services sector – including financial services – brought about an increased demand for labour. The convincing evidence of a tight labour market was the substantial increase in real wages. By the early 1970s, Hong Kong had emerged as one of the four ANIEs: having high technological and managerial capabilities. Its also developed enviable international marketing skills.

The most important recent economic event for Hong Kong was its transformation from an entrepôt economy to one based on strong manufacturing and service sectors. This transformation was achieved without planning or even premeditation. It was largely shaped by the natural reaction of the economy to adjust to exogenous forces. The process of transformation was encouraged by the influx of MNC capital and Hong Kong's highly skilled manpower.

All of China's indirect trade passed through Hong Kong, its tourist traffic came through it and all of its loan syndications were handled in Hong Kong. Due to the efficient trading services provided by Hong Kong, more of China's trade passed through Hong Kong than through Shanghai. Thus, the Hong Kong-China nexus is an old one. Since the adoption of the 'open door' policy in December 1978, more of China's trade began to be conducted through Hong Kong. In 1989, 41 per cent of China's total exports comprised re-exports from Hong Kong (Sung, 1991a). China relied heavily on Hong Kong for marketing, re-exporting and trans-shipment services. The sharp rise in China's indirect trade with Taiwan and South Korea in the recent past was one of the reasons behind China's trade expansion through Hong Kong. Indirect trade with Taiwan soared over the 1980s after China tried to attract Taiwan by abolishing all tariffs on its products, on the grounds of Taiwan being part of China.

However, the Hong Kong-Guangdong nexus is a new one, and China's open door policy has a good deal to do with it. Adoption of such a policy by a centrally planned economy was a veritable giant stride in institutional reform. A number of follow-through measures were taken in quick succession: the *renminbi* (Rmb) was substantially depreciated; a grey market for foreign exchange was introduced; foreign joint ventures and fully-owned foreign enterprises were allowed; special economic zones (SEZs) were established; and the decisions regarding foreign trade and investment were decentralised. Policy fine-timing was done on several occasions. At the time of the 14th National Congress in October 1992, the strategy of 'reform, opening to the outside world and the drive for modernisation' was reassuringly reinforced. It was made abundantly clear that the dictum of ideology must not be allowed to become an excuse for economic failure. Endeavours to establish something called a 'socialist market economy' – oxymoron unintended – were to be put in full swing. In keeping with the reform strategy, several SEZs were established, of which the best-known is Shenzhen, in the Guangdong region of China, immediately north of Hong Kong (*see Map 5.2*). It stretches for 327.5 sq. km. between Emping and Chaozhou. The area is also called the Pearl River delta. In a short span of time it has been transformed from a society of subsistence-farming peasants to an industrial powerhouse. In 1978, 90 per cent of Guangdong's total output was derived from farming and 10 per cent from industry. In 1990, the proportions were reversed, with industry accounting for Rmb 142.2 billion of the gross provincial output of Rmb 164.3 billion (Cheng and Taylor, 1991). Trade between Hong Kong and Guangdong was more than HK $ 400 billion (US $ 50 billion) in 1990, which was almost as large as the GDP of Hong Kong (Cheng and Taylor, 1991).

Cross-border economic ties were strong. Although Shenzhen has problems regarding the availability of skilled workers, engineers and some support industrial services, it has done well in terms of growth. Over the 1980–90 period its GDP increased at an average annual rate of 50 per cent and exports climbed at an annual average rate of 75 per cent. To be sure, these statistics hide the low-starting base effect. Export growth slowed to 15.4 per cent during 1991 (Cheng and Mosher, 1992). The slowdown was partly attributed to the withdrawal of some trade privileges from the SEZ because of the austerity measures. Also, changes in credit policies created financial problems for many trading and manufacturing firms operating in the region. During the boom period, infrastructure in the SEZ was found to be inadequate, and there were plans to invest heavily in infrastructure development, which was expected to improve export

Map 5.2   Sub-regional economic zones in the Asia-Pacific Region

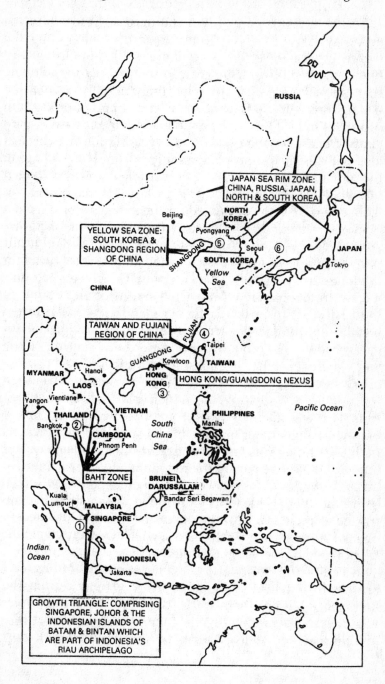

capabilities and linkages within Guangdong as well as with Hong Kong.

Just as in Singapore, when the need to restructure the economy arose in Hong Kong, instead of upgrading the labour-intensive sectors into more skilled-intensive and higher value-added sectors, firms promptly reacted to rising costs and labour scarcity by relocating across the border into Guangdong, sub-contracting the whole or part of production processes to facilities in the region. These facilities were generally created for the purpose of executing the sub-contract jobs with the help of capital resources from Hong Kong. In the parlance of the Hong Kong government, this was termed 'outward processing'. In the process, a substantial quantity of labour resources were released for the services sector, as was obvious from the sharp decline in the share of manufacturing employment in Hong Kong within a decade. Although this pace of structural adjustment was too high, it was crucial for the long-term survival of the economy. The process of transferring traditional labour-intensive and medium technology industries began in the early 1980s and accelerated in the middle of the decade. Hong Kong's outward processing spearheaded close economic integration between Hong Kong and Guangdong. The relationship strengthened fast because of the symbiosis involved in it. Other investment, other than for outward processing, also took place in Guangdong. Initially it was made by Hong Kong-based overseas Chinese but increasingly other firms followed suit. Investors' interest in the beginning was limited to export-orientated enterprises but with the conversion of the renminbi into a hard currency, investors began to invest even in Chinese enterprises as well (Fairlamb, 1993). Due to its ethnic links, Guangdong also attracted capital from Macau. Investors tapped the newly-opened stock market for 'B' shares, which were quoted in the US dollar and reserved for foreigners.

In 1990, 20 000 local factories in the Pearl River delta were busy with outward processing jobs for Hong Kong-based firms. In addition, there were 7000 Sino-Hong Kong joint ventures in operation. Together they employed over three million workers, which was about four times Hong Kong's own manufacturing workforce (Wong, 1991). The outward processing set its roots so smoothly because the process was simple and made a great deal of business sense. Armed with foreign orders, production designs, equipment and capital, Hong Kong firms contracted out the jobs in Guangdong. Many a time, the small facilities created on an *ad-hoc* basis for specific jobs were developed into medium or large-size production units, and what began as job-specific involvements frequently grew into a large projects. For the investing firm these arrangements meant quick results and little risk. However, the biggest advantage to the Hong Kong firms lay in the low wages and real estate prices in the Pearl River delta: average wages were one-seventh of the Hong Kong level, while factory-space rental was one-ninth. Small and medium-sized firms exploited the outward processing to the fullest. Starting from modest and informal arrangements, they upgraded the relationship into a large and formal one, like an equity joint venture (Wong, 1991). Outward processing facilitated the process of vertical as well as horizontal division of labour between Hong Kong and Guangdong, integrating the two economies closely.

A similar process took place on the financial side. Hong Kong's status as one of the world's largest financial and information centres benefited Guangdong. Free circulation of the Hong Kong dollar in the SEZ helped in improving its liquidity position, enabling it to overtake Shanghai as the country's largest foreign currency swap centre. In the process, strong financial ties developed between Hong Kong and Guangdong, particularly with Shenzhen. Although officially frowned upon, the Hong Kong dollar is also used for consumer purchases. According to one estimate, 20 per cent of Hong Kong's money supply in 1992 was circulating in Guangdong (Cheng and Mosher, 1992). Economists on both sides of the border concur that in future Hong Kong will be the financial and service centre for the manufacturing activity in the northern Pearl River delta. Hong Kong banks have started integrating with the economic activity in Guangdong, several large banks moving beyond conventional trade finance to lucrative advisory work. Outstanding loans maturing beyond 1977 made to China by Hong Kong-based banks amounted to HK $ 55 billion or US $ 7.11 billion at the end of 1991.[2] Hong Kong-based Japanese banks also actively participated in business with the Guangdong region.

THE TAIWAN-FUJIAN NEXUS

The capita income of Taiwan soared at a sustained 6 to 8 per cent annually over the 1970s and the 1980s and exceeded $ 10 000 in 1992, putting it also into the World Bank's category of high-income countries. Structural transformation of the economy reached the point where a mere 4 per cent of GDP was generated in agriculture. Taiwan's gross savings rate, at 30 per cent, has been among the highest in the world (Ranis, 1992). Another measure of its economic vitality was its foreign exchange reserves, that crossed $ 82 billion in 1992, and was the second-largest in the world after Germany. Taiwan's transition from a developing economy to a newly industrialising economy was vividly shown by the relative increase in industrial exports. In 1965, 54 per cent of exports originated from the agricultural sector. In 1990, 96 per cent of them originated from the industrial sectors. Its largest exports were in textiles and electrical machinery and apparatus. The structure of exports was also changing, textiles were losing ground while the importance of technology-intensive products was on the rise. Over the 1980s electronics and information technology products were gaining increasing importance in production as well as in exports.

Economic development in Taiwan followed a logical route. First, a great deal of emphasis was put on the strengthening of the agricultural sector, followed by the light industry sector and ending with the heavy and high-tech industries. Trade has been the mainstay of Taiwan's economic development. In fact, trade and growth formed a virtuous circle. A good deal of attention was constantly paid to raising the efficiency of the export sectors and keeping the product lines competitive in the international markets. This was accomplished by the diffusion of modern technology in the industrial sector and by adopting modern scientific management techniques (Wu, 1985). Taiwan's spectacular success in exports raised its export/GDP ratio from 10 per cent in the 1950s to 60 per cent in the 1980s, which exposed the economy to exogenous fluctuations, business cycles of the trade partners and neo-protectionism. What was more problematic was that Taiwan's trade has been heavily skewed towards two trading partners, the USA and Japan. In addition, its commodity composition seemed over-specialised.

However, the Taiwanese economy has been able to adjust and survive the adverse pressures. Not only its economic structure changed with growth but its export structure also altered. By the end of the 1980s, 50 per cent of its exports were in the high-tech sectors, that is, machinery and basic metals, transport equipment and precision instruments. This was a striking change of direction from the labour-intensive manufactured products of the 1960s and 1970s (Riedel, 1992). The industrial output mix not only shifted towards high-tech products but also towards the short-product cycle end of the spectrum. Also, a continuous upgradation of product quality took place. It was one of the strategies adopted to fight off the quantitative restrictions in the importing countries. Unlike Hong Kong and Singapore, Taiwan also tried hard to maintain its competitiveness in some of the labour-intensive sectors. It neither shed them readily nor moved them offshore as soon as the first symptoms of loss of comparative advantage were seen. Similarly, over the 1980s Taiwan was busy altering the concentration of trading partners. The importance of the USA slipped: it was responsible for 34 per cent of total Taiwanese trade in 1985, but in 1990 it absorbed only 20 per cent of total exports. As opposed to this, the importance of China rose considerably.

The 100-mile-wide Taiwan straits separates Taiwan and the Fujian province of China (see Map 5.2). Although 98.5 per cent of Taiwanese population came from the mainland, differences in political systems kept them apart until 1979. Since the inception of the open door policy, indirect trade between the two Chinas through Hong Kong burgeoned. To a lesser degree, it also took place through Singapore and Japan. Yet it was paltry until 1979, when Taiwan's exports to China through Hong Kong were $ 21 million, while reverse tariff was $ 55 million (Kao and Yen, 1992). Direct trade in the form of smuggling and 'minor trade' took place through the designated coast mainland ports. The Taiwanese government allowed 'minor trade' through the use of Taiwanese vessels of up to 100 tons. Other than this, it was well known that Taiwanese businesses trans-shipped large unreported consignments regularly, which was considered illegal by Taiwan. Even in 1992, Taiwan prohibited direct air and shipping links. By 1985, Taiwan's exports to the mainland through Hong Kong had risen to $ 987 million and imports to $ 116 million, resulting in a large trade balance surplus for Taiwan. Between 1985 and 1991, exports to the mainland through Hong Kong rose by almost five-fold and reached $ 4667 million, while imports rose tenfold and reached $ 1126 million. The trade balance surpluses continued to rise (Kao and Yen, 1992). The real trade figures, however, must be read as at least 25 per cent higher than the ones reported above, because they apparently do not include trade through other places and the unreported trade (Kraas, 1992). At this rate, China could replace the USA as Taiwan's biggest trading partner within a decade. The Chinese trade boom also kept Taiwan from slipping into recession with the USA and the EU. Thus, the importance for Taiwan of trade with China increased considerably over the 1980s.

The major export products from Taiwan in 1990 were synthetic fabrics and non-electric machinery, while major commodities in China's exports to Taiwan were Chinese herbal medicine, textiles and clothing. Cross trade in textiles was symptomatic of the beginning of intra-industry trade. However, the massive Chinese deficit is harmful for trade expansion between the two.

When the need to restructure the industrial sector arose, the Taiwanese government did not encourage off-shore investment immediately, for fear of hollowing out the industrial sector. First, attempts were made to rescue the declining sectors by technological upgrading. But low-technology, labour-intensive operations made little commercial sense in expensive Taiwan. The attraction of moving across the Taiwan strait was irresistable. Fujian offered labour at a tenth of the price in Taiwan and land at a thousandth of the price in Taiwan (*The Economist*, 1992). Most of the investment took place in Fujian through front companies in Hong Kong, Singapore and Bangkok. The Xiamen region of Fujian and Guangdong were the other favoured locations for Taiwanese investors. No records exist for the pre-1985 volume of investment. However, for the post-1985 period, estimates for March 1991 ranged between $ 750 million and $ 3 billion (Yu, 1992). It was difficult to obtain accurate statistics because investing firms tended to avoid reporting their 'across the straits' operations.

Taiwan's investments in Fujian was largely in small-scale labour-intensive operations producing light manufactures for exports. It included textiles, footwear, umbrellas, travel accessories and electronics. Over 80 per cent of Taiwan's footwear industry moved to the mainland (Sung, 1991b). Since Taiwan had both the technological prowess and financial muscle, a tendency towards increasing size and sophistication in investment projects was observed. Recent investments were in the areas of chemicals, building materials, automobile parts and electronic products and components, and a gigantic naphtha cracking plant was set up in Xiamen. In many cases, the output of these factories was exported to Taiwan in the form of semi-finished or finished products (Shapiro, 1992). Gradually intra-trade is expected to rise and alleviate the pressure of China's large trade deficit.

THE YELLOW SEA ZONE

The economic metamorphosis of Korea began after 1961. A remarkable pattern of sustained long-term growth followed. Measured by any of a number of parameters, its economic performance was outstanding. That apart, the brisk growth occurred without the many debilitating effects known to take their toll of growing developing economies – the 'teething pains' were missing from a large part of the Korean experience. Few can argue that a well-laid macroeconomic strategy has not been instrumental in accelerating Korean economy. The interaction between the state geared to developmental goals and the profit-maximising private sector worked rather well in Korea. The macroeconomic managers were certain that wisdom lay in choosing pragmatically between different combinations of market and non-market approaches. Korea did this with sufficient ingenuity: state intervention was non-ideological and based on economic efficiency criteria (Das, 1992).

Most analysts of the Korean scene concur that the outward-orientated development strategy and export promotion were integrally associated with its phenomenal economic growth and rapid industrialisation. Before the launch of this strategy Korea could not take advantage of gains from trade in the Heckscher-Ohlinian sense because of significant factor and product market distortions, and its comparative advantage in labour-intensive manufactures remained merely a potential one. However, once it came upon the right strategy, Korea made successful use of trade policy to determine the pace and direction of its industrialisation. This strategy also stimulated Korea's expansion into newer and more modern lines of industrial activity. Its early export success was adequately supported by the paradigm of static comparative advantage, whereas the dynamic comparative advantage was seen more in operation during the later phases (Das, 1991). In 1960, before the beginning of the Park era, exports were a mere $ 33 million and were dominated by primary goods like metallic ores, fish, hides and leather products, tobacco, vegetable materials, dried seaweeds, raw silk and so on. The only significant manufactured export product was woven cotton fabric, which constituted over half of the total exports in this category; the manufactured exports accounted for barely 14 per cent of the total. Since then export growth has accelerated considerably, reaching $ 882 million in 1970, 76 per cent of which consisted of commodities that fall between Standard International Trade Classification (SITC) code number 5 and 8 and are classified as manufactured goods. In 1980, exports rose to $ 17 billion, 86 per cent being manufactured goods, and in 1988 they reached $ 59.65 billion, 90.33 per cent being modern manufactured products. The average annual growth rate of exports was 40.1 per cent during 1961–70, 36.0 per cent during 1971–80, and 47.5 per cent during 1982–8. In 1990, they crossed the $ 65 billion mark. These averages are much higher than those of the other ANIEs and are, in fact, the highest in the world. They vindicated Korea's claim regarding successful export-orientated industrialisation. Admittedly, the manufactured exports started from a small base, but their growth rate remained very high even after they became substantial. The Korean export sector, particularly the manufactured exports sector, was the engine of growth, not its handmaiden. However, for years between 1988 and 1991, the average export growth rate fell to 9.2 per cent and over 1990–91 it was a mere 3.4 per cent. In this context it should be noted that between 1985 and 1989 the exchange rate of the won against the dollar climbed by 23.6 per cent. Wages more than doubled over the 1985–90 period and the price index soared from 100 in 1985 to 200 in 1991. The economy was ripe for structural reforms (*Bank of Korea*, 1992). By 1991, Korea's per capita GNP had reached $ 6498. Although it was the lowest among the four ANIEs, it made Korea one of the top middle-income countries. Another distinction that Korea had acquired was that it had the most sophisticated industrial technology among the four ANIEs (Sung, 1991b).

Rising wages and prices and the appreciating won made labour-intensive industries lose their comparative advantage. To cope with the situation, a two-pronged strategy was adopted by Korean firms: first, technological upgradation of the declining sector; and then relocation of industries into areas of lower factor costs. Korea also began to shift its export-market and import-sourcing patterns. Therefore, geographical proximity to China's northern provinces, particularly Shandong and Liaoning, took on a special meaning for Korea (see Map 5.2). China, hoping to attract Korean capital and technology, designated the Shandong province as an 'open area' in 1988.

Indirect trade between China and Korea commenced in a small way after 1979. Chinese tariffs on Korean products were higher than those on other countries because political limitations prohibited any bilateral trade agreement. In 1985, the two countries set up a temporary channel of communication in Hong Kong and in 1988 freight transport routes were established between them, with the proviso that vessels be registered in third countries. The following year, Korean banks were given permission to enter into correspondent bank agreements with the Bank of China, so that foreign exchange transactions could be facilitated. Passenger transport, both by sea and air, began in 1990 and the two countries set up Overseas Trade Promotion Offices in each other's capital. Finally, in August 1992 the two countries established normal diplomatic relations. Trade between them had started from a very low level. In 1980, Korea exported $ 110 million-worth and imported $ 73 million-worth of merchandise. In 1985, exports reached $ 639 million and imports $ 607 million. Thereafter growth of trade was fast and in 1988 both imports and exports crossed the $ 1 billion mark. By 1990, Korean exports had climbed to $ 1.4 billion and imports to $ 2.3 billion, with China enjoying a large trade surplus, (Sung, 1991b). This situation was the opposite of Taiwan's, against whom China had a large deficit. Korea's principal export items to China were chemicals, fertilisers, plastics, televisions, steel, medical equipment, household appliances, electrical goods and textiles. China exported mostly primary goods, which included industrial raw materials, coal, nonferrous metals as well as finished goods like textiles. Thus, as in the case of Taiwan, intra-trade existed for textiles (Kim, 1992).

Investments in the Shandong and Lioning regions started from a low base in small-scale, labour-intensive units producing electronics, toys, processed foods, apparel and household items. However, the average size of Korean investments, as well as technological sophistication, went on increasing, a situation identical to that of Taiwan. Some of the large projects that were on the anvil in the late 1980s were Hyundai's $ 4 million project to manufacture tungsten products and Tong II's $ 10 million project of manufacturing automobile components. The latter was to be a joint venture.

China wooed Korean investment in Shandong because this is where its heavy industry complexes were and this region was relatively poorly developed. It could benefit immensely from Korean technological prowess as well as from the strong industrial competitiveness of Korean products in the international markets. For Korea, moving into this region would help it in its structural transformation. Also, since its export growth rates were slumping, Korea was looking for virgin markets in the republics of the former Soviet Union. There was a tremendous surge in investment in 1991, with 110 ventures on the drawing board, involving an investment of $ 84 million (Yoshikawa, 1992). Normalisation of economic relations gave a boost to bilateral trade and investment as well as to the formation of the Yellow Sea Zone.

It is evident from the foregoing exposition that there is a wide variety in the degree of economic interaction between the three ANIEs and China, with Hong Kong being the closest to the mainland while Korea has a relatively lower degree of economic integration and Taiwan falls between the two. Hong Kong did not have any political, cultural and geographical barriers, which brought it close to the mainland economy relatively faster. The *laissez-faire* nature of its economy also provided momentum in the same direction. Political barriers were considerable in the case of Taiwan until the early 1990s, whereas they were removed for Korea in 1992.

THE JAPAN SEA RIM ZONE

The Japan Sea rim area, which was once terra incognita, is expected to become an economic zone with enormous potential for economic and technical co-operation. At present this zone is only in an inchoate state. Five countries touch the rim: China, Russia, Japan and North and South Korea (See Map 5.2). Their current (1991) trade is of the order of $ 70 billion (Guiland, 1992). Since 1988, a great deal of interest has arisen in the Japan sea rim economic zone. It has been enhanced by the Tumen delta project, which has been designed to integrate and industrialise the Tumen River estuary. The United Nations Development Program (UNDP) has provided $ 30 billion for the project to be invested over twenty years. The objective is to construct an industrial, commercial and services complex that will be a Hong Kong of north-east Asia and benefit several countries in the hinterland. The UNDP launched the project in July 1991. A trade and transport complex, which is to include eleven specialised harbours as well as a railroad hub, is to be a part of this sub-regional project.

The Tumen river forms the border between North Korea and China and, for its last 20 kilometres, the border between Russia and North Korea. The Chinese city of Hunchun, which was a harbour in the past, has been landlocked for over a century. Development of Hunchun and the area around it – where the borders of three countries meet – into a special economic zone will unlock the resource rich areas of these five countries and, to some extent, of Mongolia (Jones *et al.*, 1992). Regional co-operation would give full play to the synergies of the constituent economies. These economies are more complementary than those of Europe: South Korea and Japan are rich in capital, technology and management skills; China in labour, energy and raw materials; North Korea in labour and raw materials; and Russia in energy and raw materials. Funding is not only expected to come from multinational financial institutions, but also from banks in Japan and Korea. Each of the participants has enough of a stake in this sub-regional co-operation project. China has supported the plan and thrown its weight behind it by according Hunchun the status of an SEZ. When the Tumen delta does develop, it is expected that it will also attract Japanese economic assistance.

However, there are several snags that have slowed the project implementation down. First, China wanted to turn Hunchun into a river port by dredging the last 18 kilometres of the Tumen river, which the UNDP rejected because of its prohibitive cost. Secondly, Russia considered Vladivostoc to be ideal for such a development, and therefore was not particularly warm to the project. Thirdly, until the Kurilles island issue is resolved, Japan is not eager to give financial and technical support to the project. It has, however, shown eagerness to support the project on a smaller scale than planned. If or when these issues are resolved, the Tumen river delta has the potential to be a vibrant part of the Japan sea rim zone. Enormous potential for sub-regional integration by way of trade, investment and technology transfer exists in the zone.

CONCLUSION

In the Asia-Pacific region, market-driven, sub-regional economic zone formation has been taking place. Although it was not institutionalised, it was all the same economically, uniting various sub-regions and eventually the whole region. Intense interaction between spatial units has created functional economic zones. Economic co-operation in the form of trade and investment in these zones went on increasing during the 1980s and early 1990s. Five sub-regional economic zones have emerged so far, and there is a possibility of the creation of a sixth in the short term.

Singapore, along with the neighbouring parts of Malaysia and the island of Indonesia, has succeeded in creating a Growth Triangle. Singapore's strength lay in its capital resources, highly-skilled and trained labour force and an advanced services sector, while its weaknesses were its small territory and limited labour supply. It logically developed a symbiotic economic relationship with Malaysia and Indonesia, which had plenty of land as well as labour resources and needed Singaporean capital, technology and managerial skills. The complementarities that existed between the factor endowments of the three partners worked towards bringing them together in the form of a growth triangle.

Thailand has been actively working to create a 'baht economic zone' based on the strength of its economy as well as its currency. Laos, Cambodia, Myanmar and Vietnam were weak, unstable, inflation-ridden economies with poor financial systems. The baht was the only strong and stable currency in the region, with minimum exchange risk and easy convertibility into the US dollar and the yen. Therefore, it appeared attractive and inspired confidence among the neighbouring economies. The central bank of Thailand took several pro-active measures to encourage the use of the baht in the Indochina region. Also, Thai banks were expanding their operations and presence in the region for expanding the influence and use of the baht. The establishment of an off-shore banking centre called the Bangkok International Facility (BIBF), was under way in early 1993. It was intended to serve the whole Indochina region.

Hong Kong had an export-orientated manufacturing sector and strong service – including financial services – sector. By the early 1970s, it had emerged as one of the four ANIEs, having high technological and managerial capabilities. It had also developed enviable international marketing skills. China had long-term ties with it because virtually all of China's in-direct trade passed through Hong Kong. After China adopted its open door policy and the renminbi was substantially de-preciated, an SEZ was established at Shenzhen, north of Hong Kong. The area is also called the Pearl River delta and with the help of Hong Kong has become a modern industrial powerhouse. Despite shortages of skilled workers, Shenzhen did extremely well over the 1980s. Several labour-intensive industries were transferred from Hong Kong to the Guangdong region of China: a good deal of the sub-contracted work of Hong Kong firms was done there. In the parlance of the Hong Kong government this was called 'outward processing', and it spearheaded closer economic in-tegration between Hong Kong and the Guangdong region. Also, the Hong Kong dollar was being used in Guangdong, which improved the liquidity position in the area.

The Taiwan Straits separated Taiwan from the Fujian province of China. The two countries did have some indirect trade through Hong Kong, but by early 1990s, China had become an important trade partner of Taiwan. Also, when the need for restructuring its industrial sector arose, Taiwan first attempted to rescue the declining sectors by technological upgradation and then by moving the low-technology, labour-intensive sectors off-shore to the Fujian region. During the early 1990s, off-shore investment gained considerable momentum. Initially the investments made by Hong Kong and Taiwan were small and in low-tech products, but gradually their volume as well as sophistication increased.

In a similar vein, the Yellow Sea zone, comprising Korea and the Shandong and Lioning regions of China, began to integrate. Rising wages, prices and the appreciating won made labour-intensive industries lose their comparative advantage. To cope with the situation, a two-pronged strategy was adopted by Korean firms; first, technological upgradation of the declining sectors; and second, relocation of industries into the above-named regions of China. On its part, hoping to attract Korean capital and technology, China designated the Shandong province as an open area in 1988. China's heavy industry complexes were located in this region and it was relatively poorly developed. It stood to benefit a good deal from Korean technological prowess.

Lastly, the Japan sea rim is expected to become an economic zone of enormous potential in the future. Five countries touch this rim and the area is also a beneficiary of a large UNDP investment, called the Tumen delta project. To encourage the development of the Japan Sea rim, China has begun to develop the area around Hunchun, where the borders of three countries meet. The development of the Japan Sea rim zone will depend upon resolving several snags which have emerged and stalled progress.

6 Regionalism versus Multilateralism: The Asia-Pacific Penchant

INTRODUCTION

Although it was initiated by Viner (1950), the debate on regionalism versus multilateralism only became intense following the signing of the Treaty of Rome (1958) and establishment of two large economic blocs in Europe. The resurrection of protectionism and later on the débâcle of the Uruguay Round gave new relevance to it. There are several economic reasons why regionalism, in the form of grouping together as free-trade areas or customs unions, is a profitable strategy for the economies forming a regional group. If the regional grouping is of an open and non-discriminatory variety and does not become a defensive economic bloc, it contributes to multilateralism. Prima-facie regionalism seems an antithesis of the most-favoured-nations principle of the General Agreement on Tariffs and Trade (GATT) and a gross abuse of its Article XXIV. However, according to the last stand taken by the GATT, it is to be treated and accepted as a worthwhile supplement to multilateralism, not an alternative. There has been a great deal of growth in the intra-regional trade in the Asia-Pacific region over the 1980s. There has also been brisk growth in intra-industry trade, intra-regional investment and technology transfer, and the operation of product life cycle. A good deal of complementarity exists between the regional economies. Consequently, regional economic interaction has been intense and the play of market forces has brought the economies close together. In what follows, we shall see in the context of their rapid outward-orientated growth and intense economic interaction, which way the Asia-Pacific economies have voted. Did they lean towards regionalism or opt for multilateralism?

Alternatively, did they chalk out a new – more apt, functional and situation-specific – route for themselves?

EXPANDING REGIONALISM

Establishment of institutions like the Bretton Woods twins and the GATT, and operation of the international economy under their strategic directives, or tutelage, was accepted as a satisfactory form of multilateral economic order. As opposed to this, any deviations in the form of concentration of trade and investment in any specific region was termed 'regionalism' and, therefore, was considered antithetical to the spirit of multilateralism. Such a reaction became strong in the wake of the surge of neo-protectionism and pernicious leanings towards managed trade practices. The collapse of the Uruguay Round strengthened apprehensions of the international economy drifting towards regionalism and, therefore, fragmentation. Regionalism in the form of free-trade areas and customs unions has made a resurgence and is having a good deal of sway over the international economy. Although no comprehensive enumeration of regional preferential trading arrangements has been published by any authoritative organisation, a fairly complete listing (Fieleke, 1992, and Bergsten, 1991) given in Table 6.1 shows twenty-three relatively large arrangements, comprising 119 countries. They accounted for 82 per cent of the world's trade in merchandise. No region in the world is bereft of such arrangements. Indeed, one would be hard-pressed to find even one country that does not receive from, or grant to, other countries some form of explicit preferential treatment in international trade – the treatment need not necessarily be the kind of multilateral arrangement shown in Table 6.1. Also, many agreements, having been made, have failed or fallen into abeyance.

In all these regional groupings, the primary objective is to favour the trade of the group partners over that of non-partners. To this end, trade barriers are dismantled among members of the group forming the free-trade area, but are retained against third countries, or are harmonised in the

Table 6.1   Preferential Trading Arrangements, by Geographic Region and Year Launched

Region, title and membership	Year launched	Type of trade arrangement
Africa		
Communauté Economique de l'Afrique de l'Ouest (CEAO), or West African Economic Community: Benin, Burkina Faso, Côte d'Ivoire, Mali, Mauritania, Niger, Senegal	1959	Customs union
Union Douanière et Economique de l'Afrique Centrale (UDEAC), or Economic and Customs Union of Central Africa Cameroon, Central African Republic, Chad, Congo, Equatorial Guinea, Gabon	1964	Customs union
Southern African Customs Union (SACU) Bophuthatswana, Botswana, Ciskei, Lesotho, Namibia, South Africa, Swaziland, Transkei, Venda	1969	Customs union
Mano River Union (MRU) Guinea, Liberia, Sierra Leone	1973	Customs union
Economic Community of West African States (ECOWAS) Benin, Burkina Faso, Cape Verde, Côte d'Ivoire, The Gambia, Ghana, Guinea, Guinea-Bissau, Liberia, Mali, Mauritania, Niger, Nigeria, Senegal, Sierra Leone, Togo	1975	Common market
Preferential Trade Area for Eastern and Southern African States (PTA) Burundi, Comoro Islands, Djibouti, Ethiopia, Kenya, Lesotho, Malawi, Mauritius, Mozambique, Rwanda, Somalia, Swaziland, Tanzania, Uganda, Zambia, Zimbabwe	1981	Trade preference association
Communauté Economique des Etats de l'Afrique Centrale (CEEAC), or Economic Community of Central African States Burundi, Cameroon, Central African Republic, Chad, Congo, Equatorial Guinea, Gabon, Rwanda, São Tomé and Principe, Zaire	1981	Common market
Arab Maghreb Union (AMU) Algeria, Libya, Mauritania, Morocco, Tunisia	1989	Common market
Asia		
Association of South-east Asian Nations (ASEAN) Brunei, Indonesia, Malaysia, Philippines, Singapore, Thailand	1967	Free-trade area

Table 6.1　Continued

Region, title and membership	Year launched	Type of trade arrangement
Bangkok Agreement Bangladesh, India, Laos, South Korea, Sri Lanka	1976	Trade preference association
Australia New Zealand Closer Economic Relations Trade Agreement (ANZCERTA) Australia, New Zealand	1983	Customs union
ASEAN Free Trade Area (AFTA) The ASEAN countries named above	1991	Free-trade area
Europe		
European Union (EU) Belgium, Denmark, France, Germany, Greece, Ireland, Italy, Luxembourg, Netherlands, Portugal, Spain, United Kingdom	1957	Common market
European Free Trade Association (EFTA) Austria, Finland, Iceland, Liechtenstein, Norway, Sweden, Switzerland	1960	Free-trade area
European Community and European Free Trade Association Member countries of the EC and EFTA	1972	Industrial free-trade area
Latin America		
Central American Common Market (CACM) Costa Rica, El Salvador, Guatemala, Honduras, Nicaragua	1960	Customs union
Andean Common Market (ANCOM) Bolivia, Colombia, Ecuador, Peru, Venezuela	1969	Common market
Caribbean Common Market (CARICOM) Antigua and Barbuda, Bahamas, Barbados, Belize, Dominica, Grenada, Guyana, Jamaica, Montserrat, St. Kitts-Nevis, St. Lucia, St. Vincent and the Grenadines, Trinidad and Tobago	1973	Common market
Latin America Integration Assocation (LAIA) Argentina, Bolivia, Brazil, Chile, Colombia, Ecuador, Mexico, Paraguay, Peru, Uruguay, Venezuela.	1980	Trade preference association
Organization of Eastern Caribbean States (OECS) Antigua and Barbuda, Dominica, Grenada, Montserrat, St. Kitts-Nevis, St. Lucia, St. Vincent and Grenadines, Virgin Islands UK.	1981	Customs union

Table 6.1 Continued

Region, title and membership	Year launched	Type of trade arrangement
Southern Cone Common Market (MERCOSUL or MERCOSUR) Argentina, Brazil, Paraguay, Uruguay	1991	Common market
Middle East		
Gulf Cooperation Council (GCC): Bahrain, Kuwait, Oman, Qatar, Saudi Arabia, United Arab Emirates	1981	Common market
Middle East Africa		
Arab Common Market (ACM) Egypt, Iraq, Jordan, Lebanon, Libya, Mauritania, Syria	1964	Common market
North America		
Canada-United States Free Trade Agreement: Canada, USA	1989	Free-trade area
North American Free Trade Agreement (NAFTA) Canada, Mexico, USA	1992	Free-trade area
Oceania Australia-New Zealand Closer Economic Relations Trade Agreement (ANZCERT) Australia, New Zealand	1983	Free-trade area
Other		
Other preferential arrangements include various bilateral free trade agreements, such as that between Israel and the EU, Israel and the USA, and Chile and Mexico, and also preferential treatment for imports from less-developed countries by many countries, including the EC and the USA.		

Source: Fieleke, 1992. Recent additions made by the author.

case of a customs union, when the customs union become a common market by removing artificial or government impediments on all transactions between members, including transfers of factors of production, goods and services.

Following the unification movement in the European Union (EU), the regionalism debate took a new vigour. It began with the Milan summit in 1985 and its principal tenets were enshrined in the Single European Act of 1987. From January 1993, the EU and the European Free Trade Association (EFTA) joined hands to become European Economic Area (EEA). The EEA extended four fundamental freedoms of the EU to the seven members of EFTA. These are the freedoms of movement of goods, services, people and capital. Creation of the North American Free Trade Area (NAFTA)[1] in 1992 had the same impact on the regionalism debate. Although the Asia-Pacific economies have no formal pact of regional grouping, they have strengthened their mutual economic ties substantially – without institutionalisation – over the last two decades. Two sub-groups among them, the members of the ASEAN, and Australia and New Zealand, have signed formal free-trade agreements but they are too tiny to be treated as significant.[2] These developments have supported the tripolar international economy thinking that the international economy is ripe for fragmenting into pieces. Is this pessimistic scenario wholly overdrawn? What is happening is the repetition of a historic cycle – that is, after a liberalising period the international economy has entered a protectionist phase. There have been deterministic cycles in the international economy of liberalism following protectionism (Tumlir, 1978). The GATT discipline gradually eroded after the liberalising decades of the 1950s and 1960s, allowing neo-protectionism and regionalism to catch on (Das, 1990).

Successful launching of the EU and the EFTA created an outbreak of FTA proposals during the 1960s. The reason behind the zeal was to exploit scale economies through preferential opening of markets among the members of the FTA. A large number of these attempts remained inchoate or collapsed because the attempts to form FTAs were based on an incorrect premise. Instead of liberalising trade and letting the price mechanism guide industry allocations, potential members of the FTA were trying to deal with this issue through bureaucratic negotiations – the best way to kill any potential FTA (Bhagwati, 1968). With benediction from the GATT, regionalism returned during the 1980s. There were several reasons for its return. First, the USA that had always championed the cause of free trade made a volte-face and began to enter into FTAs with such diverse partners as Israel, Canada and Mexico. Secondly, as stated above, weakening of the GATT discipline encouraged countries to leave the multilateral route and turn to regionalism. Thirdly, the single European market and the formation of the European Economic Area (EEA) created a fear psychosis in North America and the Asia-Pacific economies and they accepted the need to form countervailing economic blocs. The USA made a general offer to the nations of South America to join it in an FTA in mid-1990, as part of an economic package to assist these nations. The response of the South American nations to the US offer was favourable. Formation of the ASEAN Free Trade Area (AFTA) in the south-east Asian region was an identical reaction on the Asia-Pacific side of the international economy. Fourthly, economic thinking in the world today has turned towards favouring the operation of market forces and deregulation. The macro-economic crises of the 1980s led to economic reform movements in many countries. Economic reforms, deregulation and market expansion are factors that have coalesced to expand regional economic ties. The Asia-Pacific economies are the best illustration of this. Several scholars have recently addressed the question of trend towards regionalism and have inferred that such a trend is indubitably under way and is likely to endure (Bhagwati, 1990, 1993; Krugman, 1993; Lawrence, 1991a).

THE RATIONALE BEHIND REGIONALISM

The liberal trading system created by the GATT did more than any other economic policy or institution to promote the extraordinary rise in global income during the first two decades after the Second World War. Yet regionalisation of world trade never lost its appeal and economies formed FTAs of various kinds. The traditional or Vinerian answer to this seeming paradox will be activism by producers' lobbies in the wake of passive consumers. The former benefit from and promote the trade-diverting preferential arrangements.

However, this traditional explanation has limited validity and none at all for the Asia-Pacific region. Non-economic or political reasons are often at work – for instance, they played an important role in the formation of the EU. The GATT-sponsored multilateral trade negotiations frustrated many a successful economy, because during the last two rounds, negotiations progressed with glacial pace. To make this scenario more dire, the Uruguay Round in which 116 countries participated, not all as contracting parties (CPs), collapsed. The Uruguay Round was the most ambitions round of multilateral trade negotiations ever launched. Its failure disappointed many who were committed to the virtues of free trade.

Against this background, interest in the regional economic activity or formation of FTAs became a natural development or *gewachsene*. Many policy intellectuals began to believe that economic and trade-related agreements can be finessed relatively easily only at the regional level. Several reasons could lead to such a situation. First, by the time of the Kennedy Round the sheer number of negotiating countries had swelled so much that formulae for negotiating tariff reductions had to be designed of necessity. Secondly, neo-protectionism involved complex grey area measures such as voluntary export restraints (VERs), orderly marketing arrangements (OMAs) and the like which tended to be difficult to monitor on a global scale. Thirdly, with eroding American hegemony, the rule-making and enforcing power of the USA has dissipated considerably. International co-operation organisations had worked better with a friendly hegemonic power. Fourthly, institutional differences among major economies had led to systemic problems in the past (Krugman, 1993). A certain set of international policy measures may yield one set of results in one major economy but a different set of results in another. For instance, winding down tariffs may open American markets more but it may have little market-opening affect on the Japanese market because of the *keiretsu* system. In such cases, one-to-one negotiations become more useful than generalised international agreements.

Since agreements regarding FTA take place in similar economies or those having similar objectives, the concessions are mutually exchanged and thereby the vexing 'free rider' problem is eliminated. So is the harmful role of the 'foot draggers'. In current trade negotiations in the trade in services this issue has a great deal of relevance because unlike in the past, the free riders are now substantial traders in their own right: their free rides have higher nuisance value now. FTAs also establish special bilateral relationships among the members. Although it is a flagrant infringement of the spirit of the GATT, partners also see FTAs as a means to redress their bilateral trade imbalances.

Scale-economies and opportunities for specialisation are also relevant considerations for FTAs. Regional arrangements enable economies of large-scale production. They improve efficiency even if they cause trade diversion. If, by entering into a FTA, a country displaces the exports of another country that had natural comparative advantage in a product, its own costs come down and its product becomes competitive due to exploitation of scale-economies. This argument is germane to the Asia-Pacific region. In addition, when large current account disequilibria exist, imports with the lowest monetary costs do not measure economic costs accurately. They, apparently, do not have the lowest opportunity costs. Trade discrimination, by creating FTAs, can help in offsetting the current account disequilibrium. This was the basic idea behind the IMF's scarce currency clause (Wonnacott and Lutz, 1989). When an FTA between Taiwan and the USA was proposed, it was intended to help the US economy with its large deficits and to gain market at the expense of the Japanese exporters.

In the EC, North America and the Asia-Pacific where regional economic ties have been strengthening, like-minded countries have been coming together. Although countries involved are far from uniform, geographical proximity, historical ties and socio-economic similarities exist between them. With enhancing regional economic ties and growing deregulation in the domestic markets, co-ordination in macroeconomic and monetary policies becomes a more achievable target. When the groups are smaller, co-operative solutions to multilateral issues become a more certain possibility. True to their nature – and to Vinerian analysis – FTAs lead to trade-creation and trade diversion. How each FTA will behave will depend entirely upon its circumstances. Empirical studies of the welfare effects of actual customs unions and FTAs have shown them as small and uncertain (Pomfret, 1988; Lloyd, 1992). To be sure, regional groupings can be designed in such a manner as to increase market size, competition and improve resource allocation.

The regional ties that grow without forming a defensive economic bloc, or which maintain a stance of open regionalism, in effect become complementary to the multilateral system. This form of regionalism enhances multilateral liberalisation. Therefore, instead of opposing the regional economic links, attention needs to be given to the quality of regional co-operation and the openness of regional arrangement (Lorenz, 1989). If the FTA is not inward-looking or trade-diverting, it is a building block not a stumbling block for an integrated world economy. (This point will be further elaborated in the next section). This kind of regionalism is akin to the old notion of the GATT-Plus, where like-minded countries group in a GATT-consistent manner to grant each other privileges. These privileges are additional to the GATT discipline. In effect, it was conditional application of the most-favoured-nation (MFN) clause, like the codes of the Tokyo Round (The Atlantic Council of the United States, 1976). Although a derogation, the GATT-Plus concept was accepted as the second-best solution. However, it was never translated into action.

Arraying the merchandise trade statistics of various preferential trading groups, one observes that in 1990 the EC accounted for 41.0 per cent of the total merchandise trade of the world, the Canada-USA FTA for 17.1 per cent, the EFTA for 6.7 per cent and the ASEAN for 4.4 per cent. Thus 69.2 per cent of the total merchandise trade of the world can be attributed to the four top preferential trading groups. Their share is so large because these trading groups comprise large trading countries. As opposed to this, there are groups like the Central American Common Market and the Economic and Customs Union of Central Africa that accounted for 0.1 per cent of world merchandise trade. The fact that a group of neighbouring countries has begun to trade intensively does not imply that countries have turned inward and they are trading more at the expense of other non-member countries (Fieleke, 1992). It is likely that they trade more because of lower transportation and communications costs. No country or region where these trends are strengthening can possibly ignore their extra-regional trade and economic links (Lawrence, 1991a).

REGIONALISM AND THE GATT

The architects of the GATT placed the principle of non-discrimination in its foundation. It is enshrined in Article I as the Most-Favoured-Nation (MFN) clause and was intended to provide the best prospects for equitable trade to all the contracting parties (CPs) in an expanding world economy. According to Article I, all CPs must be treated equally. Regional trade arrangements contravene this philosophy and seemingly undermine the GATT. Free traders, therefore, have an intrinsic negative attitude towards regional arrangements. However, the drafters of the GATT were not surprised by these developments. Regional arrangements are allowable under the GATT code: one of the articles of agreement devotes explicit attention to the issue of regional trade preferences. These articles have a clear perception of the trade dynamics involved in the formation of a regional trading and economic bloc.

The provisions of Article XXIV of the GATT allow for the formation of an FTA or a customs union or for the adoption of an interim agreement necessary for their formation (see Appendix 1). The substantive qualifications of Article XXIV include the following: first, for an FTA, the individual tariffs must not be higher than the corresponding tariffs for the constituent territories prior to the formation of the FTA; second, tariffs and other restrictive regulations have to be eliminated with respect to 'substantially all the trade' between the constituents of the FTA; third, for a customs union, the common tariff rates and other regulations of commerce must not be higher or more restrictive than the general incidence of those applicable in the constituent territories prior to the formation of the customs union (para 5). In order to ensure that the CPs abide by these specifications when they form FTAs or customs unions, they are required to notify GATT instantaneously when taking such steps (paras 6 and 7). The same article also prescribes detailed regulations regarding the fixing of new tariffs.

There are two fine points of Article XXIV which have enormous operational implications. First, Article XXIV provides that while discrimination is allowed, it must be complete, not partial or with discrimination in patches. The discriminating CPs need to eliminate, not reduce, all trade barriers on *substantially all* trade among themselves. There is good reason behind this seeming incongruity that partial discrimination is not allowable whereas complete discrimination is allowed. However, this incongruity can be explained. Partial discrimination, covering some products but not all, is likely to lead to an emphasis on trade diversion with little trade creation. CPs can pick and choose products for making preferential agreements at the cost of minimum-cost-producer third countries. In addition, partial discrimination will open the way to avoiding trade-creating tariff cuts. Thus, allowing complete discrimination protects the rights of the minimum-cost-producer third countries and helps in ensuring efficiency within the FTA. Conversely, allowing partial discrimination as an instrument of everyday commercial policy will amount to the death knell of the liberal trading system. Secondly, to be sure, discriminatory trade liberalisation will displace the exports of the non-member third countries. However, the drafters of the Articles have done some damage control work. In a real life situation, the competitiveness of exports of the non-member third countries to the members of the FTA will indubitably decline, but they may well be able to export lower volumes. At the same time, since the tariffs of an FTA or customs union cannot be higher than those of its constituent territories prior to the formation of FTA, the non-member third countries will not be able to claim loss of benefit due to trade diversion (Finger, 1993).

Opinion in this regard varies and several scholars maintain that Article XXIV has been abused and that it was only intended for small regional arrangements like the Benelux (Patterson, 1989). Creation of the EC is considered by some to be the first and the most serious such abuse. At the time the EC was born, it was subjected to extensive debate and no agreement was reached regarding the legality of the EC *vis-à-vis* the requirements of Article XXIV. At the same time, it was clear that if the EC was found to be illegal, the GATT as an institution would be dealt a mortal blow, because the formation of the EC was going forward anyway. Pragmatically, therefore, attention was shifted from the question of legality to specific and practical problems. Since then the EC has operated as if it has received the GATT's approval of its legality. The EFTA, shortly thereafter, received similar treatment. In effect, two large regional trading arrangements got away with GATT-incompatible behaviour. During the 1960s and early 1970s, the EC created a network of preferential trading arrangements with the Mediterranean countries which was injurious to US trade. In addition, preferential trade relations with the French and Belgian colonies expanded to include over sixty African, Caribbean and Pacific nations in the Lomé Convention of 1975. The EC also established an FTA in manufactured goods with the EFTA, so that Britain could come into the fold of EC. In the process, the EC had developed a 'pyramid of privileges' which flagrantly flouted the MFN principle (Stevens, 1981). The EC's MFN tariffs, which should have been applied to all the CPs, applied to six trading partners: Australia, Canada, Japan, New Zealand, Taiwan and the USA. Since all the other countries were enjoying one kind of special treatment or another, this group received something akin to the least-favoured-nation treatment (Pomfret, 1992). Little wonder that the Luetwilder Report was firmly critical of 'the exceptions and ambiguities' which were permitted, in effect, weakening the discipline and eroding the GATT system. In deviations like the EC and the EFTA, Leutwilder *et al.* saw clear evidence of 'damage to the trade interest of non-participants' (Leutwilder *et al.*, 1985).

As opposed to the above, Schott (1989) contended that bilateral trade negotiations need not be an antithesis of the multilateral process. In a way, the GATT itself is a multilateral extension of the bilateral trade agreements negotiated by the USA in the decade following the passage of the Reciprocal Trade Agreements Act of 1934 (Destler, 1986). Until the Kennedy Round, bilateral accords also played a dominant role in shaping the multilateral trade liberalisation that the GATT could achieve. After chafing under the controversy for decades, the GATT has come to a well-thought out stance in this regard. That is, it does not consider regionalism and multilateralism as rival strategies, but as two sides of the same coin. It views regionalism as a useful supplement, not an alternative, to multilateralism. When the CPs decide to enter into regional agreements within the framework of their multilateral obligations, the multilateralism and regionalism co-exist. The débâcle of the Uruguay Round made it obvious that the difficulties involved in following the multilateral route are enormous, which left regional co-operation as the only practical alternative. The GATT has given its consent to treating regional and multilateral approaches to trade liberalisaton as mutually supportive (Dunkel, 1992). It sees Article XXIV as a recognition of the fact that the process of economic integration is a continuum, not limited to a point in time. The draft Uruguay Round agreement has introduced improvements in the effects of regional agreements on the non-member third countries and has proposed modifications to control damage. There is no reason why regional agreements should not, on balance, provide gains for members and non-members alike. Open regionalism of this nature will have beneficial implications for multilateral trade in general.

MARKET-LED REGIONAL INTEGRATION

Frankel (1991), in his award-winning paper, has convincingly argued that – in spite of some symptoms – there is no clear

Table 6.2 Intra-Trade within the EU, the NAFTA and the Asia-Pacific, 1965–90

I. Intra-Trade within the EU

Year	Imports			Exports		
	Total imports ($ bn.)	Annual growth rates (%)	Selected average growth rates (%)	Total exports ($ bn.)	Annual growth rates (%)	Selected average growth rates (%)
1965	33.3			32.8		
1966	36.9	10.8		36.0	9.9	
1967	38.6	4.7		37.8	5.0	
1968	43.8	13.4		42.9	13.7	
1969	53.8	22.8		52.6	22.5	
1970	62.3	16.0		61.8	17.4	
1971	71.5	14.8		71.4	15.6	
1972	88.5	23.6		88.6	24.1	
1973	123.0	39.0		123.0	38.7	
1974	154.0	25.2		155.0	26.0	
1975	163.0	5.8		162.0	4.5	
1976	185.0	13.5		185.0	14.2	
1977	211.0	14.1		211.0	14.1	
1978	258.0	22.3		260.0	23.2	
1979	335.0	29.8		339.0	30.4	
1980	380.0	13.4	18.7 (1965–80)	384.0	13.3	18.9 (1965–80)
1981	331.0	-12.9		334.0	-13.0	
1982	326.0	-1.5		330.0	-1.2	
1983	322.0	-1.2		326.0	-1.2	
1984	325.0	0.9		330.0	1.2	

Table 6.2 Continued

I. Intra-Trade within the EU

Year	Imports			Exports		
	Total imports ($ bn.)	Annual growth rates (%)	Selected average growth rates (%)	Total exports ($ bn.)	Annual growth rates (%)	Selected average growth rates (%)
1985	349.0	7.4		352.0	6.7	
1986	445.0	27.5		450.0	27.8	
1987	553.0	24.3		559.0	24.2	
1988	623.0	12.7		626.0	12.0	
1989	667.0	7.1		674.0	7.7	
1990	818.0	22.6	11.7 (1981–90)	820.0	21.7	11.6 (1981–90)

Table 6.2 Continued

II. Intra-Trade within the NAFTA

Year	Imports			Exports		
	Total imports ($ bn.)	Annual growth rates (%)	Selected average growth rates (%)	Total exports ($ bn.)	Annual growth rates (%)	Selected average growth rates (%)
1965	12.2			11.9		
1966	14.6	20.0		14.1	18.6	
1967	16.4	12.8		15.7	11.3	
1968	19.5	18.6		18.6	18.3	
1969	22.4	14.6		21.1	13.4	
1970	23.5	5.0		22.0	4.5	
1971	26.4	12.4		24.8	12.7	
1972	31.5	19.4		29.6	19.3	
1973	39.3	24.8		36.8	24.5	
1974	51.5	30.9		48.2	30.8	
1975	52.7	2.4		49.7	3.3	
1976	60.6	14.9		56.9	14.4	
1977	66.1	9.2		61.5	8.0	
1978	75.0	13.5		69.7	13.3	
1979	93.7	24.9		84.7	21.6	
1980	110.0	17.4	15.5 (1965–80)	101.0	19.2	15.1 (1965–80)
1981	123.0	11.8		115.0	13.9	
1982	110.0	-10.6		99.8	-13.2	
1983	120.0	9.1		113.0	13.2	
1984	147.0	22.5		136.0	20.4	

Table 6.2 Continued

II. Intra-Trade within the NAFTA

Year	Imports			Exports		
	Total imports ($ bn.)	Annual growth rates (%)	Selected average growth rates (%)	Total exports ($ bn.)	Annual growth rates (%)	Selected average growth rates (%)
1985	153.0	4.1		140.0	2.9	
1986	145.0	-5.2		127.0	-9.3	
1987	160.0	10.3		155.0	22.0	
1988	189.0	18.1		182.0	17.4	
1989	207.0	9.5		200.0	9.9	
1990	219.0	5.8	7.6 (1981–90)	219.0	9.5	8.4 (1981–90)

Table 6.2 Continued

III. Intra-Trade within the Asia-Pasific Region

Year	Imports			Exports		
	Total imports ($ bn.)	Annual growth rates (%)	Selected average growth rates (%)	Total exports ($ bn.)	Annual growth rates (%)	Selected average growth rates (%)
1965	6.2			6.0		
1966	7.0	13.2		6.9	14.3	
1967	7.9	13.0		7.6	10.8	
1968	8.7	9.7		8.6	12.8	
1969	10.5	21.4		10.5	22.5	
1970	12.6	19.9		12.1	15.5	
1971	14.5	15.1		13.7	13.3	
1972	17.8	22.4		16.8	22.7	
1973	28.9	62.5		28.6	69.6	
1974	42.8	48.0		40.5	41.6	
1975	40.7	-4.9		39.4	-2.7	
1976	49.6	22.0		47.0	19.4	
1977	56.8	14.4		54.3	15.4	
1978	71.4	25.8		68.8	26.8	
1979	93.5	31.0		88.4	28.4	
1980	116.9	25.0	22.7 (1965–80)	109.9	24.3	22.5 (1965–80)
1981	129.5	10.8		120.2	9.3	
1982	125.9	-2.8		117.5	-2.2	
1983	127.6	1.4		119.4	1.6	
1984	147.3	15.4		136.4	14.2	

Table 6.2 Continued

III. Intra-Trade within the Asia-Pasific Region

Year	Imports			Exports		
	Total imports ($ bn.)	Annual growth rates (%)	Selected average growth rates (%)	Total exports ($ bn.)	Annual growth rates (%)	Selected average growth rates (%)
1985	150.6	2.3		137.2	0.6	
1986	155.8	3.4		142.8	4.1	
1987	200.0	28.4		182.0	27.5	
1988	259.5	29.8		236.5	29.9	
1989	295.3	13.8		272.2	15.1	
1991	325.3	10.1	12.0 (1981–90)	300.3	10.3	11.8 (1981–90)

Source: International Economic Data Bank, Australian National University, Canberra.

evidence of 'an evolving East Asian trade bloc centred on Japan'. Let me take some illuminating strands out of his line of logic. The share of intra-regional trade in the Asia-Pacific region, according to his computations, increased from 33 per cent in 1980 to 37 per cent in 1989. The corresponding proportions for the EC were 51 per cent and 59 per cent and for North America 32 per cent and 37 per cent, respectively. Thus, while the EC is the largest trading bloc and one of long standing, the other two regions have recorded identical proportions of intra-trade growth. Using another indicator, namely, long-term average growth rates of intra-regional exports and intra-regional imports, one observes that in the Asia-Pacific region the average annual growth rate of intra-regional imports was 22.7 per cent over 1965–80 and 12.0 per cent over 1981–90. As Table 6.2 shows, these averages were higher than those for the EC and far higher than those for the NAFTA for both the periods. The story on the intra-regional exports side is identical: the growth rate for the 1965–80 period was 22.5 per cent for the Asia-Pacific region whereas that for the 1981–90 period was 11.8 per cent. Again, these growth rates were higher than those for the EC and much higher than those recorded by the NAFTA (Table 6.2).

Since manufacturing is considered to be one of the most dynamic sectors of any economy, it is worthwhile comparing the trends in intra-trade in manufactures in the three regions. Intra-regional imports in manufactures increased at an average rate of 18.5 per cent over the 1965–80 period in the Asia-Pacific region and a rate of 12.0 per cent over the 1981–90 period (Table 6.3). These growth rates are virtually the same as those in the EC for the two periods but are considerably higher than those for the NAFTA. The growth rates of intra-regional exports in manufactured products in the Asia-Pacific region were 21.7 per cent and 14.4 per cent, respectively, for the two periods. These two averages turned out to be higher than the corresponding averages in the EC and much higher than those in the NAFTA region.

These statistics demonstrate the coming together, or integrating if you prefer, of the Asia-Pacific economies by way of trade.

Table 6.3 Intra-Trade in Manufactures within the EU, the NAFTA and the Asia-Pacific, 1965–90

I. Intra-Trade in Manufactures within the EU

Year	Imports			Exports		
	Total imports of manufactures ($ bn.)	Annual growth rates (%)	Selected average growth rates (%)	Total exports of manufactures ($ bn.)	Annual growth rates (%)	Selected average growth rates (%)
1965	22.7			22.6		
1966	25.4	11.9		25.2	11.4	
1967	26.7	5.0		26.5	5.3	
1968	30.5	14.3		30.4	14.6	
1969	38.2	25.3		37.9	24.6	
1970	45.1	18.0		44.9	18.5	
1971	52.2	15.6		52.5	16.9	
1972	64.7	23.9		65.1	24.0	
1973	88.5	36.8		88.9	36.6	
1974	109.0	23.1		110.0	23.7	
1975	115.0	5.5		115.0	4.5	
1976	133.0	15.7		134.0	16.5	
1977	151.0	13.5		152.0	13.4	
1978	187.0	23.8		189.0	24.3	
1979	240.0	28.3		244.0	29.1	
1980	267.0	11.3	18.9 (1965–80)	271.0	11.1	19.1 (1965–80)
1981	227.3	−14.9		229.6	−15.3	
1982	225.3	−0.9		228.7	−0.4	

Table 6.3 Continued

I. Intra-Trade in Manufactures within the EU

Year	Imports			Exports		
	Total imports of manufactures ($ bn.)	Annual growth rates (%)	Selected average growth rates (%)	Total exports of manufactures ($ bn.)	Annual growth rates (%)	Selected average growth rates (%)
1983	220.5	-2.2		224.5	-1.8	
1984	222.7	1.0		226.9	1.0	
1985	241.7	8.5		246.2	8.5	
1986	330.6	36.8		336.4	36.7	
1987	419.7	27.0		428.3	27.3	
1988	481.6	14.8		485.8	13.4	
1989	519.9	7.9		525.8	8.2	
1990	642.9	23.7		646.1	22.9	
			13.8 (1981–90)			13.7 (1981–90)

Table 6.3   Intra-Trade in Manufactures within the EU, the NAFTA and the Asia-Pacific, 1965–90

II. Intra-Trade in Manufactures within the NAFTA

Year	Imports			Exports		
	Total imports of manufactures ($ bn.)	Annual growth rates (%)	Selected average growth rates (%)	Total exports of manufactures ($ bn.)	Annual growth rates (%)	Selected average growth rates (%)
1965	7.8			7.4		
1966	9.8	25.9		9.3	26.6	
1967	11.6	18.2		10.9	16.6	
1968	14.0	20.4		13.0	19.6	
1969	16.5	17.8		15.1	16.4	
1970	17.0	3.0		15.5	2.6	
1971	19.5	14.6		17.9	15.0	
1972	23.1	18.8		21.0	17.8	
1973	28.3	22.4		25.8	22.7	
1974	35.8	26.5		32.6	26.2	
1975	37.2	3.9		34.4	5.7	
1976	43.5	17.0		39.8	15.8	
1977	46.9	7.7		42.8	7.4	
1978	53.0	13.2		48.8	13.9	
1979	65.2	23.0		57.4	17.8	
1980	72.3	10.9	15.5 (1965–80)	65.0	13.2	15.2 (1965–80)
1981	84.7	17.1		77.5	19.3	
1982	73.5	–13.2		64.7	–16.5	

Table 6.3 Continued

II. Intra-Trade in Manufactures within the NAFTA

Year	Imports			Exports		
	Total imports of manufactures ($ bn.)	Annual growth rates (%)	Selected average growth rates (%)	Total exports of manufactures ($ bn.)	Annual growth rates (%)	Selected average growth rates (%)
1983	81.1	10.4		75.0	15.8	
1984	104.9	29.2		94.9	26.5	
1985	111.3	6.2		100.8	6.3	
1986	110.8	-0.5		96.6	-4.2	
1987	122.4	10.4		118.7	22.9	
1988	146.8	19.9		141.6	19.3	
1989	158.7	8.1		156.2	10.3	
1990	167.1	5.3	9.5 (1981–90)	167.6	7.3	10.8 (1981–90)

Table 6.3   Intra-Trade in Manufactures within the EU, the NAFTA and the Asia-Pacific, 1965–90

III. Intra-Trade in Manufactures within the Asia-Pasific Region

Year	Imports			Exports		
	Total imports of manufactures ($ bn.)	Annual growth rates (%)	Selected average growth rates (%)	Total exports of manufactures ($ bn.)	Annual growth rates (%)	Selected average growth rates (%)
1965	3.0			2.9		
1966	3.4	14.3		3.3	14.5	
1967	4.0	17.2		3.7	11.3	
1968	4.5	12.4		4.4	20.2	
1969	5.5	21.8		5.4	22.3	
1970	6.7	21.5		6.4	18.5	
1971	7.9	17.7		7.4	16.6	
1972	9.6	22.0		9.2	23.5	
1973	15.6	61.8		15.4	67.8	
1974	22.5	44.5		21.2	37.6	
1975	21.4	–4.7		20.8	–2.1	
1976	26.1	21.6		24.9	19.7	
1977	29.9	14.9		28.5	14.7	
1978	40.2	34.2		39.9	39.9	
1979	49.7	23.7		48.7	22.2	
1980	61.0	22.7		60.6	23.0	
			18.5 (1965–81)			21.7 (1965–80)
1981	70.2	15.1		68.5	14.3	
1982	66.7	–5.0		64.3	–6.1	

Table 6.3 Continued

II. Intra-Trade in Manufactures within the Asia-Pasific Region

Year	Imports			Exports		
	Total imports of manufactures ($ bn.)	Annual growth rates (%)	Selected average growth rates (%)	Total exports of manufactures ($ bn.)	Annual growth rates (%)	Selected average growth rates (%)
1983	70.7	5.9		67.9	5.6	
1984	85.5	21.0		80.4	18.4	
1985	90.7	6.1		83.4	3.7	
1986	103.0	13.5		95.6	14.7	
1987	136.7	32.7		125.7	31.4	
1988	183.9	34.6		170.2	35.4	
1989	213.4	16.0		197.3	15.9	
1990	237.3	11.2	12.0 (1981–90)	219.9	11.4	14.4 (1981–90)

Source: International Economic Data Bank, Australian National University, Canberra.

Frankel argued that if one allows for the phenomenon that most of the Asia-Pacific economies recorded rapid growth in total output as well as in trade, it is likely that there has been no movement towards an intra-regional bias in the evolving pattern of trade. He logically stated that since the total trade of the Asia-Pacific economies, in dollar terms, increased by 108 per cent between 1980 and 1989 while world trade increased by only 53 per cent, therefore, even if there was no regional bias, the observed intra-regional share of trade would have increased by one-third due *solely* to the greater weight of the Asia-Pacific countries in the world economy. However, Frankel is not countering the coming together, or integrating, of the regional economies. His emphasis is on bringing to the fore the coming together of these economies without any policy bias or an overt attempt to integrate.

If only transport costs are taken into account, countries will tend to trade with those that are closer rather than those that are far away. Likewise, though the trade of the Asia-Pacific economies increased rapidly, it increased more rapidly with the regional economies. That is to repeat that it occurred without any institutionalised bias. A closely related issue is that of the bilateral trade of Japan with the rest of the region. Like intra-regional trade, the trade of the Asia-Pacific region with Japan increased rapidly. The *endaka* was one of the major reasons behind this (Das, 1993). Another was the reversal in decline that set in during the first half of the 1980s (Petri, 1991). Thus, this growth of bilateral trade was a totally natural outcome of the play of market forces. Lawrence (1991b) has calculated that out of the 28 per cent increase in the market share of the Asia-Pacific economies in Japanese imports over the 1985–8 period, 11 per cent is attributable to improved competition and 18 per cent to the commodity mix of their exports. There is no residual to be attributed to Japan's special endeavours in terms of institutionalisation of regional trade. Thus one can infer that countries near each other trade with each other for a myriad of economic reasons. There is no evidence of Asia-Pacific economies concentrating on trade with each other in any non-market or institutionalised manner.

Saxonhouse (1992) estimated factor, endowment-based gravity equations in order to examine more systematically the issue of regional bias in trade and investment. The results for the Asia-Pacific intra-regional exports compared with those of exports to North America and the EU were striking. The intra-regional exports appeared to be well-explained by a factor-endowment-based gravity equation. Out of a total of 2088 trade flows, Saxonhouse estimates only 325 were outside the tolerance interval. This small number of extreme observations suggested that there was little policy bias in the Asia-Pacific trade. Neither trade-related policy initiatives nor large intra-regional investments have resulted in intra-regional distortions. This conclusion is applicable not only to the whole Asia-Pacific region but also to the individual economies. None of the following regional economies had more than a small number of extreme observations: Japan, Korea, Taiwan, Hong Kong, Malaysia, the Philippines and Singapore.

Regional economies can and do integrate in a market-driven manner as well as in an institutionalised manner. The foregoing exposition clearly and convincingly established that the recent growth of economic relations among Asia-Pacific economies is an example of the former. As opposed to this, economic integration in Europe has flourished within a formal and institutional framework, and discriminates against economies outside the EU. The Asia-Pacific is not a discriminatory FTA but is wedded to the concept of *open regionalism* which – as we saw – is GATT–consistent. It is a regionalism of functional variety, not a formal variety. Since these economies benefited immensely from international trade and are dependent on it, they have a great deal at stake in the maintenance of an open international trade regime. Their interest encompasses all the issues that are presently under negotiation in the Uruguay Round. Their collective voice in its support gives them an important multilateral role.

If the Asia-Pacific region chooses to adopt formal regionalism, rejecting the open, functional kind, it will not be easy to establish an EC-like regional framework in the Asia-Pacific region. This is because in the process of brisk growth, some barriers to international transactions were taken off in some economies, but others were raised or introduced anew; many were not removed in the first place. Brisk growth and equally brisk changing comparative advantage necessitated structural adjustments in the regional economies. Their general record in this regard has been good (Drysdale and Garnaut, 1989b). But this cannot be taken to mean that there are no examples of tariffs and non-tariff barriers blocking the structural adjustment process. Several notable instances of high trade barriers are to be found in industries that were losing comparative advantage as a result of economic change. Conspicuous among them are the foodstuffs industry in Japan, Korea and Taiwan and the labour-intensive and standard-technology manufacturing industry in Australia. Although recent policy initiatives have brought them down, Australia and New Zealand had the highest average tariff levels of all OECD countries on manufactured goods. Contrary to international perception, Japan has the cleanest import system for manufactured goods among OECD countries, lowest tariffs and the least formal non-tariff barriers (NTBs). Yet, it does have powerful conservative biases that slow down large-scale imports. The NTBs were high on manufactured imports in Korea and Taiwan, although both economies were taking liberalising measures. Similarly, manufacturing output was highly distorted by tariffs, quantitative restrictions and local content regulations in China and the ASEAN countries. Although liberalisation efforts have been made by them, a good deal remains to be done. This state of affairs will not be conducive to the formation of a formal FTA in the short term. An open and informal regional integration arrangement that came into being almost on its own fits the region well (Drysdale and Garnaut, 1992). My contention is that the deepening Asia-Pacific economic integration and its open regionalism of the *de facto* variety will continue to co-exist and reinforce each other. The concept of *de jure* regionalism of the discriminatory EU variety does not gel with the Asia-Pacific region. This kind of open regionalism has the potential to become complementary to the multilateral system and enhance economic liberalisation. Thus, to answer the question raised in the first section of this chapter, the region – propelled by market forces – has devised for itself a functional and situation-specific framework. The regional economies have been integrating themselves in a market-driven manner. This mode is not only GATT-consistent but is also an antithesis of the closed regionalism of the EU-variety.

CONCLUSION

The free-traders consider regionalism to be a contravention of the principle of non-discrimination and the MFN clause of the GATT. Yet no region in the world is presently without a regional trading arrangement. The upsurge in neo-protectionism and the débâcle of the Uruguay Round have raised international interest in regionalism again. Except for two minor formal agreements, the Asia-Pacific region is so far without a comprehensive regional grouping. Several economic benefits are seen in a regional economic and trading arrangement by the member economies. This leads to both trade creation and trade diversion. However, if regional economic ties grow without forming a defensive economic bloc, and if the countries of the Asia-Pacific maintain a stance of open regionalism, such regional economic ties do not harm the interests of the non-members and, in addition, become complementary to the open multilateral economic system.

Regional arrangements are allowed under the provisions of Article XXIV of the GATT. However, members of an FTA have to eliminate, not reduce, all trade barriers on substantially all trade among themselves; partial discrimination is not allowed. The GATT has given its consent to treating regional and multilateral approaches to trade liberalisation as mutually supportive strategies that can co-exist.

Since economic ties have strengthened a great deal among the Asia-Pacific economies, one gets an impression that this region is also heading towards forming an EU-like bloc. However, economic integration in the Asia-Pacific was market-driven, and took place without any conscious policy bias. It is difficult for the region to adopt an EU-like regional stance. It has, over the years, adopted the principle of open regionalism which is GATT-consistent. It is a regionalism of functional variety, not a formal variety, and it does not harm the interests of the non-members.

Appendix: Article XXIV of the GATT

Territorial Application – Frontier Traffic – Customs Unions and Free-Trade Areas

1. The provisions of this Agreement shall apply to the metropolitan customs territories of the contracting parties and to any other customs territories in respect of which this Agreement has been accepted under Article XXIV or is being applied under Article XXXIII or pursuant to the Protocol of Provisional Application. Each such customs territory shall, exclusively for the purposes of the territorial application of this Agreement, be treated as though it were a contracting party; *Provided* that the provisions of this paragraph shall not be construed to create any rights or obligations as between two or more customs territories in respect of which this Agreement has been accepted under Article XXVI or is being applied under Article XXXIII or pursuant to the Protocol of Provisional Application by a single contracting party.

2. For the purposes of this Agreement a customs territory shall be understood to mean any territory with respect to which separate tariffs or other regulations of commerce are maintained for a substantial part of the trade of such territory with other territories.

3. The provisions of this Agreement shall not be construed to prevent:

    (a) Advantages accorded by any contracting party to adjacent countries in order to facilitate frontier traffic;
    (b) Advantages accorded to the trade with the Free Territory of Trieste by countries contiguous to that territory, provided that such advantages are not in conflict with the Treaties of Peace arising out of the Second World War.

4. The contracting parties recognize the desirability of increasing freedom of trade by the development, through voluntary agreements, of closer integration between the economies of the countries parties to such agreements. They also recognize that the purpose of a customs union or of a free-trade area should be to facilitate trade between the constituent territories and not to raise barriers to the trade of other contracting parties with such territories.

5. Accordingly, the provisions of this Agreement shall not prevent, as between the territories of contracting parties, the formation of a customs union or of a free-trade area or the adoption of an interim agreement necessary for the formation of a customs union or of a free-trade area; *Provided* that:

(a) with respect to a customs union, or an interim agreement leading to the formation of a customs union, the duties and other regulations of commerce imposed at the institution of any such union or interim agreement in respect of trade with contracting parties not parties to such union or agreement shall not on the whole be higher or more restrictive than the general incidence of the duties and regulations of commerce applicable in the constituent territories prior to the formation of such union or the adoption of such interim agreement, as the case may be;

(b) with respect to a free-trade area, or an interim agreement leading to the formation of a free-trade area, the duties and other regulations of commerce maintained in each if the constituent territories and applicable at the formation of such free-trade area or the adoption of such interim agreement to the trade of contracting parties not included in such area or not parties to such agreement shall not be higher or more restrictive than the corresponding duties and other regulations of commerce existing in the same constituent territories prior to the formation of the free-trade area, or interim agreement, as the case may be; and

(c) any interim agreement referred to in sub-paragraphs (a) and (b) shall include a plan and schedule for the formation of such a customs union or of such a free-trade area within a reasonable length of time.

6. If, in fulfilling the requirements of sub-paragraph 5 (a), a contracting party proposes to increase any rate of duty inconsistently with the provisions of Article II, the procedure set forth in Article XXVIII shall apply. In providing for compensatory adjustment, due account shall be taken of the compensation already afforded by the reductions brought about in the corresponding duty of the other constituents of the union.

7. (a) Any contracting party deciding to enter into a customs union or free-trade area, or an interim agreement leading to the formation of such a union or area, shall promptly notify the CONTRACTING PARTIES and shall make available to them such information regarding the proposed union or area as will enable them to make such reports and recommendations to contracting parties as they deem appropriate.

(b) If, after having studied the plan and schedule included in an interim agreement referred to in paragraph 5 in consultation with the parties to that agreement and taking due account of the information made available in accordance with the provisions of sub-paragraph (a), the CONTRACTING PARTIES find that such agreement is not likely to result in the formation of a customs union or of a free-trade area within the period contemplated by the parties to the agreement or that such period is not a reasonable one, the CONTRACTING PARTIES shall make recommendations to the parties to the agreement. The parties shall not maintain or put into force, as the case may be, such an agreement if they are not prepared to modify it in accordance with these recommendations.

(c)   Any substantial change in the plan or schedule referred to in paragraph 5 (c) shall be communicated to the CONTRACTING PARTIES, which may request the contracting parties concerned to consult with them if the change seems likely to jeopardize or delay unduly the formation of the customs union or of the free-trade area.

8.   For the purposes of this Agreement:

(a)   A customs union shall be understood to mean the substitution of a single customs territory for two or more customs territories, so that

    (i)   duties and other restrictive regulations of commerce (except, where necessary, those permitted under Articles XI, XII, XIII, XIV, XV and XX) are eliminated with respect to substantially all the trade between the constituent territories of the union or at least with respect to substantially all the trade in products originating in such territories, and,

    (ii)   subject to the provisions of paragraph 9, substantially the same duties and other regulations of commerce are applied by each of the members of the union to the trade of territories not included in the union;

(b)   A free-trade area shall be understood to mean a group of two or more customs territories in which the duties and other restrictive regulations of commerce (except, where necessary, those permitted under Articles XI, XII, XIII, XIV, XV and XX) are eliminated on substantially all the trade between the constituent territories in products originating in such territories.

9.   The preferences referred to in paragraph 2 of Article I shall not be affected by the formation of a customs union or of a free-trade area but may be eliminated or adjusted by means of negotiations with contracting parties affected. This procedure of negotiations with affected contracting parties shall, in particular, apply to the elimination of preferences required to conform with the provisions of paragraph 8 (a) (i) and paragraph 8 (b).

10.   The CONTRACTING PARTIES may by a two-thirds majority approve proposals which do not fully comply with the requirements of paragraphs 5 to 9 inclusive, provided that such proposals lead to the formation of a customs union or a free-trade area in the sense of this Article.

11.   Taking into account the exceptional circumstances arising out of the establishment of India and Pakistan as independent States and recognizing the fact that they have long constituted an economic unit, the contracting parties agree that the provisions of this Agreement shall not prevent the two countries from entering into special arrangements with respect to the trade between them, pending the establishment of their mutual trade relations on a definitive basis.

12. Each contracting party shall take such reasonable measure as may be available to it to ensure observance of the provisions of this Agreement by the regional and local governments and authorities within its territory.

GATT exists no more. It has been supplanted by the World Trade Organisation (WTO). Yet, Article XXIV continues to exist and in a strengthened and updated form, it forms a part of the WTO agreement. The clarifications of the Article, Ministerial declarations, decisions and understandings, which spell out further obligations and commitments for WTO members, are as follows:

Territorial Application – Frontier Traffic – Customs Unions and Free-trade Areas

1. The provisions of this Agreement shall apply to the metropolitan customs territories of the contracting parties and to any other customs territories in respect of which this Agreement has been accepted under Article XXVI or is being applied under Article XXXIII or pursuant to the Protocol of Provisional Application. Each such customs territory shall, exclusively for the purposes of the territorial application of this Agreement, be treated as though it were a contracting party; *Provided* that the provisions of this paragraph shall not be construed to create any rights or obligations as between two or more customs territories in respect of which this Agreement has been accepted under Article XXVI or is being applied under Article XXXIII or pursuant to the Protocol of Provisional Application by a single contracting party.

2. For the purposes of this Agreement a customs territory shall be understood to mean any territory with respect to which separate tariffs or other regulations of commerce are maintained for a substantial part of the trade of such territory with other territories.

3. The provisions of this Agreement shall not be construed to prevent:

    (a) Advantages accorded by any contracting party to adjacent countries in order to facilitate frontier traffic;

    (b) Advantages accorded to the trade with the Free Territory of Trieste by countries contiguous to that territory, provided that such advantages are not in conflict with the Treaties of Peace arising out of the Second World War.

4. The contracting parties recognize the desirability of increasing freedom of trade by the development, through voluntary agreements, of closer integration between the economies of the countries parties to such agreements. They also recognize that the purpose of a customs union or of a free-trade area should be to facilitate trade between the constituent territories and not to raise barriers to the trade of other contracting parties with such territories.

5. Accordingly, the provisions of this Agreement shall not prevent, as between the territories of contracting parties, the formation of a customs union or of a free-trade area or the adoption of an interim agreement necessary for the formation of a customs union or of a free-trade area; *Provided* that:

    (a) with respect to a customs union, or an interim agreement leading to a formation of a customs union, the duties and other regulations of commerce imposed at the institution of any such union or interim agreement in respect of trade with contracting parties not parties to such union or agreement shall not on the whole be higher or more restrictive than the general incidence of the duties and regulations of commerce applicable in the constituent territories prior to the formation of such union or the adoption of such interim agreement, as the case may be;

(b) with respect to a free-trade area, or an interim agreement leading to the formation of a free-trade area, the duties and other regulations of commerce maintained in each if the constituent territories and applicable at the formation of such free-trade area or the adoption of such interim agreement to the trade of contracting parties not included in such area or not parties to such agreement shall not be higher or more restrictive than the corresponding duties and other regulations of commerce existing in the same constituent territories prior to the formation of the free-trade area, or interim agreement as the case may be; and

(c) any interim agreement referred to in subparagraphs (a) and (b) shall include a plan and schedule for the formation of such a customs union or of such a free-trade area within a reasonable length of time.

6. If, in fulfilling the requirements of subparagraph 5(a), a contracting party proposes to increase any rate of duty inconsistently with the provisions of Article II, the procedure set forth in Article XXVIII shall apply. In providing for compensatory adjustment, due account shall be taken of the compensation already afforded by the reduction brought about in the corresponding duty of the other constituents of the union.

7. (a) Any contracting party deciding to enter into a customs union or free-trade area, or an interim agreement leading to the formation of such a union or area, shall promptly notify the CONTRACTING PARTIES and shall make available to them such information regarding the proposed union or area as will enable them to make such reports and recommendations to contracting parties as they may deem appropriate.

(b) If, after having studied the plan and schedule included in an interim agreement referred to in paragraph 5 in consultation with the parties to that agreement and taking due account of the information made available in accordance with the provisions of subparagraph (a), the CONTRACTING PARTIES find that such agreement is not likely to result in the formation of a customs union or of a free-trade area within the period contemplated by the parties to the agreement or that such period is not a reasonable one, the CONTRACTING PARTIES shall make recommendations to the parties to the agreement. The parties shall not maintain or put into force, as the case may be, such agreement if they are not prepared to modify it in accordance with these recommendations.

(c) Any substantial change in the plan or schedule referred to in paragraph 5(c) shall be communicated to the CONTRACTING

PARTIES, which may request the contracting parties concerned to consult with them if the change seems likely to jeopardize or delay unduly the formation of the customs union or of the free-trade area.

8. For the purposes of this Agreement:

   (a) A customs union shall be understood to mean the substitution of a single customs territory for two or more customs territories, so that

   (i) duties and other restrictive regulations of commerce (except, where necessary, those permitted under Articles XI, XII, XIII, XIV, XV and XX) are eliminated with respect to substantially all the trade between the constituent territories of the union or at least with respect to substantially all the trade in products originating in such territories, and,

   (ii) subject to the provisions of paragraph 9, substantially the same duties and other regulations of commerce are applied by each of the members of the union to the trade of territories not included in the union;

   (b) A free-trade zone shall be understood to mean a group of two or more customs territories in which the duties and other restrictive regulations of commerce (except, where necessary, those permitted under Articles XI, XII, XIII, XIV, XV and XX) are eliminated on substantially all the trade between the constituent territories in products originating in such territories.

9. The preferences referred to in paragraph 2 of Article I shall not be affected by the formation of a customs union or of a free-trade area but may be eliminated or adjusted by means of negotiations with contracting parties affected. This procedure of negotiations with affected contracting parties shall, in particular, apply to the elimination of preferences required to conform with the provisions of paragraph 8(a)(i) and paragraph 8(b).

10. The CONTRACTING PARTIES may by a two-thirds majority approve proposals which do not fully comply with the requirements of paragraphs 5 to 9 inclusive, provided that such proposals lead to the formation of a customs union or a free-trade area in the sense of this Article.

11. Taking into account the exceptional circumstances arising out of the establishment of India and Pakistan as independent States and recognizing the fact that they have long constituted an economic unit, the contracting parties agree that the provisions of this Agreement shall not prevent the two countries from entering into special arrangements with respect to the trade between them, pending the establishment of their mutual trade relations on a definitive basis.

12. Each contracting party shall take such reasonable measures as may be available to it to ensure observance of the provisions of this Agreement by the regional and local governments and authorities within its territories.

Article XXV

Joint Action by the Contracting Parties

1. Representatives of the contracting parties shall meet from time to time for the purpose of giving effect to those provisions of this Agreement which involve joint action and, generally, with a view to facilitating the operation and furthering the objectives of this Agreement. Wherever reference is made in this Agreement to the contracting parties acting jointly they are designated as the CONTRACTING PARTIES.

2. The Secretary-General of the United Nations is requested to convene the first meeting of the CONTRACTING PARTIES, which shall take place not later than March 1, 1994.

3. Each contracting party shall be entitled to have one vote at all meetings of the CONTRACTING PARTIES.

4. Except as otherwise provided for in this Agreement, decisions of the CONTRACTING PARTIES shall be taken by a majority of the votes cast.

5. In exceptional circumstances not elsewhere provided for in this Agreement, the CONTRACTING PARTIES may waive an obligation imposed upon a contracting party by this Agreement; *Provided* that any such decision shall be approved by a two-thirds majority of the votes cast and that such majority shall comprise more than half of the contracting parties. The CONTRACTING PARTIES may also by such a vote
    (i) define certain categories of exceptional circumstances to which other voting requirements shall apply for the waiver of obligations ....

11. The consulting Member shall prepare a Basic Document for the consultations which, in addition to any other information considered to be relevant, should include; (*a*) an overview of the balance-of-payments situation and prospects, including a consideration of the internal and external factors having a bearing on the balance-of-payments situation and the domestic policy measures taken in order to restore equilibrium on a sound and lasting basis; (*b*) a full description of the restrictions applied for balance-of-payments purposes, their legal basis and steps taken to reduce incidental protective effects; (*c*) measures taken since the last consultation to liberalize import restrictions, in the light of the conclusions of the Committee; (*d*) a plan for the elimination and progressive relaxation of remaining restrictions. References may be made, when relevant, to the information provided in other notifications or reports made to the WTO. Under simplified consultation procedures, the consulting Member shall submit a written statement containing essential information on the elements covered by the Basic Document.

12. The Secretariat shall, with a view to facilitating the consultations in the Committee, prepare a factual background paper dealing with the different aspects of the plan for consultations. In the case of developing country Members, the Secretariat document shall include relevant

background and analytical material on the incidence of the external trading environment on the balance-of-payments situation and prospects of the consulting Member. The technical assistance services of the Secretariat shall, at the request of a developing country Member, assist in preparing the documentation for the consultations.

Conclusions of Balance-of-Payments Consultations

13. The Committee shall report on its consultations to the General Council. When full consultation procedures have been used, the report should indicate the Committee's conclusions on the different elements of the plan for consultations, as well as the facts and reasons on which they are based. The Committee shall endeavour to include in its conclusions proposals for recommendations aimed at promoting the implementation of Articles XII and XVIII:B, the 1979 Declaration and this Understanding. In those cases in which a time-schedule has been presented for the removal of restrictive measures taken for balance-of-payments purposes, the General Council may recommend that, in adhering to such a time-schedule, a Member shall be deemed to be in compliance with its GATT 1994 obligations. Whenever the General Council has made specific recommendations, the rights and obligations of Members shall be assessed in the light of such recommendations. In the absence of specific proposals for recommendations by the General Council, the Committee's conclusions should record the different views expressed in the Committee. When simplified consultation procedures have been used, the report shall include a summary of the main elements discussed in the Committee and a decision on whether full consultation procedures are required.

Understanding on the Interpretation of Article XXIV of the General Agreement on Tariffs and Trade 1994

Members,

Having regard to the provisions of Article XXIV of GATT 1994;

Recognizing that customs unions and free-trade areas have greatly increased in number and importance since the establishment of GATT 1947 and today cover a significant proportion of world trade.

Recognizing the contribution to the expansion of world trade that may be made by closer integration between the economies of the parties to such agreements;

Recognizing also that such contribution is increased if the elimination between the constituent territories of duties and other restrictive regulations of commerce extends to all trade, and diminished of any major sector of trade is excluded;

Reaffirming that the purpose of such agreements should be to facilitate trade between the constituent territories and not to raise barriers to the trade of other Members with such territories; and that their formation or enlargement the parties to them should to be greatest possible extent avoid creating adverse effects on the trade of other Members;

Convinced also of the need to reinforce the effectiveness of the role of the Council for Trade in Goods in reviewing agreements notified under Article XXIV, by clarifying the criteria and procedure for the assessment of new or enlarged agreements, and improving the transparency of all Article XXIV agreements;

Recognizing the need for a common understanding of the obligations of Members under paragraph 12 of Article XXIV;

Hereby *agree* as follows:

1. Customs unions, free-trade areas, and interim agreements leading to the formation of a customs union or free-trade area to be consistent with Article XXIV, must satisfy, *inter alia*, the provisions of paragraphs 5, 6, 7 and 8 of that Article.

Article XXIV:5

2. The evaluation under paragraph 5(a) of Article XXIV of the general incidence of the duties and other regulations of commerce applicable before and after the formation of a customs union shall in respect of duties and charges be based upon an overall assessment of weighted average tariff rates and of customs duties collected. This assessment shall be based on import statistics for a previous representative period to be supplied by the customs union, on a tariff-line basis and in values and quantities, broken down by WTO country of origin. The Secretariat shall compute the weighted average tariff rates and customs duties collected in accordance with the methodology used in the assessment of tariff offers in the Uruguay Round of Multilateral Trade Negotiations. For this purpose, the duties and charges to be taken into consideration shall be the applied rates of duty. It is recognized that for the purpose of the overall assessment of the incidence of other regulations of commerce for which quantification and aggregation are difficult, the examination of individual measures, regulations, products covered and trade flows affected may be required.

3. The 'reasonable length of time' referred to in paragraph 5(*c*) of Article XXIV should exceed 10 years only in exceptional cases. In cases where Members parties to an interim agreement believe that 10 years would be insufficient they shall provide a full explanation to the Council for Trade in Goods of the need for a longer period.

Article XXIV:6

4. Paragraph 6 of Article XXIV establishes the procedure to be followed when a Member forming a customs union proposes to increase a bound rate of duty. In this regard Members reaffirm that the procedure set forth in Article XXVIII, as elaborated in the guidelines adopted on 10 November 1980 (BISD 27S/26-28) and in the Understanding on the Interpretation of Article XXVIII of GATT 1994, must be commenced before tariff concessions are modified or withdrawn upon the formation of a customs union or an interim agreement leading to the formation of a customs union.

5. These negotiations will be entered into in good faith with a view to achieving mutually satisfactory compensatory adjustment. In such negotiations, as required by paragraph 6 of Article XXIV, due account shall be taken of reductions of duties on the same tariff line made by other constituents of the customs union upon its formation. Should such reductions not be sufficient to provide the necessary compensatory adjustment, the customs union would offer compensation, which may take the form of reductions of duties on other tariff lines. Such an offer shall be taken into consideration by the Members having negotiating rights in the binding being modified or withdrawn. Should the compensatory adjustment remain unacceptable, negotiations should be continued.

Where despite such efforts, agreement in negotiations on compensatory adjustment under Article XXVIII as elaborated by the Understanding on the Interpretation of Article XXVIII of GATT 1994 cannot be reached within a reasonable period from the initiation of negotiations, the customs union shall, nevertheless, be free to modify or withdraw the concessions; affected Members shall then be free to withdraw substantially equivalent concessions in accordance with Article XXVIII.

6. GATT 1994 imposes no obligation on Members benefiting from a reduction on duties consequent upon the formation of a customs union, or an interim agreement leading to the formation of a customs union, to provide compensatory adjustment to its constituents.

Review of Customs Unions and Free-Trade Areas

7. All notifications made under paragraph 7(a) of Article XXIV shall be examined by a working party in the light of the relevant provisions of GATT 1994 and of paragraph 1 of this Understanding. The working party shall submit a report to the Council for Trade in Goods on its findings in this regard. The Council for Trade in Goods may make such recommendations to Members as its deems appropriate.

8. In regard to interim agreements, the working party may in its report make appropriate recommendations on the proposed time-frame and on measures required to complete the formation of the customs union or free-trade area. It may if necessary provide for further review of the agreement.

9. Members parties to an interim agreement shall notify substantial changes in the plan and schedule included in that agreement to the Council for Trade in Goods and, if so requested, the Council shall examine the changes.

10. Should an interim agreement notified under paragraph 7(a) of Article XXIV not include a plan and schedule, contrary to paragraph 5(c) of Article XXIV, the working party shall in its report recommend such a plan and schedule. The parties shall not maintain or put into force, as the case may be, such agreement if they are not prepared to modify it in accordance with these recommendations. Provision shall be made for subsequent review of the implementation of the recommendations.

11. Customs unions and constituents of free-trade areas shall report periodically to the Council for Trade in Goods, as envisaged by the CON-

TRACTING PARTIES to GATT 1947 in their instruction to the GATT 1947 Council concerning reports on regional agreements (BISD 18S/38), on the operation of the relevant agreement. Any significant changes and/or developments in the agreements should be reported as they occur.

Dispute Settlement

12. The provisions of Articles XXII and XXIII of GATT 1994 as elaborated and applied by the Dispute Settlement Understanding may be invoked with respect to any matters arising from the application of those provisions of Article XXIV relating to customs unions, free-trade areas or interim agreements leading to the formation of a customs union or free-trade area.

Article XXIV:12

13. Each Member is fully responsible under GATT 1994 for the observance of all provisions of GATT 1994, and shall take such reasonable measures as may be available to it to ensure such observance by regional and local governments and authorities within its territory.
14. The provisions of Articles XXII and XXIII of GATT 1994 as elaborated and applied by the Dispute Settlement Understanding may be invoked in respect of measures affecting its observance taken by regional or local governments or authorities within the territory of a Member. When the Dispute Settlement Body has ruled that a provision of GATT 1994 has not been observed, the responsible Member shall take such reasonable measures as may be available to it to ensure its observance. The provisions relating to compensation and suspension of concessions or other obligations apply in cases where it has not been possible to secure such observance.
15. Each member undertakes to accord sympathetic consideration to and afford adequate opportunity for consultation regarding any representations made by another Member concerning measures affecting the operation of GATT 1994 taken within the territory of the former.

Understanding in Respect of Waivers of Obligations under the General Agreement on Tariffs and Trade 1994

Members hereby *agree* as follows:

1. A request for a waiver or for an extension of an existing waiver shall describe the measures which the Member proposes to take, the specific policy objectives which the Member seeks to pursue and the reasons which prevent the Member from achieving its policy objectives by measures consistent with its obligations under GATT 1994.
2. Any waiver in effect on the date of entry into force of the WTO Agreement shall terminate, unless extended in accordance with the procedures above and those of Article IX of the WTO Agreement, on

the date of its expiry or two years from the date of entry into force of the WTO Agreement, whichever is earlier.

3. Any member considering that a benefit accruing to it under GATT 1994 is being nullified or impaired as a result of:

    (a) the failure of the Member to whom a waiver was granted to observe the terms or conditions of the waiver, or

    (b) the application of a measure consistent with the terms and conditions of the waiver

may invoke the provisions of Article XXIII of GATT 1994 as elaborated and applied by the Dispute Settlement Understanding.

Notes and References

1 The Changing Morphology of the Asia-Pacific Region

1. The term 'country' is being used somewhat loosely for expositional convenience, although not all the Asia-Pacific countries qualify for it. 'Korea' without exception stands for the Republic of Korea.
2. That is, people's determination to pull their country up by its boot-straps.
3. Little, I. M. D., T. Scitovsky and M. Scott (1990) *Industry and Trade in Some Developing Countries: A Comparative Study*, New York: Oxford University Press.

2 From Economic Integration to Economic Co-operation: Institutional Initiatives

1. The latest stage in European integration was marked on 7 February 1992 with the signing of the Maastricht Treaty on European Union. Consequently the title European Economic Community (EC) underwent a change and European Union (EU) is currently used.
2. Somewhat tactlessly worded because it sounds like the guilt-ridden and discredited concept of the Greater East Asia Co-prosperity Sphere of the interwar and wartime periods.
3. Under the chairmanship of Professor Gunal Kansu, the Kansu report was jointly sponsored by the UN Department of Economic and Social Affairs, the Economic Commission for Asia and Far East, Food and Agriculture Organisation and the UN Conference on Trade and Development.
4. He made this call while addressing the Korean Business Association, in Seoul, in January 1989. Therefore the APEC is said to have emanated from the Hawke initiative.
5. This list of basic principles was set out in the Chairman's summary of the first APEC meeting held in November 1989 in Canberra.
6. The Bangkok declaration talks at length about it. See the *Bangkok Declaration*, Asia-Pacific Economic Co-operation, September 1992.

3 The Ascension of the Japanese Economy to Pre-eminence

1. It was named after the first mythical Emperor of Japan.
2. Iwato was the cave in which the goddess of the sun, Amaterasu, hid because she was offended by the misdeeds of her younger brother.
3. It was named after the god who created the Japanese archipelago by dipping his spear in the sea.
4. See my book *The Yen Appreciation and the International Economy*, London: Macmillan 1993.
5. For detailed treatment see Das (1993). Chapter 1.

6.   GATT statistics cited by Kojima (1977). (See Table 1.3).
7.   Source: Japan Industrial Robot Association, Tokyo.
8.   Tatsuno (1990). Chapter 1.
9.   For detailed treatment refer to Helon 1991.
10. The results of this survey were reported in the *Nikkei Weekly*, 25 April 1992.

4 Market-led Integration in the Asia-Pacific Region

1.   An earlier study than Yamazawa's 1987 study was conducted under the aegis of the Institute of Developing Economies, and yielded similar results. This was published in the December 1983 issue of the *Developing Economies*. See Yamazawa *et al.*, 1983.

5 Undercurrents of Integration

1.   Consensus regarding the creation of AFTA was reached between the ASEAN economies during their summit meeting in January 1991.
2.   Estimated by Morgan Stanley Asia. Published in *Far Eastern Economic Review*, 24 September 1992, p. 58.

6 Regionalism versus Multilateralism: The Asia-Pacific Penchant

1.   The pact was signed on 7 October 1992. It must be ratified by each nation's legislature to take effect on 1 January 1994. The USA, Canada and Mexico will phase out barriers over a 15-year period after that.
2.   These two agreements are the ASEAN Free Trade Area (AFTA) and the Australia New Zealand Closer Economic Relations Trade Agreement (ANZCERTA), respectively.

Bibliography

Abegglen, J. C. and G. Stalk (1985) *Kaisha: The Japanese Corporations*, New York: Basic Books.

Adachi, F. (1992) 'The Position of Small and Medium-Sized Firms in Japan's 'Foreign Direct Investment'. *Regional Development Dialogue*. vol. 13, no. 2, Summer pp. 27–42.

Akamatsu, K. (1962) 'A Historical Pattern of Economic Growth in Developing Countries', *The Developing Economies*, no. 1. Mar.–Aug.

Amsden, A. H. (1989) *Asia's New Giant*, New York: Oxford University Press.

Anderson, K. and B. Smith (1981) 'Changing Economic Relations between the Asian ADCs and Resource Exporting Advanced Countries', in W. Hong and L. B. Krause (eds) *Trade and Growth of the Advanced Developing Countries in the Pacific Basin*, Seoul: Korea Development Institute.

Arndt, H. W. (1989) 'Industrial Policy in East Asia', *Industry and Development*. no. 22, Vienna: United Nations Industrial Development Organisation.

Asian Development Bank (ADB), The (1971) *Southeast Asia's Economy in the 1970s*, London: Longman.

Asian Development Bank (ADB), The (1993) *Subregional Economic Co-operation*, Manila, Feb.

Asian Finance (1991). 'Rising Sun Holds Key to Asia's Development', 15 Sep. pp. 66–8.

Atlantic Council of the United States, The (1976) *GATT Plus: A Proposal for Trade Reforms*, Report of the Special Advisory Panel to the Trade Committee of the Atlantic Council, Washington DC.

Australian Government Publishing Service (1986) Fourth Report, Senate Standing Committee on Industry and Trade, Canberra.

Australian Government Publishing Service (1989) 'The Impact of the Australia New Zealand Closer Economic Relations Trade Agreement'. Research Report no. 29, Bureau of Industrial Economics, Canberra.

Balassa, B. (1986) 'Japan's Trade Policies', *Weltwirtschaftliches Archiv*, Band 112, Heft 4, pp. 745–90.

Balassa, B. and M. Noland (1988) *Japan in the World Economy*, revised edn, Washington DC: Institute of International Economics.

Balassa, B. and J. Williamson (1990) *Adjusting to Success: Balance of Payments Policy in the East Asian NICs*, Washington DC: Institute of International Economics.

Bank of Japan (1987) 'Adjustment of Japanese Economies under Strong Yen', Special Paper no. 149, Tokyo, Mar.

Bank of Japan (1988) 'Balance of Payments Adjustment Process in Japan and the United States', Special Paper no. 162, Tokyo, Mar.

Bank of Korea (1992) *Monthly Statistical Bulletin*, Seoul, Oct.

Barbone, L. (1988) 'Import Barriers: An Analysis of Time Series Cross section Data', *OECD Economic Studies*, no. 11, Autumn.

Bergsten, C. F. (1991) 'Comment on Krugman', in *Policy Implications of Trade Currency Zones*.

Bergsten, C. F. and W. R. Cline (1988) *The United States–Japan Economic Problems*, Washington DC: Institute of International Economics.

Berger, P. L. and H. H. M. Hsiao (eds) (1988) *In Search of an East Asian Development Model*, New Brunswick: Transaction Books.

Bhagwati, J. N. (1968) 'Trade Liberalisation Among LDCs, Trade Theory and GATT Rules', in M. Wolfe (ed.), *Value, Capital and Growth: Papers in Honour of Sir John Hicks*, Edinburgh: University of Edinburgh Press.

Bhagwati, J. N. (1990) 'Regional Accords Be: GATT Trouble for Free Trade', *Wall Street Journal*, 5 Dec.

Bhagwati, J. N. (1993) 'Regionalism and Multilateralism: An Overview', in J. De Melo and A. Panagariya (eds) *New Dimensions in Regional Integration*, Cambridge: Cambridge University Press.

Bradford, C. I. and W. H. Branson (1987) 'Pattern of Trade and Structural Change', in C. I. Bradford and W. H. Branson (eds) *Trade and structural Change in Pacific Asia*, Chicago: University of Chicago Press.

Byrnes, M. (1992) 'Changing Faces: Sweeping Changes', *Financial Review*, 24 Oct.

Campbell, B. O. (1986) 'Trade between Asian Developing Countries: Record and Prospects', *Asian Development Review*, vol. 4. no. 2.

Chandler, C. (1991) 'Japanese GNP Grew in Quarter at the Rate of 11.2 Per Cent', *Asian Wall Street Journal*, 19 Jun.

Chang, H. J. and A. Singh (1992) 'Public enterprises in developing countries and economic efficiency', UNCTAD Discussion Paper no. 48, Geneva: United Nations Conference on Trade and Development.

Chen, E. (1979) *Hypergrowth in Asian Economies*, New York: Holmes & Meier.

Chenery, H. B. and M. Syrquin (1975) *Pattern of Development 1950–70*, Oxford: Oxford University Press.

Cheng, E. and S. Mosher (1992) 'Free for All: Economic Strategy Inspired by Hong Kong', *Far Eastern Economic Review*, 14 May, pp. 24–9.

Cheng, E. and M. Taylor (1991) 'Delta Force', *Far Eastern Economic Review*, 16 May, pp. 64–7.

Cheng, T. and S. Haggard (1987) *Newly Industrialising Asia in Transition: Policy Reforms and American Response*, Berkeley: Institute of International Studies.

Chintayarangsan, R. *et al.* (1992) 'ASIAN Economies: Macro-economic Perspective', *ASEAN Economic Bulletin*, Mar., pp. 353–75.

Chiu, L. C. and C. Chung (1992) 'An Assessment of Taiwan's Indirect Investment Towards Mainland China', Taipei. Taiwan: Chung-Hua Institute for Economic Research, Occasional Paper no. 9201, Jan.

Chang, M. K. (1990) 'ASEAN's Institutional Structure and Economic Co-operation', *ASEAN Economic Bulletin*, Mar., pp. 268–82.

Corbo, V. *et al.* (1985) *Export Oriented Development Strategies: The Success of Five Newly Industrialising Countries*, Boulder, Colo: Westview Press.

Crawford, J. G. and S. Okita (1976) *Australia, Japan and Western Pacific Economic Relations*, Canberra: Australia Government Printing Service.

Das, Dilip K. (1990) 'Erosion of the GATT Discipline', in H. W. Singer *et al.* (eds) *Trade Liberalisation in the 1990s*, New Delhi: Indus Publications.

Das, Dilip K. (1991) *Korean Economic Dynamism*, London: Macmillan.

Das, Dilip K. (1992) 'The Invisible Hand Versus the Visible Hand: The Korean Case', *Seoul Journal of Economics*, vol. 5. no. 2.

Das, Dilip K. (1993) *The Yen Appreciation and the International Economy*, London: Macmillan.

Denison, E. F. (1962) *The Sources of Economic Growth and the Alternatives before the US*, New York: Committee for Economic Development.

Denison, E. F. and W. K. Chung (1976) *How Japan's Economy Grew So Fast?* Washington DC: Brookings Institution.

Destler, I. M. (1986) *American Trade Policies: System Under Stress*, Washington DC: Institute of International Economics.

Dore, R. (1987) *Taking Japan Seriously*, London: Athlone Press.

Drysdale, P. (1978) 'An Organisation for Pacific Trade, Aid and Development: Regional Arrangements and the Resource Trade', in L. B. Krause and H. T. Patrick (eds) *Mineral Resources in the Pacific Asia*, San Francisco: Federal Reserve Bank of San Francisco.

Drysdale, P. (1988) *International Economic Pluralism*, Sydney: Allen & Unwin.

Drysdale, P. and R. Garnaut (1989a) 'A Pacific Free Trade Area?', in J. J. Schott (ed.) *Free Trade Areas and the US Trade Policy*, Washington DC: Institute of International Economics.

Drysdale, P. and R. Garnaut (1989b) 'A Pacific Free Trade Area?', *Pacific Economic Papers*, no. 171, Canberra: Australia-Japan Research Centre, Australian National University.

Drysdale, P. and R. Garnaut (1992) 'The Pacific: A General theory of Economic Integration', Twentieth Pacific Trade and Development Conference, Institute of International Economics, Washington DC. 10–12 Sep. (mimeo).

Drysdale, P. and H. T. Patrick (1979) *An Asian-Pacific Regional Economic Organisation: An Explanatory Concept Paper*, Congressional Research Service, Washington DC: US Government Printing Office, Jul.

Dunkel, A. (1992) 'Regionalism and Multilateralism are two Sides of the Same Coin', Geneva: GATT Press Communique, 21 Aug.

Economic Planning Agency, The (1992) *Economic Survey of Japan 1991–1992*, Tokyo, Jul.

Economic Planning Agency, The *Annual Report on National Accounts*. Tokyo, various issues.

Economist, The, (1991) 'What Makes Yoshio Invent?' 12 Jan., p. 71.

Economist, The (1992a) 'Deng's Last Show', 10 Oct., pp. 13–14.

Economist, The (1992b) 'A Change of Face: A Survey of Taiwan', 10 Oct.

Economist Intelligence Unit, The (1991) *Japan in the 1990s*, London: Special Report no. 2083, Jul.

Economist Newspaper Ltd, The (1983) *Japan*, London.

Elek, A. (1990) 'The Outlook for World Trade: The Asia-Pacific Regions' Trade Policy Interests and the Role of the GATT beyond the Uruguay Round', Canberra: Australia National University, Oct.

Elek, A. (1992) 'Pacific Economic Co-operation: Policy Choices for the 1990s', *Asia-Pacific Economic Literature*, vol. 6, no. 1 (May) pp. 1–15.

Emmott, B. (1992) 'Japan's Global Reach after the Sunset', *Pacific Review*, vol. 5, no. 3, pp. 232–40.

Fairlamb, D. (1993) 'Surging, Churning China', *Institutional Investor*, Jan., pp. 35–46.

Far Eastern Economic Review (1991) 'Pouring Money into the Region', 10 Oct.

Financial Review (1992) 'Japanese Investment in ASEAN Region to Grow', 19 Jun.

Fieleke, N. S. (1992) 'One Trading World, or Many: The Issue of Regional Trading Blocs', *New England Economic Review*, May/Jun., pp. 3–20.

Finger, M. J. (1993) 'GATT's Influence on Regional Arrangements', in J. De Milo and A. Panagariya (eds), *New Dimensions in Regional Integration*, Cambridge: Cambridge University Press.

Frankel, J. (1991) 'Is a Yen Bloc Forming in Asia?' in R. O'Brien (ed.) *Finance and the International Economy*, Oxford: Oxford University Press.

Fujii, H. (1989) 'Japan's Foreign Policy in an Interdependent World', *Japan Review of International Affairs*, vol. 3, no. 2, pp. 119–44.

Fujii, H. (1992) 'The Growing Weight of Services in Economic Growth', *Japan Research Quarterly*, Autumn, pp. 28–34.

Fujigane, Y. and P. Ennis (1990) 'Keiretsu: What They are Doing', *Tokyo Business Today*, Feb., pp. 26–30.

Garnaut, R. (1988) *Asia's Giant*, Adelaide: University of Adelaide.

Garnaut, R. (1989) *Australia and the Northeast Asian Ascendance*, Report to the Prime Minister and the Minister of Foreign Trade, Canberra: Australia Government Printing Service.

General Agreement on Tariffs and Trade (1992) 'What Would a Uruguay Round Deal Contain?' Uruguay Round of Multilateral Trade Negotiations, Geneva, 10 Nov.

Gibney, F. (1992) *The Pacific Century*, New York: Maxwell Macmillan International.

Guiland, W. (1992) 'Prospects of Economic Co-operation in Northeast Asia', *Intereconomics*, Sep.

Hanazaki, M. (1989) 'Industrial and Trade Structure and the International Competitiveness of Asia's Newly Industrialising Economies', Japan Development Bank Research Report no. 15, Tokyo, Aug.

Harris, O. (1989) 'Regional Economic Co-operation', *Pacific Review*, vol. 4, no. 4.

Hayashi, F., T. Ito and J. Slemrod (1987) 'Housing Finance Imperfections and National Savings: A Comparative Simulation Analysis of the US and Japan', NBER Working Paper no. 2272, Jun.

Heller, H. R. (1968) *International Trade: Theory and Empirical Evidence*, Englewood Cliffs, NJ: Prentice Hall.

Helou, A. (1991) 'The Nature and Competitiveness of Japan's Keiretsu', *Journal of World Trade*, Jun., pp. 99–131.

Higashi, C. and G. P. Lanter (1990) *The Internationalisation of the Japanese Economy*, Boston: Kluwer Academic Publishers.

Higgott, R. *et al.* (1991) 'Co-operation Building in the Asia-Pacific Region: APEC and the New Institutionalism', Australia-Japan Research Centre, Pacific Economic Papers, no. 199, Australian National University, Sep.

Hirono, R. L. (1988) 'Japan: Model for East Asian Industrialisation', in H. Hughes (ed.) *Achieving Industrialisation in East Asia*, Cambridge: Cambridge University Press, pp. 241–59.

Ho, Y. P. (1992) *Trade, Industrial Restructuring and Development in Hong Kong*, London: Macmillan.

Hoon, S. J. (1992) 'Looking Ahead: Looking Abroad', *Far Eastern Economic Review*, 13 Aug.

Horioka, C. Y. (1985) 'A Survey of the Literature on Household Saving in Japan: Why is the Household Saving Rate So High?' Kyoto: Kyoto University (mimeo).

Hughes, H. (1991) 'Does APEC Make Sense?' *ASEAN Economic Bulletin*, vol. 8, no. 2, Nov.

Hyun, J. T. and K. Whitmore (1989) 'Japanese Direct Foreign Investment: Patterns and Implications for Developing Countries', Washington DC: World Bank, Industry Series, paper no. 1, Feb.

Ito, T. (1992) *The Japanese Economy*, Cambridge, Mass.: MIT Press.

The Japan Center for Economic Research (1992) *The Coming Multipolar Economy*, Tokyo.

Johnson, C. (1982) *MITI and the Japanese Miracle*, Stanford, Calif: Stanford University Press.

Joint Statement (1992) 'Asia-Pacific Economic Co-operation Forum', Fourth Ministerial Meeting, Bangkok, 10–11 Sep.

Jones, R., R. King and M. Klein (1992) 'The Chinese Economic Area: Economic Integration without a Free Trade Area', OECD Economic Department, paper no. 124, Paris.

Kahn, H. (1970) *The Emerging Superstate*, Englewood. NJ: Prentice-Hall.

Kahn, H. (1979) *World Economic Development: 1979 and Beyond*, London: Croom Helm.

Kao, C. and T. T. Yen (1992) 'The Current Conditions and Development Trend of Economic Exchange Across the Taiwan Straits', Taipei: Chung-Hua Institute for Economic Research, Jan. (mimeo).

Kazutomo, I. (1990) 'Changes in the Japanese Economy', Tokyo: Research Institute of International Trade and Industry, Discussion Paper no. 90, Feb.

Kim, D. Y. (1992) 'Economic Co-operation between Korea and China', *Korea Trade and Business*, Nov., pp. 19–20.

Kindleberger, C. P. (1986) 'A Pacific Economic Community and Asian Developing Countries', *Hitotsubashi Journal of Economics*, Jun., 1966. pp. 17–37.

Kodama, F. (1991) *Analysing Japanese Technologies: The Techno-Paradigm Shift*, London: Pinter.

Kojima, K. (1968) 'Japan's Interest in Pacific Trade Expansion', in K. Kojima (ed.) *Pacific Trade and Development*, vol. 1, Tokyo: Japan Economic Research Centre.

Kojima, K. (1971) *Japan and the Pacific Free Trade Area*, London: Macmillan.

Kojima, K. (1976) 'An Organisation for Pacific Trade, Aid and Development: A Proposal', *Australia-Japan Economic Relations Research Project*, Research Paper no. 40. Canberra: Australian National University. Sep.

Kojima, K. (1977) *Japan and a New World Economic Order*, Boulder, Colo: Westview Press.

Korean Development Bank, The (1992) 'Recent Trends in Korea's Overseas Investment', Seoul, Jun.

Kosai, Y. (1986) *The Era of High Speed Growth*, Tokyo: University of Tokyo Press.

Kosai, Y. and Y. Ogino (1984) *The Contemporary Japanese Economy*, London: Macmillan.

Kraas, L. (1992) 'Asia's Hot New Growth Triangle', *Fortune*, 5 Oct., pp. 54–8.

Krause, L. B. (1987) 'The Structure of Trade in Manufactured Goods in the East and Southeast Asian Region', in C. I. Bradford and W. H. Branson (eds) *Trade and Structural Change in Asia Pacific*, Chicago: University of Chicago Press.

Krause, L. B. *et al.* (1987) *The Singapore Economy Reconsidered*, Singapore: Institute of Southeast Asian Studies.

Krugman, P. (1991) 'The Move Towards Free Trade Zones', in *Policy Implications of Trade and Currency Zones*, A symposium sponsored by the Federal Reserve Bank of Kansas City, Jackson Hole, Wyoming, Aug., pp. 7–42.

Krugman, P. (1993) 'Regionalism vs. Multilateralism: Analytical Note', in J. De Melo and A. Panagariya (eds) *New Dimensions in Regional Integration*, Cambridge: Cambridge University Press.

Kubo, I. (1992) 'Symbiotic Growth: Japanese Firms in Asia', *Tokyo Business Today*, Jun., pp. 30–35.

Kuznets, S. (1966) *Modern Economic Growth: Rates, Structure and Speed*, New Haven, Conn.: Yale University Press.

Langhammer, R. J. (1989) 'Trade in manufactures between Asian Pacific Rim Countries', *ASEAN Economic Bulletin*, vol. 6. no. 1, pp. 94–109.

Lau, L. J. (1990) (ed.) *Models of Development: A Comparative Study of Economic Growth in South Korea and Taiwan*, San Francisco, Calif: Institute for Contemporary Studies Press.

Lawrence, R. Z. (1987) 'Imports in Japan: Closed Markets or Minds?' Brookings Papers on Economic Activity, vol. III, no. 2, pp. 517–54.

Lawrence, R. Z. (1991a) 'Scenario for the World Trading System and their Implications for Developing Countries', Technical Paper no. 47, Paris: Development Centre, Organisation for Economic Co-operation and Development.

Lawrence, R. Z. (1991b) 'An Analysis of Japanese Trade with Developing Countries', Brookings Discussion Paper no. 87, Apr.

Lawrence, R. Z. (1991c) 'How Open is Japan?' in P. Krugman (ed.) *Trade with Japan: Has the Door Opened Wider?*, Chicago: University of Chicago Press.

Leutwilder, F. *et al.* (1985) *Trade Policies for a Better Tomorrow: Proposals for Action*, Geneva: General Agreement on Tariffs and Trade.

Lincoln, E. J. (1988) *Japan Facing Economic Maturity*, Washington DC: The Brookings Institution.

Linder, S. B. (1986) 'The Pacific Century', Stanford, Calif: Stanford University Press.

Lloyd, P. J. (1992) 'Regionalization and World Trade', Paris: Organisation for Economic Co-operation and Development (mimeo).

Lorenz, D. (1989) 'Trends Towards Regionalisation in the World Economy', *Intereconomics*, Mar./Apr., pp. 64–70.

MacFarquhar, R. (1990) 'The Post-Confucian Challenge', *The Economist*, 9 Feb., p. 67.

Machlup, F. (1976) 'A History of Thought on Economic Integration', in F. Machlup (ed.) *Economic Integration: Worldwide, Regional, Sectoral*, London: Macmillan.

Malaysian Institute for Economic Research (MIER) (1989) 'Johor Economic Plan, 1990–2005', Kuala Lumpur.

Ministry of International Trade and Industry (1971) 'The Basic Direction of Trade and Industry', Tokyo, Nov.

Ministry of International Trade and Industry (1990) 'White Paper on International Trade 1990', Tokyo, Jun.

Ministry of Industry and Trade (1992a) 'Vision for the Economy of the Asia-Pacific Region in the Year 2000 and Tasks Ahead', Tokyo, Aug. (mimeo).

Ministry of International Trade and Industry (1992b) 'White Paper on International Trade 1992', Tokyo.

Mirza, H. (1986) *Multinationals and the Growth of the Singapore Economy*, London: Croom Helm.

Mitsumori, K. and K. Meshino (1992) 'China Maps Capitalist Road on Japan's Economic Model', *Nikkei Weekly*, Oct.

Morita, A. (1993) 'Japan Should Globalise on its own Initiative', *Nikkei Weekly*, 28 Jan., p. 7.

Morris-Suzuki, T. (1992) 'Japanese Technology and the New International Division of Labour', in S. Tokunaga (ed.) *Japan's Foreign Investment and Asian Economic Interdependence*, Tokyo: University of Tokyo Press.

Murakani, Y. and Y. Kosai (1986) *Japan in the Global Community*, Tokyo: University of Tokyo Press.

Muton, H. (1986) *Industrial Policies for Pacific Economic Growth*, Sydney: Allen & Unwin.

Myrdal, G. (1968) *Asian Drama: An Enquiry into the Poverty of Nations*, New York: Pantheon Books.

Nakajima, A. (1992) 'MITI's Enlarging Role in Asia', *Nikkei Weekly*, 4 Apr.

Nelson, R. R. (1990) 'Acquiring Technology', in H. Soesastro and M. Pangestu (eds) *Technological Challenge in the Asia-Pacific Economy*, Sydney: Allen & Unwin.

Ng, C. Y. and P. K. Wong (1991) 'The Growth Triangle: A Market Driven Response?', Tokyo: Asian Club Paper no. 2, May.

Nikkei Weekly (1992) 'Growth Triangle Targets Japanese as Key Investors', 29 Aug.

Noguchi, Y. (1988) 'Japan's Economic Policies and their Regional Impact', in R. A. Scalapino *et al.* (eds) *Pacific-Asian Economic Policies and Regional Interdependence*, Berkeley: University of California Press.

Noland, M. (1990a) *Pacific Basin Developing Countries*, Washington DC: Institute of International Economics.

Noland, M. (1990b) 'An Econometric Investigation of International Protection', Washington DC: Institute of International Economics (mimeo).

Nomura Research Institute (1993) *Quarterly Economic Review*, 1st Quarter, p. 3.

Ohkawa, K. and H. Rosovsky (1973) *Japanese Economic Growth in Trend Acceleration in the Twentieth Century*, Stanford Calif: Stanford University Press.

Ogasawara, C. (1992) 'Baht Zone: Reality or Fantasy?' *Nikkei Weekly*, 15 Feb.

Okita, S. (1990) *Approaching the 21st Century: Japan's Role*, Tokyo: Japan Times.

Orr, R. M. (1989) 'The Rising Sun: What Makes Japan Give?' *International Economy*, Sep./Oct., pp. 80–83.

Otani, I. and D. P. Villanueva (1988) 'Determinants of long-term growth performance in developing countries', IMF Working Paper 88/97, 7 Nov.

Owens, C. (1993) 'Thailand Clears Offshore Facility', *Asian Wall Street Journal*, 3 Mar.

Ozawa, T. (1985) 'Japan', in J. H. Dunning (ed.) *Multinational Enterprises, Economic Structure and International Competitiveness*, New York: John Wiley & Sons.

Ozawa, T. (1989) *Recycling Japan's Surpluses*, Paris: Organisation for Economic Co-operation and Development.

Park, Y. C. and W. A. Park (1991) 'Changing Japanese Trade Patterns and the East Asian NICs', in P. Krugman (ed.) *Trade with Japan: Has the Door Opened Wider?*, Chicago: Chicago University Press.

Patrick, H. (1977) 'The Future of Japanese Economy', *Journal of Japanese Studies*, Summer, pp. 230–59.

Patrick, H. and H. Rosovsky (1976) 'Japan's Economic Performance: An Overview', in H. Patrick and H. Rosovsky (eds) *Asia's New Giant*, Washington DC: The Brookings Institution.

Patterson, G. (1989) 'Implications for the GATT and the World Trading System', in J. J. Schott (ed.) *Free Trade Areas and US Trade Policy*, Washington DC: Institute of International Economics.

Petri, P. (1991) 'Japanese Trade in Transition: Hypotheses and Recent Evidence', in P. Krugman (ed.) *The United States and Japan: Has the Door Opened Wider?*, Chicago: University of Chicago Press.

Phongpaichit, P. (1990) *The New Wave of Japanese Investment in ASEAN*, Singapore: Institute of Southeast Asian Studies.

Pomfret, R. (1988) *Unequal Trade: the Economics of Discriminatory International Trade*, Oxford: Blackwell.

Pomfret, R. (1992) 'Regionalisation in the World Economy', Paper presented at the conference on the *Global Perspective: Forces for Regionalism in World Trade*, 19–21 Jul., Flinders University, South Australia.

Porter, M. E. (1990) *The Competitive Advantage of Nations*, London: Macmillan.

Ranis, G. (1992) 'From developing to Mature Economy', in G. Ranis (ed.) *Taiwan: From Developing to Mature Economy*, Boulder Colo.: Westview Press.

Riedel, J. (1984) 'Trade as the engine of growth in developing countries: Revisited', *Economic Journal*, Mar., 94(373), pp. 56–73.

Riedel, J. (1992) 'International Trade in Taiwan's Transition from Developing to Mature Economy', in G. Ranis (ed.) *Taiwan: From Developing to Mature Economy*, Boulder Colo.: Westview Press.

Saxonhouse, G. R. (1992) 'Pricing Strategies and Trading Blocs in East Asia', in J. Frankel (ed.) *US and Japan in Pacific Asia*, Chicago: University of Chicago Press.

Saxonhouse, G. R. (1983) 'The Micro- and Macro-economics of Foreign Sales to Japan', in W. R. Cline (ed.) *Trade Policies in the 1980s*. Washington DC: Institute of International Economics, pp. 259–304.

Schott, J. J. (1989) *More Free Trade Areas?*, Washington DC: Institute of International Economics.

Scott, B. R. (1985) 'National Strategies: Key to International Competitiveness', in B. R. Scott and G. C. Lodge (eds) *US Competitiveness in the World Economy*, Boston, Mass.: Harvard University Press.

Sekiguchi, S. (1991) 'The International Economy and Japan in 2000', Tokyo: The Japan Center for Economic Research, Jul. (mimeo).

Shapiro, D. H. (1991) 'Seeking Partners for Mainland China', *Asian Wall Street Journal*, 20 May.

Shapiro, D. H. (1992) 'Taiwan Expands Regional Investment', *Far Eastern Economic Review*, 15 Oct., pp. 34–5.

Smith, M. *et al.* (1985) *Asia's New Industrial World*, London: Methuen.

Stevens, C. (1981) *EEC and the Third World: A Survey*, London: Hodder & Stoughton.

Sung, Y. W. (1991a) *The China-Hong Kong Connection*, Cambridge: Cambridge University Press.

Sung, Y. W. (1991b) 'The Economic Integration of Hong Kong, Taiwan and South Korea with Mainland China', in R. Garnaut and L. Guogang (eds) *Economic Reforms and Internationalisation*, London: Allen & Unwin.

Tai, H. C. (1989) 'The Original Alternative', in H. C. Tai (ed.) *Confucianism and Economic Development*, Washington DC: The Washington Institute Press.

Takenaka, H. (1991) 'The Japanese Economy and the Pacific Development', in M. Ariff (ed.) *The Pacific Economy*, Sydney: Allen & Unwin.

Tatsuno, S. M. (1990) *Created in Japan*, New York: Harper & Row.

Tejima, S. (1992) 'Japanese Foreign Direct Investment in the 1980s and its Prospects in the 1990s', *EXIM Review*, Jul., pp. 25–51.

Tinbergen, J. (1962) *Shaping the World Economy: Suggestions for an International Economic Policy*, New York: Twentieth Century Fund.

Tokunaga, S. (1992) 'Japan's FDI-Promoting systems and Intra-Asia Networks: New Investments and Trade Systems Created by the Borderless Economy', in S. Tokunaga (ed.) *Japan's Foreign Investment and Asian Economic Interdependence*, Tokyo: University of Tokyo Press.

Tumlir, J. (1978) 'National Interest and International Order', London: Trade Policy Research Centre.

Ungphakarn, P. (1992) 'Asia-Pacific Economic Group to Establish Permanent Secretariat', *Nikkei Weekly*, 4 Jul.

Vatikiotis, M. (1992) 'The Mahathir Paradox', *Far Eastern Economic Review*, 20 Aug.

Vernon, R. (1966) 'International Investment and International Trade in the Product Cycle', *Quarterly Journal of Economics*, vol. 80, no. 2, May.

Viner, J. (1950) *The Customs Union Issue*, New York: Carnegie Endowment.

Vogel, E. F. (1984) 'The Advent of the Pacific Century', *Harvard Business Review*, 6(5), Mar.

Vogel, E. F. (1986) 'Pax Nipponica', *Foreign Affairs*, Spring, pp. 752–67.

Watanabe, T. (1988) 'Japan, the US and the NICs in the Age of Western Asia', *Toyo Keizai*, May (in Japanese; cited in Takenaka, 1991).

Watanabe, T. and H. Kajiwara (1983) 'Pacific Manufactured Trade and Japan's Options', *The Developing Economies*, Dec. pp. 313–39.

Wong, J. (1991) 'Economic Integration of Hong Kong and Guangdong', Singapore: Institute of East Asian Philosophies, Oct. (mimeo).

Wonnacott, P. and M. Lutz (1989) 'Is there a Case for Free Trade Areas?' in J. J. Schott (ed.), *Free Trade Areas and US Trade Policy*, Washington DC: Institute of International Economics.

World Bank (1885) *China: Economic Structure in International Perspective*, Washington DC.

World Bank (1989) *Economic Prices for Project Evaluation in China*, Washington DC.

World Bank (1992) *World Development Report 1992*, Washington DC.

Woronoff, J. (1986) *Asia's Miracle Economies: Korea, Japan, Taiwan, Singapore and Hong Kong*, New York: M. E. Sharp.

Wu, Y. (1985) *Becoming an Industrialised Nation*, New York: Praeger.

Yamazaki, H. and B. Clifford (1992) 'MITI Sharpens Asian Focus in Policy'. *Nikkei Weekly*, 20 Jun.

Yamazawa, I. (1987) 'Japan and Her Asian Neighbours in a Dynamic Perspective', in C. I. Bradford and W. H. Branson (eds), *Trade and Structural Change in Pacific Asia*, Chicago: University of Chicago Press.

Yamazawa, I., K. Taniguchi and A. Hirata (1983) 'Trade and Industrial Adjustment in Pacific Asian Countries'. *The Developing Economies*, Dec., pp. 281–312.

Yan, T. K. *et al.* (1992) 'ASEAN and Pacific Economic Co-operation'. *ASEAN Economic Bulletin*, vol. 8, no. 3, Mar. pp. 209–330.

Yoshikawa, K. (1992) 'South Korea Sinks Roots Deep in Chinese Economy', *Nikkei Weekly*, 5 Sep.

Yoshitomi, M. (1989) 'Japan's Savings and External Surplus in the World Economy', New York: Group of Thirty, occasional Paper no. 26.

Yasutomo, D. T. (1986) *The Manner of Giving*, Lexington: Lexington Books.

Yu, T. S. (1992) 'The Two Sides of Taiwan Straits: Economic Interdependence and Co-operation', Taipei: Chung-Hua Institution for Economic Research, Occasional Paper no. 9203, Mar.

Yuan, L. T. (1991) *Growth Triangle: The Johor-Singapore-Riau Experience*, Singapore: Institute of Southeast Asian Studies.

Index